DISTRIBUTED BY
Vedanta Press
1946 VEDANTA PLACE • HOLLYWOOD, CALIF. 90068

MAN AND HIS MIND

Swami Nihsreyasananda

Sri Ramakrishna Math
Mylapore, Madras-600 004.

Published by :
© The President,
Sri Ramakrishna Math,
Mylapore, Madras 600 004.

Second Impression
II-3M 3C-5-95
ISBN 81-7120-643-3

Printed in India at
Sri Ramakrishna Math Printing Press,
Mylapore, Madras 600 004.

PUBLISHER'S NOTE

Swami Nisreyasananda, was an eminent monk of the Ramakrishna Order, well-known for his depth of scholarly thinking.

Born in 1899, at Trichur in the State of Kerala, he joined the Ramakrishna Order at its branch at Trichur. He was a disciple of Swami Shivanandaji, known as 'Mahapurush Maharaj', a disciple of Sri Ramakrishna and the second President of the Order from 1922 to 1934. The Swami was ordained a monk by his Guru in 1932.

The Swami worked in the Trichur, Ceylon and Madras centres of the Order. At Madras, he was the Asst. Editor of the monthly magazine *Vedanta Kesari*. In 1939, he started the Visakhapatnam centre in Andhra Pradesh. He was the head of the Mauritius centre from 1948 to 1951 and also the Editor of *Prabuddha Bharata*, another monthly journal of the Order for two years, 1957 and 1958. Later he went to Africa and worked hard to spread the message of Vedanta and Ramakrishna-Vivekananda in Zimbabwe, Zambia and South Africa. His ministry in these countries from 1959 till his passing away in November 1991 attracted quite a number of devotees to the message of the Great Master and his disciple, Swami Vivekananda.

The present book is a collection of the editorial articles written by the Swami every month during 1957-58, in *Prabuddha Bharata*. They have been rearranged under classified headings. The footnotes have been taken to the end of the book. These quotations, mostly from the Vedantic scriptures, reveal the depth of scholarship of the Swami. These articles deal with man's struggles with his own mind. The author shows how an undisciplined and uncontrolled mind is the cause of numerous problems, not only for the individuals, but for the society as well. The Swami, through apt illustrations and quotations from Ramakrishna, Vivekananda, Sri Sarada Devi and the scriptures, depicts the ways and means of bringing the mind under control.

We are grateful to Mr. R.L. Kashyap of the U.S.A. for his contribution towards subsidizing this publication.

Madras.

Akshaya Tritiya

25 April 1993 PUBLISHER

CONTENTS

Publisher's Note iii

I Discipline

1. Educative Value of Philosophic Discipline 1
2. Goal and Plan of Inspired Guides 15
3. Seeds and Sowing for Inner Harvest 30
4. Unified Outlook through proper Discipline 43
5. Scope of Personal Exertion 56

II. Word-power

6. Catchwords for Correcting Perspective 69
7. Uplifting Power behind Words and Acts 83
8. Scriptural Aids to end Afflictions 98
9. Picturesque Reminders 110

III. Reflection

10. Synthesis through Deeper Reflection 123
11. Reflection and Control of Reactions 137

IV. Vision

12. Spiritual Ascent through Art and Worship 152
13. Intention's Penetrative Power 167
14. Vision that Supplements and Balances 180
15. Refinement of Reactions 194
16. Towards Fuller Vision 206

V. Guidance

17. Creation of Interest and Certainty 218
18. Awakening and Grouping of Talents 231
19. Formula of Rousing and Refining 241
20. Graded Forms and Levels of Aid 257
21. Opening up of Inner Springs 270

VI. Service

22. Coordinated Insight and Service 283
23. Mental Preparation for Efficient Services 294

VII. Attainment

24. Attainment, Delight, and Non-Swerving 307

I. DISCIPLINE

1. Educative value of philosophic discipline

It is knowledge alone that will save us in every department of life—in knowledge is worship. The more we know the better.

Swami Vivekananda

I

A Little analysis will convince us that our usual round of activities is prompted, among other things, by two main desires. One aims at bringing out our best as quickly as possible. When consciously directed, it releases a tremendous amount of energy to go forward, and overcomes the obstacles that beset our path. But often it fails to operate properly, and in forgetful moments we glide down into childish levels and waste our precious time in running after pleasures that deaden finer perceptions. Often, too, the sight of the difficulties confronting us and of the successes of our neighbours in apparently similar circumstances, throws us off the main track. And then, instead of putting forth creative efforts to eliminate our troubles, we permit our minds to become the dancing ground of destructive emotions like envy, anger, or despair. Even if they are not actively present, the craving for securing quick results holds the field. It does much harm. In most cases it is responsible for making us skip over important facts. Unless checked in time, it produces the chronic inability to discern just those subtle forces and events—in ourselves and in our environment—on whose proper control our forward movement depends. Without sharp observation and steady habits, none can climb high or achieve anything worthy. And this means rigorous discipline.

The second desire, which analysis reveals, aims at using our best gifts for participating in an intimate and beneficial manner in whatever world movement we can conveniently contact. This is a very commendable tendency. The fact that different parts of the world have come close together in a number of ways provides ample scope for the fulfilment of this desire. Men of talent, original thinkers, inventors, planners, business executives, administrators, and specialists in every field, including religion and philosophy, are in demand everywhere. For the world's needs are many, and they go on multiplying from day to day. To satisfy them competent men and women are wanted in constantly increasing numbers. This, again, means rigorous discipline.

Mass production of gifted individuals, with strength and purity combined, is not an easy task. How often we witness the sad spectacle of experts in certain fields, able to fulfil their own limited duties well, turning out to be hopelessly inefficient, if not unreliable and even corrupt, in their general dealings in departments of social activity for which they had not the requisite training or qualification! Such tragedies take place because of the lack of suitable and timely exercises in character formation. There are four factors, which have, somehow or other, become dominant in shaping people's attitudes at the present day. They are: race, language, geographical position, and nationality. Each of these can, up to a certain extent, assist in calling forth the finest sentiments from within, and in canalizing them for the betterment of the world. The achievements of any individual, naturally, can be the result of invoking the past glory of any of these. Such achievements can also, in their turn, enhance the prestige of any or even all of these four, with which he is connected. But there are dangers too where the person concerned has serious defects in his character, existing side by side with his special talent. By such a person's getting of his own accord, or being officially sent, into areas involving large-scale contacts with the public, the benefits accruing from his talents are, as we often see, neutralized by the disturbances and explosions he creates. In a simple domestic field the damage will be acute, no doubt, but limited in extent. But the damage becomes incalculable indeed in the national and international fields, now open to those who can supplement their single talent with plenty of the capacity to elbow their way forward. Democracy's greatest merit is that it can give an individual a fair chance to rise to his full stature by his own efforts. But democracy, as a framework of the external environment, cannot guarantee that every individual develops his character properly before entering into the general—and—quite often, unscrupulous—struggle for power and position. What is it, then, that can—negatively—prevent calamities and—positively—enable us to draw inspiration from our racial, linguistic, national and geographical associations, so as to express that inspiration in ways that promote the world's welfare? It is only our own conscience, our own sense of what is right, reasonable and dignified, our own highest estimate about ourselves and others, in short, our philosophic outlook. Its acquisition and retention too depend upon rigorous discipline.

II

Life enforces some discipline or other. In fact, from early childhood, the behaviour of an individual gets adjusted to certain patterns, although for the most part, unaccompanied by that controlled combination of language and reasoning which we learn to use as we grow older. It is not uncommon to see indulgent parents permitting their pet children to evolve a kind of formula, viz. of persistent crying, for securing all that they want! At school, however, where the parents and the home atmosphere are replaced by the teacher, fixed bours of instruction, and the presence of diligent companions getting credit for greater proficiency, the crying formula is discovered to be totally useless. As a result of close observation of the conduct of every one in his new environment, the child slowly learns to put forth its best efforts, to compete with other students, and to pick up knowledge as fast as they do. Crying and fighting are not dropped altogether, but are reserved for employment wherever they might succeed. After studies are finished and the adult enters service, he finds it necessary to modify the formula of competitive learning and adapt himself for quick and efficient discharge of the responsibilities officially put on him. The fear of punishment and the hope of promotion play a great part in prompting him to acquire the required skills without delay, and in avoiding open corruption or fights. When, in due course, he marries and sets up a separate house, love compels him to evlove a totally new formula, in which crying and competition are automatically ruled out, and the attitude of cooperation and of a healthy give-and-take becomes the dominant element. Competition and fights survive even now, but are reserved for modified application to forge ahead in official and social fields, particularly with the aim of making his own family more prosperous than the rest. Even the latest formula is, however, seen to be inadequate when he is blessed with children of different capacities and temperaments, and he is thrown into the need for forgiving, teaching, protecting, and even praying for, them.

When a formula is repeated, specially with satisfaction, a number of times it becomes a habit. And unless it is neutralized by opposing formulas through conscious effort, it creates new channels of expression, like pentup waters making breaches wherever resistance is less. What happens, then, to the formulas of noisy cries, of competition and of fighting which find limited utility in certain contexts yet? Their roots lie safely imbedded in the subconscious or the habit-level—the secluded expanse of the personality affording them facilities to make alliances for common purposes. We know that the piling up of armaments is likely to be followed by some explosion somewhere, even on slight provocations. Habits of a lower cultural value also follow the same law. If allowed to remain entrenched without conscious control, they become capable, whenever occasions arise, of invading areas of conduct where they can secure victories without immediate detection or effective resistance. The manifold contacts, which the complicated national and international relationships of the present day offer, often become the 'no man's land' where the unsublimated formulas of the individual can make periodic inroads, while on the domestic front his latest-evolved formula of love and cooperation, of forgiveness and prayer, holds its ground and is realized to be eminently satisfying.

What is called common sense or worldly wisdom certainly imposes restrictions on wild behaviour. What we are concerned with here is the essential worth of the reasoning or calculation that compels us to impose them. If actual deeds alone are controlled, and not their sources in the thought world, and that too when danger is scented, viz. exposure or punishment for us as individuals, or loss and bloodshed for the community as a whole, the relatively steady platform from which we launch the controlling force is really low indeed. If our basic formula is that we shall not withdraw from self-seeking so long as gains flow in, or until dangers threaten us, our inner development does not rise much above that of the cow that approaches us when grass is held in her front, but runs away the moment we brandish a stick.[1] Such a formula, moreover, is definitely inferior to that of the pious man who refrains from bad conduct owing to his fear of hell fire, and who scrupulously observes every detail of formal worship because of the pleasure God may give him in heaven. In the latter case, the formula has the decided merit of incorporating the concept of God in some form to dignify his daily round of activities. As against it, in the former there is the sordidness of keeping aggrandisement and expediency as the principal factors. Finer sentiments can never take root in our personality as long as we wish to entertain them only for a diplomatic handling of the situations external to us. The case is similar to that of poetry or painting, in which a person rises to the fullest creative heights, not when he resorts to it because of compulsion from others, but only when he realizes that the taste for it is part of his mental make-up, and that he should dedicate all his energy to develop it to perfection even if others obstruct him.

Nowadays we rightly honour the man who detects oil deep down in the earth, or dares to climb up a peak which baffled man's approach hitherto. Compared with these activities, it must be the most stimulating adventure for us to dive into the personality itself and explore its farthest reaches, just because we have been associated with it from our birth, and it accompanies us in every situation like a faithful friend and multipurpose instrument. A thorough investigation of its highest possibilities and appropriate adjustments to them constitute, in a sense, the most fundamental of all sciences. To give it a minor importance, or to discontinue it in any community or in any generation will allow imperfect values and discordant forces to vitiate human relationships, and to that extent lead to the misuse of the benefits the other sciences confer. In accepting such a research we are only making a vital extension of the very principle of evolving new training formulas that made the baby grow into the loving parent. When followed up to its sublimest range, it gradually transfroms sectional-minded, struggling men and women into integrated personalities, in whom conceptual differences of oneself, others, nature, and divinity become equally effective springboards, nay, sacred means, for manifesting perfect unity and rendering loving service. By philosophic discipline we mean all the efforts involved in this change of direction and values.

III

When we stop talking about the utility of such a comprehensive discipline and turn to the field of philosophy proper for picking up some suitable practical steps from it, we are confronted with a variety of systems, which ordinarily provide sufficient material for three or four years of intensive study even for one whose lowest aim is to get a general view of them and to equip himself for transmitting that veiw to others! We cannot say definitely to what extent the propounder of each system—especially if he was not a clergyman—struggled to trasform his own personality in the light of the picture of the universe and of his place in it. which he found coherent in the course of his diligent and long-continued search.

To put it roughly, each system serves the purpose of a map, having its own pattern to arrange the diverse elements and forces, operating outside as well as inside the human being, and regarded by the founder as essential for a correct understanding of the universe. Most often one of the categories is shown as the dominant factor, or the supreme cause, and the rest as subordinate to it, or flowing from it in different streamlets as its modifications or results. If any system includes what religions call God, it is natural to expect essential powers attributed to Him, and His grace indicated as descending at some stage to complete the transformation of the spiritually advancing seeker. If, however, the system eliminates God completely—as certain types of government do with kingship—we can find that the other categories share those powers among themselves in varying proportions, so that on the whole it becomes possible to account for the current running of the universe, as pictured in that system.

The progress of science in the different fields of its inquiry is exerting its own influence on philosophy's map-making, and on the interpretation of certain aspects of existing maps. Referring to 'standard philosophical discussions' of problems like causality and free will, or of materialism and mentalism, Sir James Jeans says towards the close of his book, *Science and Philosophy* that they 'are based on an interpretation of the pattern of events which is no longer tenable', 'the scientific basis of these discussions' having been 'washed away'. He hastens to add that 'this does not mean that the conclusions reached were necessarily wrong. But it means that the situation must be viewed afresh. Everything is in the melting-pot and we must start anew and try to discover truth on the basis of the new physics ... Apart from our knowledge of the pattern of events, our tools (for such discovery) can only be probable reasoning and the principle of simplicity'. From the standpoint of physics, particularly, he says that 'there is no longer the dualism of mind and matter, but of waves and particles; these seem to be the direct, although almost unrecognizable, descendants of the older mind and matter. The two members of this dualism are no longer antagonistic or mutually exclusive; rather they are complementary'. 'for one controls the other—the waves control the particles, or in the old terminology, the mental controls the material'. Though these remarks cannot be taken as positive statements about mind, they can be taken as indications of the way in which the facts of scientific research are altering the total landscape on our maps, showing some familiar hills submerged and new ones emerging in unexpected areas. One thing is clear; the mansized world is now standing between two unimaginably vast and wonderful worlds, that of the atom with its minute size and tremendous energy on one side, and the astronomical bodies with their fantastic speeds and distances on the other. We have only to add to these the advances made in departments like biology and psychology, to understand the difficulty of evolving a coordinated picture of the universe on the basis of science itself.

How does man look in this present setting? The complexity of this problem was seen by thoughtful people even before atomic research reached its present phase of development. As early as 1935, Dr. Alexis Carrel wrote in *Man the Unknown* (ch. 1 and 2) that 'It is impossible... to make use of the mass of information accumulated by the specialists. For no one has undertaken to coordinate the data already obtained, and to consider the human being in his entirety... Mechanical, physical, and chemical sciences are incapable of giving us intelligence, moral discipline, health, nervous equilibrium, security and peace... The science of man... the most difficult of all sciences... will be the task of the future... Such a synthesis cannot be obtained by a simple roundtable conference of specialists. It requires the efforts of one man, not merely those of a group... The synthesis needed for our knowledge of man should be elaborated in a single brain'.

IV

In these days numbers count and the tendency to think in terms of mass movements is on the increase. Hence a formula like that of 'working for the welfare of the world' captures the imagination, and is likely to create in each person, irrespective of his fitness, the picture of himself as the glorious instrument to benefit as many as he can contact. While the enthusiasm evoked is certainly valuable, it has to be supplemented by the clear recognition that actual work must be based, as in any department of scientific activity, on a careful study of all the forces involved. The first duty is to collect relevant facts about the section to be benefited, its requirements, our own capacities to serve as instruments for creative work, and the potentialities inherent in the particular time and place. This must be followed by the formulation of a realizable goal, in which all the facts are harmonized, and also by the laying down of a series of steps leading to it. Last comes the actual carrying out of the planned steps,—a course often revealing facts previously not observed. The basic condition leading to success in this complicated undertaking is the development and harmonization of our own personalities. We all know that a tar-brush is not the proper instrument for painting walls white. And yet most of us plunge, or dream of plunging, into the midst of activities affecting numbers of people, without first purifying our own motives by systematic discipline, and increasing our 'visibility', or power of accurate perception, in the field of the subtle forces regulating human relationships. In other words, in the mental world we rub ourselves against others with much tar flowing with our motives! The wise have declared as Tamasic, or born of inner darkness, the types of action started without calculating one's own ability to push it through to success, or the evil consequences that may arise from it, viz. deterioration in the total situation, and needless pain to those who do not deserve it.[2]

Taking, then, the harmonization of our own inner powers and the heightening of our capacity to grasp subtler forces as the basic requirements for future good, either of ourselves or, through us, of others, it is easy to see that every philosophic (and religious) system becomes valuable as a good map for intending travellers. Since each one of us is guided by a selective impulse from within, a comparative study of the various systems is bound to evoke a natural response from that interior agency, and help us in choosing that system which suits our temperament, as much as a variety store enables the purchaser to select the article that very nearly answers his needs. Here we make a wise approach to philosophy itself: instead of allowing the structure of each system to remain apart pointing to a torch-like intellectual conclusion at its top, we propose to traverse the steps, take the torch and introduce it into all the intricate movements of life, as we live it, verifying its lighting power as we proceed. The selected system thus becomes a conceptual ladder, by climbing whose rungs our emotional awareness of what we call love, goodwill, beauty, prayer, peace and so on can be established on sublimer levels, and raised to such an intensity that it can penetrate egoistic walls in the same way as electricity in the form of light can penetrate glass and become available to those who wish to take advantage of the transmission. If philosophic principles are employed for graded creative work within our own personalities, we shall find the different systems, not contradictory, but highly useful, each in its own way, to master particular forces.

The sincere seeker can easily choose from the material supplied by each system, and prepare for his use, a graded system of disciplines for bridging that vast gulf that has, on one side, ignorance, laziness, selfishness, fear or duplicity, and, on the other side, corresponding virtues like wisdom, fervour, generosity, courage, or truthfulness. As the wide span becomes covered, sectional terms like mysticism, idealism, materialism, humanitarianism, dualism, non-dualism, or 'other-worldliness' will be found inadequate to express the nature of the process involved or the transformation achieved internally and externally. Quarrels stop when we reach higher levels and visibility increases.

2. Goal and plan of inspired guides

> May He, the Lord of all, strengthen me with wisdom. May I be the possessor of the wisdom that leads to immortality. May my body become fit. May my tongue become extremely sweet. May I hear much (auspicious and helpful) with my ears. ...Protect that which I have heard.

This is a prayer from the *Taittiriya Upanishad* (1.4.1). It will not be difficult to find in the extant literature of every religion prayers containing these or similar ideas. There are, no doubt, some systems that do not accept God, Personal or Impersonal, and therefore do not prescribe prayers in the sense of petitions addressed to any extraneous Power. Instead of stressing an attitude of supplication, they lay down various disciplines and affirmations calculated to purify the stream of thoughts and emotions. The underlying principle is that when the mind is kept clean and unruffled, truth shines in it, as in a mirror free from dust. Rightly has it been said that 'neither father nor mother nor kindred can confer greater benefits than does the well-directed mind.'[1]

I

In Buddhist teachings, particularly, 'there recur continually three categories, to some extent like the headings of three chapters on ethic: uprightness, self-concentration, and wisdom'[2] The wise ones are described as 'ever meditative and ever putting forth strong effort' to attain Nibbana, 'the incomparable (state of) security'.[3] 'Wakeful among the heedless, keenly vigilant among the sleeping ones, the wise man forges ahead, even as a charger outdistances a horse of lesser strength'.[4] The earnest seeker is instructed to consider his mind to be strong like a fortress and to fight the Evil One with the sword of knowledge, and to guard his conquest without hankering.[5] Such a person alone can be respected as a knower of truth, 'who is pre-eminent, superior to all others, a hero, a great sage, a conqueror, free from craving, cleansed of sin, an Enlightened One'.[6] Indeed in this world there is nothing purifying like knowledge.[7]

Taking the Buddha and Jesus as two representatives of the great founders of religions, let us make a reverent study of them from two important angles. First as regards their advent and illumination: That the Lord Himself came down, or that He sent His own Son and Messenger for guiding mankind, or that the Time-Spirit or Cosmic need evolved personalities of such extraordinary power and wisdom, are some of the ways in which devotees have tried to account for the manner of their births and the nature of their precepts. Why they appeared among men can be judged only from what they did and from the creative forces that streamed from their teachings. One thing that stands out clearly is that they had nothing to do with wars of aggression or of retaliation. In fact, they did not enter into any kind of struggle to overcome enemies and secure their own survival: In a way, the dangers created by foreign invasions have a great share in whipping up heroism among the defenders and in evolving the skill and tactics of their commanders in the field. To that extent we may say that military abilities are evolved by the struggle itself. In a similar sense we may concede that the pressure exerted by the pitiable sight of sinners made these large-hearted prophets retire into solitude and struggle for insight—for a 'revelation' that naturally expressed itself as a special formula for teaching and as the power to transform those who were sensitive enough to respond. But this theory will leave many points unexplained. For example, it fails to show why they turned 'inward' for a solution, resolutely avoiding every conventional source of strength or redress—relatives, wealth, arguments, military organization, and the like. They not only rejected these readily available supports, but considered them as great impediments and steered their sense organs and intellect in a direction altogether different. Compassion can be accepted as one of the reasons for the main drive, for the determination not to relax their efforts till a solution came. But it does not account for the conviction that all energy, attention, and aspiration should be mobilized and concentrated to probe the very foundation of life and thought. If such a swing of the entire personality is also to be included in the category of the struggle for successful existence, that struggle certainly belongs to a rare variety, since it is absolutely uncontaminated by the least trace of the usual competition for personal enjoyments, safety or survival.

The outside environment is undoubtedly a challenge. It demands new responses. These, in their turn, lead to new outlooks and new habits, resulting gradually in appropriate changes in the physical and other levels of existence. We can grant this and at the same time incorporate the lives of great prophets into a more comprehensive principle of evolution. To do this we have only to ask ourselves why we inwardly revere these Saviours of old as well as those among our contemporaries who risk their precious lives to rescue others from danger. Our honest reply would be that 'progress in the rational human kingdom cannot be achieved, like that in the animal kingdom, by the destruction of others'. The highest evolution of man is effected through sacrifice alone. 'A man is great among his fellows in proportion as he can sacrifice for the sake of others, while in the lower strata of the animal kingdom, that animal is the strongest which can kill the greatest number of animals'. The truth, thus, is that the struggle theory is not equally applicable to both kingdoms. We find that man's struggle lies in the mental sphere and that his struggle is measured in terms of the control he has over his feelings and emotions. 'The struggle which we observe in the animal kingdom for the preservation of the gross body obtains in the human plane of existence for gaining mastery over the mind or for attaining the state of balance'.[8]

At the back of important conscious efforts, there is always the perception of a gap between what is actually secured and what is expected to give greater satisfaction if got. In the early stages of the growth of the personality, these gaps relate mostly to the numerous objects found in the environment. Even the feeling of love is, at this stage, prompted by the motive of drawing the attention of others to oneself than by the joy, that a maturer man has, of dedicating his best to serve everyone coming within his orbit. Let us suppose that all desirable objects and relationships are somehow obtained. Will this be a guarantee against the opening up to view of fresh and more serious gaps in subtler fields? We know that the framework in which our life is cast is limited in many ways. Thus, even if by ingenious tricks we manage to make our surroundings conform more or less to our tastes, we shall not be able to retain that state for long. Nature has in her stock the forces of decay, separation, and death to play havoc with our nice arrangements, And the result is that sooner or later gaps will appear, complelling us to learn new lessons. It is not without sufficient reason that when scripture wishes to make us see that there are grades of joy and bliss, it takes the lowest unit to be the sum total of those very conditions which men without discrimination ordinarily regard as ideal. 'Let there be a good youth,' says the *Taittiriya Upanishad* (2.8) 'a student of the sacred texts, well disciplined, very firm and very strong. Let the whole earth be full of wealth for him. This is one joy of man'. The idea is that the joy of a prosperous ruler of men can very well be taken as a standard unit for comparisons. We can conceive of many other units, each later one a hundredfold more intense than its predecessor, in an ascending order. All of them would have this similarity that they depend upon a continuous struggle to bring about a sort of relationship between the perceiving ego and particular object found in its field of perception. The intention of scripture is to show that all these joys must be placed over against the unbroken bliss of a wise man, which is unaffected by the duality involved in the normal processes of perception and reflection. The utmost we can do is to plot a series of points to indicate the increasing manifestations of this abiding Perfection in different observable fields, and from them frame our law of evolution, recognizing at the same time that this Perfection does not evolve at all.

II

So much about the theory; but the more important question is: How can we make it practical, so that we can experience that evolution in our own personalities? What falls within our competency in this matter is to provide the most favourable conditions for manifesting more and more of it. Our own normal ways of reacting can give us some useful clue. We do not evolve a better formula for our aspirations and conduct in exact proportion to the harassment that our neighbours give us; they too will not start a campaign of that kind, imagining it to be the proper means to make us evolve! The chances of their success are brighter if they can show us the essential worth and utility of a better pattern, especially if it be the one they themselves follow. Education has ever been the best and safest remover of all obstacles. Competition and struggle, in which one survives at the cost of another, only create setbacks and throw in hindrances, whose elimination would call for additional effort. Still, even today, 'some say that if man did not fight with man, he would not progress'! Actually, however, 'every war has thrown back human progress by fifty years, instead of hurrying it forwards. The day will come when men will study history from a different light and find that competition is neither the cause nor the effect' of progress, but 'simply a thing on the way, not necessary for evolution at all'.[9] 'In man there is the potential god, kept in by the locks and bars of ignorance. When knowledge breaks these bars, the god becomes manifest'. 'Even when all competition has ceased, this perfect nature behind will make us go forward until everyone has become perfect'.[10]

It was on this inward Perfection that the prophets, impelled by their inborn temperaments, focussed their thoughts and aspirations till they became established in it. The majority of us, on the contrary, continue to be in the thick of the competitive scramble for sense pleasures. To us it appears as if there is plenitude only in the familiar functioning of awareness. Hence we imagine the moves of the prophets towards spiritual harmony to have been a misguided retreat into a narrow aloofness, in which many of the beauties of life as well as chances of dynamic action were sadly shut out! Because of our holding fast to the idea that their attitude was negative, we find it hard to explain how what is claimed to be 'revelation' in their case could result in a downpour of unsurpassed power, wisdom, and love, for which their personalities became effective channels forthwith. We are not right in regarding these determined souls as exceptions. Their disciplines meant, in reality, an extension in awareness, a transcendence of the limitations under which our ordinary cognition works. If we could learn to use our mental apparatus, as they did, there is nothing to prevent us from getting the illumination they had. The fact is that they did not fritter away their energies, as we do. So within a short time they achieved the maximum possible evolution, and thus they were able to manifest in their daily life the fullness latent in every-one of us. Our progress cannot but be slow, since we aim only at such knowledge as may help us to run after perishable goods. The object of well thought out disciplines is to reduce the period of evolution. In this sense the prophets have indeed set a model for us. For, 'in one span of life they lived the whole life of humanity, traversed the whole length of time that it takes ordinary humanity to come to perfection'.[11] They are truly our standard-bearers. Having marched ahead and reached the goal of inner development, they are beckoning to us to advance. If we are earnest and prudent, we can adopt their plan and pace, as much as our inborn temperaments require and permit.

III

The second angle for observation is intended to cover the methods of teaching the great Masters have followed. Their medium of instruction was almost invariably the spoken word, made living by their personal example. It was impossible for them to have a 'closed fist' policy. Their vision of the unity and sanctity of all life was so intensely real that petty ideas of reserving certain secrets for themselves and some favourites, while presenting only diluted principles to others, could never find entrance into their minds. The wisdom they received, they freely gave. They always remained well poised in the midst of those creative forces which expressed themselves as the changing tastes and intellectual powers of different individuals. So they could spontaneously adjust their movements and talks to benefit those who were at heart willing to cooperate. There were in their days, as there are even today, many who stood behind self-made mental barricades, and peeped and listened, only to mock or find fault later. After every contact, they took back just what they had brought with them! But there were large numbers of others, who were familiar with the rituals and traditions current at the time, but who longed to have new formulas to rouse their faith and give them certainty. Of the diverse approaches that could be employed to make them grasp spiritual truths, a few at least were sure to answer, now and then, the pressing problems of individual listeners. Each approach gained a sanctity to the extent that it aided the awakening of deeper insight, and the consequent clearance of badly-associated opinions and emotions. Abstract truths have a limitation; they do not directly enable all students to neutralize the pictures of false values that imagination conjures up by sheer habit. Counter imaginations have to be created; and this can be easily done through stories and parables. Ancient masters knew this perfectly well. What the Buddha is said to have felt within himself, while discoursing to such people, may be taken as fairly representative of the methods which most teachers adopted. The Blessed One had taught the truth, excellent in the beginning, middle, and end; but simple as it was, the people, he thought, might not understand it. 'I must speak to them, ' said he to himself, 'in their own language; I must adapt my thoughts to their thoughts. They are like childeren, and love to hear tales. Therefore I will tell them stories to explain the glory of the Dharma. If they cannot grasp the truth in the abstract arguments by which I have reached it, they may nevertheless come to understand it, if it is illustrated in parables'.[12] This is the excellent teaching principle behind all religious stories and mythologies. People often study them exclusively from the standpoints of history, or geography, or of political or social institutions, and reject as worthless those portions that do not fit into their departmental pursuits. By such a study we ruin the chances of utilizing those books as aids in the assimilation of moral and spiritual values, which they were originally intended to inculcate.

The majority of religious people lived in their own homes, and as is the case now, contacted teachers whenever they appeared in public and gave discourses.

But as the latter, in their large-heartedness, willingly went in search of 'lost sheep' and freely taught, it was possible for sincere seekers, irrespective of wealth or social position, to meet them individually and get spiritual help. Under suitable conditions words could be minimized. For, the consciousness of spiritual unity, which the teachers habitually enjoyed, created a specially charged field around them, facilitating the transmission of faith and virtue as easily as the ordinary atmosphere permits the transmission of sound, heat, or light. The economy effected in the lifting up of values can be roughly indicated by the story of the centurion who got his servant healed through an inflow of grace. His own share in it was to carry with him the firm conviction that there was no need for Jesus to walk and go 'under' his 'roof' ; it was enough if the Master only 'spoke the word'.[13] Not unoften a devotee's need of urgent help, inwardly felt, but impossible to convey orally owing to various causes, became automatically registered in the teacher's mind and made him, either through conscious deliberation or otherwise, proceed to give the required help. The *Mahabharata* illustrates this where it describes Yudhishthira finding Krishna wrapt in deep meditation. The king wondered what could have happened in the world, necessitating such a complete withdrawal of the Lord's senses and mind from their usual spheres. After a time Krishna returned to the normal waking consciousness. He then explained that Bhishma, lying on his 'bed of arrows' had been intently thinking of him, and that he had therefore gone to his side to bless him. In a reminiscent mood, he continued to enumerate the virtues of the fallen hero. each time adding significantly, 'Mentally I was with him'.[14]

Leaving such extreme cases aside, it is possible to get from the *Mahabharata* and other Indian books, including the Upanishads, a few useful glimpses into ancient educational arrangements. We see from them that some of the illumined persons lived as whole-time teachers, while others occupied different places in the social order. The latter, among whom were eminent kings and dutiful wives, also taught aspirants as and when situations arose. As the whole of life was looked upon as a God-given occasion for realizing and manifesting perfection, there was no time-bar for starting on the path leading to it. The usual custom was to entrust fairly grown up children to the care of wise elderly men, or to retired couples who lived in 'hermitages,' which in a sense functioned as educational colonies. All the students whom any teacher could conveniently look after became members of his household and actively participated in the duties pertaining to its upkeep. These duties formed part of what was called 'attendance upon the teacher'. To show that this 'attendance' was 'more important than all other duties,' the *Chandogya Upanishad* (8.16) specially points out that formal study of sacred texts was to take place only 'during the time that is left after the performance of the duties to the teacher'.[15] The idea was that education received in such centres should be a complete preparation for leading an active and worthy life. Care was, therefore, taken to see that the students combined their intellectual appreciation of moral and spiritual values with the ability and resourcefulness to translate them into practice in their daily life as citizens. The discharge from the teacher's household could normally take place only when the teacher was fully satisfied that the student was fit to be entrusted with the responsibilities of domestic life and of teaching his children as well as those who might go to him. As princes too in general followed the same routine, provision was made in such centres for instruction in important subjects like military science.

Middle-aged people, well versed in different fields of knowledge, also repaired to the retreats of perfected souls. But they too had, like the younger pupils, to undergo purificatory disciplines and 'attend upon the teacher' in order to heighten their capacity to realize subtler truths with minimum outside help. In this work of opening up higher vision by self-effort, older aspirants, like Saunaka, 'the great householder' of the *Mundaka Upanishad,* had a definite advantage over younger ones, in whom a certain amount of playfulness was bound to persist. Hence within a short period elderly men could achieve substantial inner evolution. This can be seen from the *Prasna Upanishad,* where the sage is described as suggesting to his six students only one year's extra 'attendance'.[16] As for the variety of subjects in which a diligent student might obtain proficiency, without a corresponding improvement in spiritual satisfaction, we find in the *Chandogya Upanishad* quite a good long list given by Narada to Sanatkumara, whom he chose as his preceptor. In addition to the Vedas, this list is found to include mathematics, astronomy, logic, ethics, politics, all the fine arts, and the sciences of time and of war.[17] One could go to different teachers to learn different subjects. Sri Suka, for example, is shown as having got his wisdom by attending upon his own father, upon Brihaspati, and, finally, upon king Janaka.[18] To him in whose heart humility and purity reside, the joys of the receiving and transmitting poles of wisdom appear like equally delightful manifestations of the play of supreme Bliss.

In most of the examples cited above, there were more or less permanent establishments where the teachers and the students lived together. But available religious literature also gives us pictures of teachers who had no fixed abode. Jesus, and in his early days of preaching, the Buddha, for instance, kept moving from place to place. Attracted by their wisdom and greatness, some went into homelessness like them and plunged themselves into the pursuit of spirituality. From the start they were fully convinced that the hand that protected the birds of the air and clothed the lilies of the field would supply them with the little that they needed for daily maintenance. Freed from anxiety they could, therefore, throw themselves heart and soul into the task of inner transformation wherever they liked to stay or wander. In this small compact group the teacher played the part of a loving elder brother who had ample opportunities for moulding their personalities through graded disciplines. Love and trust provided a most enjoyable setting, speeding up the assimilation of higher values by the disciples even when their conscious attention was engaged only in serving the Master or sharing with him the alternating comforts and privations that homelessness carried with it.

Generation after generation of earnest people, from all walks of life, have thus been engaged in perfecting themselves and accumulating creative energy. It is this total inner wealth, got by the fusion of mastered values, that has become expressed not merely as the well-known religious movements of the present day, but also as the spirit of dedication behind the advances made in almost every field of human activity.

Is there any aspect of life that wisdom and illumination cannot ennoble or enrich?

3. Seeds and sowing for inner harvest

I

Everyone is creative in his own way. Even a flower show or common exhibition makes this clear. The cultivator who gets the first prize for the best rose, vegetable or fruit deserves it because of the hard work he has done in two directions. He has, first, carefully observed the peculiarities of the soil, manure and seeds at his disposal. Secondly, he has learned the art of combining them to evolve a progressively higher type of yield. What the experimental station, at the Governmental level, does is to carry on the same work in a more organized way. It has the advantages that a scientific training and a well-equipped laboratory can give to the people concerned.

To start with, the research worker gathers all the 'facts' related to the elements and forces that account for the present state, form and qualities of the object under experiment. From there he extends his study to cover all possible developments that can be effected by deliberately altering the proportions of those elements and forces. Details of the past and present states are wisely fitted into a programme for making greater values available in the future. The results have been considerable; for example, the evolving of fruits with less fibre and more kernel, or of grains with greater power to resist the havoc wrought by floods or droughts. The limit to improvement is evidently imposed not by Nature herself, but only by our own inability to know what further qualities can yet be manifested and the steps we have to take to bring them out whenever we want. In short, the given structure of anything is not final and rigidly fixed. It can be altered for the better along certain lines. Wisdom lies in discovering and controlling them.

When we come to human beings, the problem becomes complicated. A material object, a plant, or an animal stays or moves within a framework which is comparatively easy to control and observe. But it is not so easy to control and observe man. His bodily conditions can be analysed with tolerable accuracy. This has led to spectacular advances in the diagnosis and treatment of various diseases. There is also an increasing awareness everywhere of the disastrous consequences of mental tensions and unworthy emotions on physical health. The result has been a growing interest in a planned alignment of thought-forms, including memories of past events, and of emotional drives. The main centre of attention, however, continues to be the retention of bodily vigour that permits reckless eating, drinking and pursuit of sense pleasures. Most people include in the last category the freedom to indulge, as fancy bids, in falsehood, misrepresentation, greed and rapacity. On the individual and domestic scale these, as we know, end in law courts or the prison, and in wars and mass destruction on an international scale. It is only when the movements of bodily limbs and of ideas fail to synchronize with the visible outcome of deeds and of accelerated ambition that anyone ordinarily thinks of resorting to mental analysis, either by himself or with the aid of others. Even then, as soon as minimum repairs are made and his personality-car is declared road-worthy, off he goes again into his accustomed ways with redoubled speed. For he is eager to make up for the time 'lost' in the workshop! His so-called dynamic life is thus a re-enactment of the twists and turns for which his vehicle is not intended and which must cause a breakdown more rapidly next time.

II

We know the part played by sense organs. They register sights, sounds and so on. But what should be the essential worth of the experiences they help to produce in us? By looking into their structure we cannot find it out. Dazzling lights blind us for a time; so we should not look at with bare eyes unusually bright objects. Apart from such negative limits, there is nothing in the organs themselves to indicate positively the best way of utilizing their services. Here the mind steps in with its tastes, desires and plans, constantly suggesting what to see and hear. If we consider mind to be the sixth sense and continue the same argument, we can readily understand why the sheer ability to use the mind vigorously does not ensure uniform peace and goodwill. For there is nothing in this internal apparatus itself to show unmistakably what the best plans are. If there had been automatic indicators, like fixed guides, rollers, meters, or built-in view-finders as in many modern machines, there would have been no failure anywhere, no breakdown, no wrong 'shot'. Each person would have not merely planned his life, but actually lived it nobly and artistically. But the fact is that such planning and living can be done only by constant vigilance and supreme effort. To the extent that mind acts like an instrument, it does not of its own accord turn in the direction of all desirable plans and purposes. Even when shifted to any relatively correct angle, it has, as everyone knows, a most disconcerting way of slipping away from it. In such moments it exhibits a strange elusiveness and freedom which we did not consciously give it, but which somehow seems to be inherent in it. No doubt, it bends in accordance with our pull. But when we relax our grip, it resiles from us without our knowledge and lets in a stream of ideas, perhaps familiar imdividually, but surely in sequences unexpected and totally unpredictable. They come in from all directions, through ever-open doors, as it were, and monopolize the entire stage for a time to enact irrelevant and even painful scenes. There would be no serious harm if the effects of the drama end in the mind itself. But unfortunately mental movement is a prelude to the physical; and the destruction that unchecked thoughts and selfishness can cause by a chain reaction in the world of human relationships can be so serious that it may take decades to repair the damage done. What shapes it has taken whenever it crossed the limits of families and excited passions within the same country or among different nations is writ large in the pages of recorded history.

Mind as we know it, however, is much more than an ingenious and tricky instrument. Just as energy exists in two states, potential and kinetic, so mental forces too function in two levels, the sub-conscious and the conscious. They are not two separate compartments, though for purposes of study at particular stages, it may be useful to picture them to be so. For example, we may wish to know why our thoughts wander far away from any central idea or familiar 'scene' on which we decide to keep them fixed for a given time. Such an exercise, by the way, is quite helpful from various standpoints. For one thing, it teaches us conclusively that if our own mind repeatedly defies our own intention and control within a few seconds, the same phenomenon must be happening in the minds of other persons as well. What right have we to become unduly irritated when their thoughts show evidences of dodging and disobeying what, a little earlier, they said they would certainly carry out? The forces that deflect their inward currents from chalked out courses operate with no less power within our own personalities minute after minute. Systematic readings of these amazing jumps within ourselves must confer on us a twofold benefit.

First, we shall realize how difficult it is to co-ordinate right intention with actual performance, both in letter and in spirit. Secondly, the discovery of the absence of synchronization within us must knock down our superior airs and teach us true humility. For the first time, then, we shall begin to look upon the failings of others with the same sympathy and forgiveness we wish to see extended to us. Nay, as selfishness becomes attenuated, we shall learn to react in a uniformly gentle and creative manner to all discrepancies between earlier decisions and subsequent deviations from them, observed either in ourselves or in our neighbours. And that reaction will be to keep up a steady and fervent, though often silent, aspiration for the attainment of perfection.

III

Even in the matter of stepping up our aspiration, it is necessary to view thought movements from different helpful angles. It is natural to feel perplexed and discouraged when our ideas flit across the field of awareness, the transition from one to another being too quick for any preventive scrutiny on our part. If we like, we may compare them to a succession of tiny sparks, flying about in all directions in an otherwise pitch dark night. The spacing of the sparks, their formation, and the fantastic designs they trace are the inevitable expressions of the working out of a unit of force depending on burning coal and the atmospheric currents surrounding it. We know that they cannot but subside when that force is exhausted. So too, any of our emotions, aims, or values, when once rendered 'active', is capable of releasing a unit of energy that must continue to operate till it is completely spent up.

We may ask what it is that, relatively speaking, corresponds in us to the stirring of the dormant fire outside. It can be any sense impression from the external world. It can be our own bodily state or actual contact with objects. For example, we may be digging in our garden to plant a rose. This simple act can suggest other bodily movements like going to the office an hour later, or other things to be planted like vegetables for the kitchen, or even other diggings by others elsewhere, say, in a churchyard after someone's death. The possibilities are almost endless. For the world of memories across which the wave of excited thrill may run its course is immeasurably vast. Thus, while the digging goes on without a break,—our hands, eyes, and legs taking over the work like a 'transferred subject' and executing it as if under strict supervision—there may be enacted in our internal stage a strange drama in which any memory or emotion may join or from which it may drop out at any time without warning. Its plot need be nothing more than what can be developed with the extempore talks and moods of any actor likely to wake up from sleep on the slightest tremor occurring in his vicinity. Let us for convenience call this entire interlude—unwanted, unplanned, and unpredictable—a 'succession'.

Since 'succession' is a single wave, we cannot undertake anything creative till it subsides of its own accord. When it moves off, we are ordinarily startled into an unpleasant realization that our mental energy had slipped out of control for some time. We had failed to supply it with a tight programme of absorbing interest. So it had exercised its little freedom to enjoy a short flight away from the field of physical work, without seriously hampering it. The only question that ought to arise next is about the best way of utilizing the calm interval that reigns before another side-tracking movement begins. There is no point in feeling unduly sorry for what has happened. Time is irreversible and we shall never be able to relive those seconds in a better manner. Besides, dejection or self-deprecation charges the present moments themselves with an undesirable content. When repeated, this also would enter the subconscious and make the cleaning process more difficult. Wisdom lies in recognizing that all pains of the past fall outside the category of those that can be 'avoided' by any kind of effort in the present.[1] This particular experience of being made to forget the Ideal, within a minute of honestly resolving to remember it, is no exception to this rule. What we have to do is to charge the present with only those values which we wish to see firmly established in the habit level, in place of the base and worthless 'associations' now operating there.

An objection may be raised that this seesaw of remembering and forgetting too will sink into the subconscious and get a permanent foothold there by constant repetition. And if the oscillations become more frequent, as they are bound to, with the passage of time, they might cause a chronic state of mental instability—let alone the chances of strengthening virtues or attaining spiritual insight. The reply is that all corrections of mistakes, as in grammar or in mathematics, in singing or in dancing, do exhibit the features of a seesaw to some extent. But we never cut a cross-section of our experience in those fields of knowledge in such a way as to imply that each correction compelled another mistake, or that the larger the number of errors eliminated the greater became the follies that stepped in to replace them. Every correction is always a new truth perceived, a new relationship learned. Hence repetition of this process must result in the growth of a habitual outlook that arrives at the truth in every context with a minimum of effort. If we apply this principle to the problem of unwanted 'successions', we shall easily see that the internal movements must be put in a more reasonable order thus: first a unit of active remembrance; then the rest, viz. the fading of interest due to various causes like monotony; resultant waywardness in the shape of a wave; its disappearance owing to the persistence of the Ideal contained in the first act of remembrance, although in a submerged condition; and lastly, a deliberate and intelligent regrouping of old thoughts round the Ideal in newer and more attractive patterns. When looked at in this way, we shall be convinced that every wave that passed means one useless 'association of ideas' exposed and dismissed. We shall also see in every calm interval following it an excellent opportunity to rearrange available units of mental energy round the Ideal in more compact and significant ways. In the re-planting of the mental field, such intervals are the right times and the virtues described in religious books the right seeds.

IV

It is true that no two religions, teachers, or sacred books present desirable qualities in the same order. This by itself need not become a great stumbling block; rather it is as it ought to be. It is now being increasingly recognized that each person has certain inborn traits which should be kept in view in all matters connected with his development. In giving secular education, in enabling people to choose their vocations aright, and even while selecting drugs to cure diseases, the tendency is to study the peculiar characteristics different 'individuals' exhibit. We see that in some systematic manner, though unknown to us at present, a person takes from his food the pigment 'natural' for his body. What we have to do is to apply the same principle to matters relating to his intellectual, emotional, moral and spiritual growth. Where the 'suggestions' given and the 'disciplines' prescribed match his inborn tastes, his reactions will as a rule be favourable, and he will speed along the path of virtue and knowledge. Where, on the other hand, the proffered advice goes against the pattern of virtuous qualities ready to sprout up within him, it will blunt his sensitivity and hamper his growth. Thus, while every quality mentioned in a system is doubtless necessary for all-round progress, adequate provision has also to be made for the individual's 'right of choice' regarding the order in which he would find it economic to cultivate them. When he is encouraged to experiment with them, he is sure, after some trial and error, to discover the one quality which, when strengthened, will give him a steady basis for the advancement of the rest.[2] Viewed in this light, all systems appear equally beneficial, though each step as it stands in any of them may not suit everyone in an equal measure at all stages of his onward march.

Some may have a predominantly devotional type of mind. Their programmes will be centred round the attainment of the grace of God. But even they have to 'exert' in a number of ways—for example, by studying sacred books, by worshipping God with the aid of symbols, by learning to meditate on Him and, finally, by 'surrendering' themselves into His protecting hands. All these or other 'disciplines' mean intense 'self-effort,' whatever the goal or the direction may be. This 'exertion' is not to be understood as a denial of humility or of a spirit of dedication. It is the direct opposite only of the laziness and inertia that finds it convenient to invoke, in words, the gratuitous aid of outside agencies without doing anything positive or useful. Exertion is the spontaneous expression of the determination to plough one's inner field properly, select and sow right seeds, pull out weeds, and do everything else for raising an excellent harvest, helpful to men and pleasing to God.

Says the *Yoga Vasishtha:* 'Had there not been the folly of idleness in this world, what man would fail to be either rich or learned? It is by reason of idleness that this earth is filled to its utmost limit of the sea with indigent and beastly men'.[3] 'It has been seen, known, heard and experienced that success comes as the result of proper acts done from one's younger days onwards. They are indeed dull-headed who think of obtaining it from fortune or by chance'.[4] 'The mind is the soul and cause of all acts which men call the doings of destiny. It is verily the mind that makes the man. It acts as it desires and enjoys accordingly the fruits thereof: it is the same thing as destiny. Know that the mind, heart, desire, action and destiny are synonymous terms, and applied by the virtuous to the 'unascertainable soul' (evolved into these forms). Whatever the 'so-named soul' undertakes to do *continually* and *with a firm resolution,* it obtains the fruits thereof accordingly. It is by means of the activity or exertion of this soul, and *by no other means,* that it attains everything'.[5] 'If you will be guided now by the pure desires of your nature, you will be gradually led by means of your good acts to secure everlasting welfare. But if your wrong inclinations tend to lead you to difficulties, you must try your best to overcome them by sheer force of will and unwavering determination'.[6] 'The current of our desires is flowing betwixt the two channels of good and evil. By duly exerting our powers we must become its masters and turn it always to the right course'.[7] Exertion should not involve haste or violence. For even in its wayward condition, the mind is sensitive and tender like a child. The pressure used has to be steady, no doubt, but gentle. It must be uniform and gradual, not haphazard and hurried. Control must have the characteristics of an adventure or an exciting game which children like, and which enables them to face all rigours in a sports-man-like spirit.[8] It is faulty actions done in the past that appear as obstacles and temptations in the present. Judicious actions of the present, however, can help us to neutralize them and make the future bright. 'Actions of the past and the present' may thus be looked upon as 'two fruit trees growing in the garden of humanity. Of these, the one that is cultivated best thrives and fructifies the most'.[9] Hence the importance of the 'living present'.

4. Unified outlook through proper discipline

I

'Mind,' as we ordinarily know it, moves 'matter'. The simplest proof is that we can make our physical body obey us. When we resolve aright, our heavy frame clambers up a mountain side or faces destruction in the field of battle. It is not necessary that the initial suggestion should originate in our 'own' mind. It can emanate from anyone with whom we are in contact. It is thus that professors convey knowledge to students, salesmen persuade intending purchasers, or politicians gain votes. When conditions are adjusted properly, views put forth by others become accepted as our own. The result is precisely what it would have been if they had sprung up independently within ourselves. The body proceeds to express them through relevant activities.

Looked at from this angle, physical movements fall into a wider perspective in which the decisive role is played by thoughts. The world, to this extent, is not so much material, but mental. If we systematically alter the pattern of thoughts, the consequences must, in due course, penetrate into appropriate material levels. If those patterns are such as rouse unhealthy passions, like hatred or greed, the outcome at the tangible end must turn out to be disastrous. We shall find ourselves dragged into war, small or big, as history has amply shown. If and when it comes, the cultural achievements of a few decades or centuries prior to us would be wiped out within a short time. The serious question, therefore, is not whether we should accept 'matter' as the basic reality, but whether we are, in our ignorance, indulging in thoughts which must condense inevitably into painful material combinations. Do we not remember what Shakespeare put into the sorrowing Capulet and Montague? Said the Prince:

See what a scourge is laid upon your hate,
That Heaven finds means to kill your joys with love.
And I, for winking at your discords too,
Have lost a brace of kinsmen:— all are punished.

When tragedy has taken its toll, it is poor compensation to say:

...I will raise her statue in pure gold;
That while Verona by that name is known,
There shall no figure at such rate be set
As that of true and faithful Juliet.

The Prince's pathetic rebuke can be lifted from its limited setting of tragic family feuds and applied to all important contexts of the modern world. If thoughts that carry disruption in seed form are left to themselves, they are bound at their own speeds to sprout, grow up, and bear fruits to poison the very atmosphere people breathe. What is worse, these fruits will, in their turn, scatter fresh batches of seeds, thereby extending the evil to vaster areas and generations yet to come.

Every religion has some texts that enumerate injurious thoughts. Often they are spoken of as marks of a 'demoniac nature'. Through attractive stories they are presented as 'attributes of living men' who act under their influence and bring about calamities. This is a useful device. 'For it is only when we can recognize evil in visible shapes that we can take steps to avoid it'.[1] If we prepare a list of the main undesirable characteristics, it can serve as a standard of reference to check our own mental movements. That will benefit us directly, and the rest of the world indirectly in the course of our dealings with it. We may start with the general statement that people of the demoniac type 'do not know what acts they should undertake to achieve human welfare'—technically called 'aims of man,' individual and collective. Naturally 'they also fail to see from what acts they should abstain in order to avert evil'. There is a kind of ignorance which is due to want of opportunities for study. That too leads to pain. That ignorance, however, is pardonable. But demoniac people stand in a different category. They are not innocent. They are clever and have used their intellectual faculties for evolving a formula of 'power and pleasure,'[2] According to them, virtue and vice do not act as invisible causes to produce joys and sorrows, or success and failure, as religious people believe. The universe, they argue, is only the resultant of 'blind forces'. Why should not man confidently manipulate them as dictated by his ego and permitted by the range of his abilities? There is no motive power behind the universe except desire. In its most sensuous form it produces physical bodies, while in its subtle form as aggressive and ruthless ambition it leads to 'success'. Knowledge occupies an important place, since without it one may not understand how to secure pleasure. There is no need for God in this scheme; and beyond the limit called 'death,' there is nothing enjoyable for which one should practise self-control now.

Regular introspection alone can show how often we are releasing into the total world of mind the destructive forces of the 'power and pleasure' formula. Scriptures condemn the narrow and perverse reasoning behind it. They point out that it can create only endless plots and frustrations in its follower's mind, and irreparable losses and sufferings in the lives of his victims, individually or collectively. Those who adopt it violate the Divinity present in themselves and in the rest.

II

We are, however, so constituted that we can, if we so desire, deal with inner forces more efficiently than with external ones. To the extent we step up and coordinate internal values, our thoughts can also acquire a rare penetrative power to tap the sources of all-round development in the field of our daily work. That is what scriptures teach. It is immaterial, for the sake of analysis, whether we say that God regulates this acceleration as a mark of His grace, or that Nature herself does it through some of her higher laws, set in motion automatically by our sustained aspiration. Of all the people in the world,—physical culturists, artists, wealth-producers, moral instructors, scientists, and politicians, to mention only a few—there is none who stresses the value of aspiration more than the religious person does.

It may be that the aspiration advances along a conventionally accepted devotional path alone. In other words, the meditator may be engaged only in directing his love to the Supreme Being, thought of as endowed with a form and a set of qualities appealing to him most. He may, for example, visualize himself as seated in the very presence of his Chosen Ideal. By creative suggestions from within, he may next train his mental eye to gaze on the beauty of the Lord's limbs, mentioning them by name one after another. Likewise, the mental ear may listen to assuring words uttered by Him, and mental service may be offered either at an altar or in the presence of His numerous creatures. In such exercises, it is advantageous to control physical movements which divert attention from the main purpose. But mental movements of the right sort are welcomed and systematically intensified. The one vital difference is that they are focussed on the Lord as the Indweller of all. Later, even when the physical body deals promptly with its legitimate objects, the loving remembrance of the Ideal, as fully immanent in the total environment, is diligently kept up with special effort. The cumulative result of repeated endeavours in this line must be to give the seeker an unwavering conviction that he is in the protecting arms of the Divine—guided by Him to play noble, though sometimes painful, parts in the situations created by His inscrutable power. Prayer and work then blend harmoniously. While we may see him serving society, he himself views his action only as worship—as religious ritual of a different variety. He may not claim any result for himself out of it. But results are bound to follow, and in all probability in a far greater measure than expected.[3] If by watering the root of a tree, its trunk and branches are able to get the necessary nourishment without water being poured directly on them, is it not reasonable to find the welfare of everyone, including oneself, brought about by the worship of the One Being who creates, sustains, and protects all?[4]

That is how the devotee may proceed and interpret his experiences. To get a fuller view, we may turn to the sacred texts which show that certain developments, not consciously aimed at, do normally take place in the personality of the sincere aspirant. Has not the Lord been residing in his heart all the while? It was indeed under His benign look and silent prompting that the meditator could succeed in emptying his mind of attachments for petty sense objects. What is, then, more fitting than that the Lord Himself should deign, at the proper time, to light the lamp of wisdom and place it, unasked, in the chamber of His devotee's heart where stormy passions rage no more? That would be a happy consummation of his labours and self-surrender. As one commentator says, it will be the lamp fed by the oil of pure devotion, and fanned by the gentle breeze of earnest meditation. Right intuition will act as its wick, and it will remain purified by the cultivation of piety and other well-known virtues.[5]

We may account for the inflow of discrimination thus: Consciouness or the 'current of thought,' as we know it, contains within it all the elements required to make us attain perfection. We experience delays because many of our desires and purposes point to a contrary direction. Intentions and attitudes act like adapters, whether we know it or not. They select particular aspects from the general current, and in due course help to manifest them in tangible forms, i.e. in the world of the senses, including our physical body. Obstacles and pains confront us because wrong adapters have been inserted. Except sheer 'ignorance'. there was no 'reason,' especially of a 'compelling' nature, for our having 'introduced' them earlier. But since they have taught us what pains to expect from them, let us hasten to put in new adapters capable of picking up the elements that can bring about the good of all. In other words, let us make universal good the one aim of all future efforts.

Some may find universal good to be too vague a concept. We can, if we like, use other terms like love, service, truthfulness and so on instead, But even these terms have an apparent mutual exclusiveness. The resulting intellectual pictures may probably make us think that supplementary exercises would have to be undertaken later for achieving all-round perfection. There is, however, no reason for anxiety on that score. For, irrespective of conceptual limitations, occasioned by words—even the best chosen ones—the general aspiration itself will, as it gathers momentum, blossom forth in all desirable directions. It will supply, from 'outside' as it were, whatever additional qualities are required. Thus, what is deemed pure devotion at the commencement ultimately gets widened and harmonized with discrimination as well as practical efficiency in daily life.[6] This Wisdom that is gained can never be divorced from love or service, as commonly feared by beginners, or by critics who 'make no beginning' at all. On the other hand, it will come as the much needed corrective to the vicious formula of 'power and pleasure'. Henceforth it will be the province of wisdom to decide how power should be secured, what type of pleasure gained, and for whom.

III

To be convinced about the merits of a unified outlook is one thing; but the actual improvisation of disciplines to achieve it is a totally different thing. And yet, without such improvisation, theories can have no practical value.

Among the aspirants who intend seriously to make experiments, there may be some who are temperamentally inclined to put all 'controllable' changes into one big category called Nature. There may be others who are prepared to accept, in addition, categories, like individual souls, infinite in number and a Supreme Being, with different meanings attached to each term. Disputations among these groups may not carry any of them very far. It is much more profitable to see that all systems—whatever be the number and implications of their categories—agree on one vital principle, viz. that all humanly controllable mental impurities must be eliminated. Until that is done there is no hope of attaining perfection which, according to one group, is inherent in Nature's subtlest realms and, according to the rest, is either the 'essential form' of individual souls, or realizable as a 'gift' from the Almighty. It is certainly reasonable to hold that when every 'controllable' change is effected, Perfection which must be, by its very nature, beyond changes in the sense of increase, decrease, or grudging, is sure to register itself on well prepared and sensitive grounds. And all religions agree that what we call 'thought' can be made sensitive to that point.

There is, thus, no harm if thought is treated as a product of Nature's evolution, and the ultimate, unified, all-loving outlook itself as a much finer and later product. Nor is there any harm if mind also is declared to be matter of a very subtle kind. What is essential is the recognition that the means adopted now, or at any stage, must hold in seed form the properties expected to appear in developed forms at subsequent stages. If brotherhood and compassion are to be realized in ourselves and in others whom we contact, at least two main conditions should be fulfilled. To use negative terms, systematically we have to detect and root out exclusiveness and hatred from the one area ever at our disposal, viz. our 'own' current thinking, willing, and feeling. Is there anything more likely to yield to control than these? Matter, energy, and mind are all there in a 'portable' state. They follow us as an ever-open laboratory for verifying the validity of the truths we proclaim for the improvement of others. Next, to use positive terms, we have to examine thoughts till we can sense, pick up, and strengthen the virtues typical of the integrated vision that confers benefits on all alike. When once we learn to handle major inner forces, we shall also acquire the art of maintaining a single, even, and expectant pressure of aspiration, whatever may be the character of the subsidiary disciplines carried on from time to time—whether they come under the literal meanings of the negative or positive terms we use.

One point to be remembered about these disciplines is that the gains that might accrue from them will be predominantly qualitative in character and verifiable within the personality of the aspirant. They are not directly intended to produce that kind of quantitative improvement in all sectors of public life which constitute the pronounced objectives of agricultural, economic, political, or military departments of a modern State. What mental disciplines can offer is the prospect of achieving inner stability and discrimination that nothing can shake. There can be harmonization of rare alertness, absolute fearlessness, habitual trust in the goodness of man and Nature, and quiet capacity to add to the totality of benevolent infuences operating in any context. Is it a small matter to fashion, out of a well-meaning but hesitant seeker, a personality that can swing into position in its entirety at a moment's notice—one that can exert an unfailing, though often imperceptible, pull on its environment—through words and deeds at opportune moments, and through a creative invocation of highest values at all times?

IV

Among the disciplines indicated by sacred books, one of the most comprehensive is based on the study of the personality itself. We find it poetically described in the *Taittiriya Upanishad.* The approach there is fivefold. It is meant primarily for persons conversant with scriptural texts and yearning to widen their already acquired knowledge into a unified outlook. Even those who regard the habit of questioning as the special mark of modernity can profitably take up this study. They can find therein enough scope to exercise their powers of reasoning: first, to see where the original passages lead; and secondly, to overcome the inner resistances to their getting out of accustomed, narrow, mental grooves. The commentator sets the ball rolling by asking why man, and not external Nature as such, is taken as the starting point. We are free to assign reasons satisfying to us. He simply leads the way by giving the traditional reply. All creatures, he reminds us, are born out of food, i.e. matter. In other words, matter itself is so arranged as to function as a body capable of unfolding higher values. All that is in the external world is therefore 'potential' in the embodied man. Man is pre-eminent among creatures, as all can see. 'He alone is competent to perform actions (to manifest all latent powers) and to acquire Wisdom' 'The Self is expressed in its full glory only in man. He is endowed with intelligence. He speaks what is known; he sees what is known. He knows what is to come. He understands the visible and invisible worlds. He desires to realize immortality by appropriate means. Thus endowed is man'.[7] All men have not evolved sufficiently to exemplify everything that is mentioned here; but the diligent and painstaking ones can evolve. That is why scripture has taken the trouble to make so many statements.

But why should we proceed slowly, climbing up five steps, as it were, instead of making a through flight to the highest level? 'Man's intelligence is at present tied up with the habit of looking upon particular external forms as the Self—which they are not. It cannot be enabled at once to turn upon the innermost or subtlest Principle, the Self, and rest upon the Unconditioned without taking the aid of familiar conditions. Hence the fiction of a visible body is assumed for the purpose of leading the aspirant by degrees to the real knowledge of the Self—as in the case of some one who is to be shown the (crescent)moon hidden behind the branches of a tree'.[8]

Thus, in the first approach, we are asked to start with the most patent 'personal' possession, the physical body. It has its well known head, arms, trunk and the like with which we are naturally identified from our birth. From there we are to move on to grasp the significance of the entire field of Matter which may be called an unrecognized cosmic body. The little body is the name given to a temporary configuration of the matter of the bigger one, moving in and out. The comparison of the lower limbs of the human frame to 'the tail' is a poetic figure,[9] deliberately used. It shows that we must adopt the poet's eyes to catch, and take full advantage of, inward visibility. Intellectual concepts of debating philosophers will only hide the light. If this exercise is rightly carried out, the defects of inordinately clinging to the perishable body will disappear by themselves. In their place will come a constant awareness of the total fund of Matter—the basis for the birth, development, and final withdrawal of all beings in the universe.

In the second stage, the same process is repeated, starting from the limited vital energy functioning as the individual life, and gradually integrating its value with Cosmic Energy. This has to be done in such a way that the earlier outlook gained by examining Matter is not lost, but enriched and widened. It is Energy itself that is viewed as Matter, individual or Cosmic.

The third stage starts from the individual mind and envisages the Cosmic. The study will give due consideration to what is conscious to the individual and what falls outside it. This is the plane which, when properly handled, helps latent values like truth and goodwill to be made 'habitual'. And the disciplines involve the careful coordination of what is accepted from scriptures and the living teacher with one's own practices and direct perception.[10]

5. Scope of personal exertion

The fruit of following scripture, of walking in the footsteps of the virtuous and of adopting beneficial local usages is well known to all. (It is the attainment of supreme insight.) Make the yearning for it rise in your heart. Let it fill the heart to overflowing and alter the current of your thoughts till it tingles in all your limbs and leads you steadily onward. That course is what the wise call personal exertion.

By diligent exertion control the mind that is addicted to evil ways and habituate it to virtuous thoughts and deeds. This is the long and short of all scriptural teachings.

Creatively use your mind, senses, and physical body. Sharpen your power of judgement by staying in the company of the virtuous and by studying scripture. In this way lifting yourself by self-effort, attain the supreme goal of life.[1]

I

Why does the mind run after various objects? Any thoughtful person must sooner or later begin to put this question to himself or to others. Even if he gets an answer from others, he can arrive at a certainty only by looking into his own experiences. For they alone constitute the surest and most easily accessible field for experiments and verification.

The explanation that is usally given is that each object fulfils some of our needs. Food, for example, satisfies hunger. And as hunger is found to recur at regular intervals, it is natural that the mind should be devising measures to assure a constant and abundant supply of food. We may extend the idea of food and use it as a symbol of all our wants, as when we speak of our search for intellectual or spiritual food. The fact is that the human personality is so made that it is subject to different strong urges, and the external world acts as a storehouse of objects that can satisfy them at least for the time being. What is, then, more reasonable than that the mind should be engaged in seizing and enjoying objects—in planning, pursuing, possessing and storing them, and in eating them at leisure? To complete the picture, we may add the modern notion that progress is to be measured by the rise in the standard of living. To most people this means only the use of diverse costly gadgets, of articles of luxury, of mere pomp or of pageantry. And as all can see, the attempt to produce these creates further complications in the spheres of labour, raw materials, industrialization, transport, commerce, exchange, markets, and competition which has till now led only to national enmities, war, and destruction. When these have come, the standard of life for the victor and the vanquished has received a crushing blow. That may be called the external result, while internally, in the matter of emotions and values, the survivors have had to suffer more serious afflictions than they had to face before.

Even if dire calamities do not threaten us, the very recognition that time is irreversible and that opportunities misused can never be got back is bound to rouse us into self-examination some day or other. We shall then ask what we have managed to achieve through past efforts and what may yet be achieved before dreaded death steps in and removes us from the scene. In the course of such examination we shall pass in review the objects on which we bestowed our precious time and energy. They could attract us only because we had assumed, rightly or wrongly, that they possessed certain qualities and that we stood badly in need of them for our peace and advancement. The enquiry would then move on to the nature of the means we adopted to gain our objectives. Lastly, there would be a summing up: What has been the net result of the whole adventure? How far has it brought us nearer to the ideal of the man who has harmonized in himself strength, alertness, deep insight and unbounded goodwill for all? It is clear that in such a person energy, which we squander away in harmful competition, would be carefully conserved and consecrated to the service of others. And his service would undoubtedly cover the widest possible range—from little acts of kindness like feeding the hungry to the most far-reaching one which other helpers can hardly hope to render, viz. the opening, through imperceptible touches, of the inner eye of sincere men and women, so that they can afterwards take their bearings independently and march forward without falling into serious dangers any more.

II

The first question is whether we are ordinarily inclined to view any object from all the angles needed to judge its worth aright. While advising others, we may enthusiastically remind them that 'all that glitters is not gold'. But when it comes to our own practice we often ignore this sound maxim. Instead we allow ourselves to be lured by objects that have an attractive exterior. Carelessness or immaturity of understanding prevents us from noticing that, like everything else in Nature, each object which we covet has its harmful or troublesome aspects as well. So when they begin to confront us—as they must when closer relations are established—we become unnerved, dejected, or irritated. Take landed property, for example. It has its definite uses. But the greater the extent of this property, the heavier must turn out to be the responsibilities to be shouldered by its owner. Unless he works strenuously, there will be no profits; and if he ceases to be vigilant, either the property would be ruined or the profits would find their way into the pockets of ever-watchful cheats and thieves! Thus it is with every other object, the more so with subtle ones like name, fame, or influence in the social, political, religious and other fields. There is no benefit that has not its counterpart in the shapes of difficulties, deterioration, losses. pains, and dangers. It matters little whether our activities come under what are commonly labelled secular or spiritual. The law of success is the same. We have to acquire the capacity to feel and wield the invisible subtle forces that condense into visible desirable results in due course. It means, again, that we must put forth persistent efforts to know the essentials and reject the non-essentials. One big difference, however, should never be lost sight of. He whose view is bound up with perishable sense pleasures, demanded by his puffed up ego, will have a tough uphill task before him. He will have to devise suitable methods to extricate his awareness from the clamour of his ego that has as yet not known what control means. And as a purely negative withdrawal is psychologically impossible, he will have to frame a positive ideal and make his emotions gradually centre round it. The very movement toward higher values will have as an indirect result a slow but steady withdrawal from lower ones.

The main obstacles to progress come from the forces lurking in the subconscious. To the beginner, the subconscious must appear to be a most baffling source of disturbance. For when he tries to hold on steadfastly to any new idea, the old ones he has loved and encouraged so far are not likely to leave him free. No impression, once formed in the conscious mind, can ever utterly die out. When it disappears, it only sinks into the subconscious level, waiting to rise up and take its place again in the conscious field. Meanwhile, it gains in strength by combining itself with allied impressions that are already there and that enter there as deposits later. The resultant bundles or Samskaras constitute creative energy in a potential state. It is in their very nature to seek ways of expressing themselves in some physical activity or other.

There is no guarantee, however, that the programmes improvised and their timings would be consistent with moral values. They may not even have any rational connection with the actual state of affairs in the external world. Most tragedies occur because people are so obsessed with the superiority of their claims, plans, and strategy that they plunge headlong into action with no further thought. An effort falls into a context, a seed into a soil, and an idea into a hearer's mind. Unless the soil, the mind and so on are in a fit condition and pregnant with higher possibilities, the sowing, talking and other activities cannot produce any worthwhile result. On the contrary, if they are in an unfit condition, treacherous like quicksand, or ready to catch fire, the slightest improper meddling may end in disaster. That is from the side of the environment; but are we sure that the effort put in is itself of the type that can evoke a healthy response? Take talking as an example. Do we not know how often it becomes a potent source of mischief? Ideas may be compared to subtle limbs and weapons with which the speaker hits his listeners. If these fall indiscriminately, they must cause reactions of varying intensity, first to ward off the blows, and later to tie up the offender. It makes little difference whether he is ignorant or deliberately brutal. Thus even to carry on day to day affairs with tolerable safety and comfort, we are forced to study the environment and our own impulses from as many angles as we can. It is in the nature of the mind to erect thought-structures as objects and events appear in front and desires spring up within. But we have to learn the art of getting out of these structures at will in order to examine whether the foundations, walls and supporting beams are cracked or loosely held. We must acquire the skill to stand aside from thought movements, note the assumptions that have shaped their courses, and introduce such elements into the sub-conscious to weave more satisfactory patterns there.

III

One may ask: Are not thought-structures breaking down of their own accord now and then, giving us the chance to detect mistakes and rectify them? The reply is that casual glimpses of that kind are not enough. As in scientific research, we need sustained and repeated observation, and that too, under controlled conditions. Imagine children at school running all over the place and playing wild pranks. One step in observation will no doubt be to take detailed statistics of the frequency of their fights, their efficiency in grouping themselves for games or dramas, and so on. But, if our object is to bring out all their latent talents to perfection, we must start controlled experiments beginning with the employment of a competent teacher to engage them in positive ways. To this extent, the question, 'Why do children cause an uproar?' is answered best by actually putting someone to train them and thereby introducing a constructive force to attract them into new fields. When useful items are repeated, they will develop better habits, and the joy they derive by the change will make them set their faces towards virtue ever afterwards. If we then ask the question, 'Why were they so tumultuous before?,' the simple answer must be: 'Because they were not helped to get better knowledge earlier'. In other words, badness was not inherent in them. Had it been so, it would not have been replaced by goodness. On the other hand, we have to conclude that goodness was latent in them all the time, like fire in dry wood. Education brought it into manifestation, like adequate friction or the application of a lighted match to the dry wood.

Indian systems often use the example of the mirror whose reflecting surface is obscured by dirt. The meaning is that the vagaries of our mind or the defects of our character have to be looked upon as mere dirt. They are not necessary components of the human personality. If they are organic parts, like bones in the arm or the leg, they cannot be removed without impairing normal functioning of the personality. How can we then speak of its improvement and harmonization? The status of evil or ignorance is thus difficult to specify. Surely, we do find it operating now; for thoughts work havoc like storms. But saints and sages, men and women like ourselves, have controlled them and used them to realize the Kingdom of Heaven within and to bring down its blessings upon ignorant and sorrowing millions without. We find in them personalities 'freed' from evil, 'liberated' from the least touch of ignorance. They have demonstrated by their very lives that the human soul is free and full of bliss—made in the image of Perfection Itself. All scriptures stress the importance of seeking the company of the virtuous. By watching them, the aspirant easily becomes convinced that the 'natural' state of the soul is precisely what is indicated in 'revealed' books. He sees also that it is possible through graded disciplines to remove the layers of dirt that at present hide its supreme effulgence. That makes him plunge into spiritual exercises with redoubled vigour and in due time arrive at the Truth where holy texts, the example of preceptors, and his own attainment mean the same thing.

IV

In some places, Patanjali makes pointed references to the force of Samskaras. Before dealing with them, it may be proper to emphasize a point or two about the philosophy behind this mental science. Many people jump to the conclusion that samadhi or trance imply some queer device to stop the thinking process altogether. This is because they fail to grasp the significance of the technical terms used. They also fail to relate them to the transformations achieved by 'directed thinking' in Nature, internal and external. Mental training, if it is to be placed on a verifiable footing, must always keep up the distinction of a field and an observer. Every effort and its result—physical, mental, moral and spiritual—must be included in the field. The observer of it has to be accepted as invariably remaining outside it, distinct from it, and absolutely uncontaminated by it. In other words, all the movements which constitute 'evolution'—particularly the oscillation between the opposing poles of selfishness and selflessness, fear and courage, doubt and certainty, ignorance and wisdom, or bondage and liberation—must be within the field alone, and not in the Witness which must be Intelligence itself. If this is understood well, we have to find out why limitless intelligence does not manifest as such within our personality. The explanation is that the components of the personality, not excluding the thinking apparatus, contain three principles—the coarsest being Tamas, mostly found in bodily tissues; the next higher being Rajas, mainly appearing in egocentric passions; and the finest being Sattva, whose ascendancy makes us see truths face to face. Disciplines are so framed that we can react to every situation by opening the flood-gates of Sattva. Its creative energy will then flow without any hitch through the channels of the purified ego and an obedient physical frame.

What will be the consequence when disciplines are completed? A window is opened through which we can have a peep at the indescribable glory of spiritual insight. We are told that 'Knowledge becomes infinite when rid of all impurities—of affliction and (non-discriminated) action'. The essence of Knowledge seldom shines forth when it is veiled by Tamas. The activity of Rajas makes it somewhat capable of recognition. But when all the impurities are removed, Knowledge attains the infinity which is its all along. When Knowledge is realized as infinite, little remains to be known further. In fact, conceptual knowledge, picked up or used, as life unrolls afterwards, will appear like the fire-fly emitting its feeble light in the wide expanse of the sky.[2] It sheds some light no doubt, but only within a very small field. It rather serves to reveal its own littleness in striking contrast to the vastness of the unlighted area all around. This is during night. With the noonday sun overhead, what does the poor insect contribute with its negligible flicker? The point of comparison is that whatever knowledge the senses and the intellect may take in later cannot add anything to the glory of the perfected sage's illumination. But the latter will spontaneously show up everything reasonable and beneficial. The technical term for this attainment is 'Dharmamegha', the Cloud of Virtue, 'inasmuch as it pours forth showers of light upon all the virtues of things to be known'.[3]

This total development, however, does not take place without continuous effort. For even after false values are combated in the surface mind, they will not stop harassing the aspirant from the Samskara level. That will serve as their headquarters till they are neutralized there as well. This is pointed out by the commentator who says in effect: We take it that the mind of the seeker is already inclined towards discriminative knowledge. It is running along the stream of real cognitions about the eternal purity of the Purusha and about the fact of Sattva reflecting it during 'controlled' periods. Still, when such control is relaxed, i.e. when it has not become part and parcel of the personality by penetrating to the Samskara level, there must be the troublesome emergence of other thoughts, such as 'I am', 'This is mine', 'I know', etc., carrying previous attachments and hatreds. This is because of old Samskaras whose sprouting power is being currently burnt up.[4]

Samskaras, as habits, are neutral, neither good nor bad. For they only show that an arrangement exists to receive any chosen value at various times and under varying conditions and accumulate the energy of scattered dribblets into a reliable, substantial fund. It then goes into a 'safe' area of the personality. Even if we do not purposefully repeat it afterwards, it becomes capable of entering into the surface mind of its own accord to rouse up emotions and induce appropriate action. Thus while by repetition a harmful thought digs itself in as a pernicious habit, the repetition of a virtuous formula not only converts itself into a stable Samskara, but also gradually acquires the power to outvote the opposites effectively operating hitherto.

To illustrate with a familiar story: Sage Visvamitra once had lust and anger in his habit level. When Menaka came to tempt him, lust burst into manifestation in full force. But after Sakuntala's birth, he sublimated it by suitable repetition of the vow of chastity and turning the new motto into lasting knowledge or the principle of control. Later, when confronted with Rambha who too intended to drag him down, he remained chaste without any inward struggle, but flew into a rage and inflicted a severe curse on her! Soon, however, he understood what was still wrong with him, and by repetition on the idea of working for the welfare of others, sublimated the tendency to cause injury out of unchecked anger. What was the result of these new controls? Lust and anger remained as mere memories, but their seed-power or capacity to produce his earlier reactions became burnt or destroyed. If the same Menaka or

Rambha approached him again, his only response would have been to give them a spontaneous welcome and shower heart-felt blessings on them. He would see in them the very pure Self, free and perfect, that he saw in himself, the perception of their physical charms notwithstanding. Philosophically speaking, the perception of Nature in the form of separate bodies and egos has *vanished* for him. The Purusa is 'established in its own self'. The transformation of values has been achieved by the virtue of intelligent repetition.

This is the significance of the Sutra: 'By potency comes its undisturbed flow'. Says the commentator: 'Undisturbed flow comes to the mind by the deftness of practice in the generating of the potencies of checking, involved in meditative controls. In case these potencies are weak, the controlling agencies are overpowered by the strength of former outgoing tendencies'.[5] But when the flow of thought is not overpowered by disturbing energy, Rajas, and inertia, Tamas, the essence of Sattva stands with all the veils of impurity removed. The sage's 'intellectual vision, then, becomes clear with regard to objects *as they exist, irrespective of all sequence*'. 'Having reached the stage of intellectual luminosity, the wise man, no longer an object of compassion, looks upon and compassionates others—as one from a hill-top views those upon the plains'.[6]

II. WORD-POWER.

6. Catchwords for correcting perspective

I

Each age has its catchwords. They help to focus public attention on the most pressing problems of the day. Hearing them causes a quick recollection of the essentials. and a serious attempt, however short-lived, to drop the non-essentials for all-round progress. During the last War, as everyone knows, one positive formula was 'Grow More Food'. Even the supply of paper decreased considerably during the period. So most people learned to open envelopes carefully and use them again by pasting economy labels. In fact 'War economy' affected every field of life.

Brief, attractive formulas have had extensive application in times of peace as well. Some commonly used now are Export Drive, Technical Aid, Five Year Plan, Programme for Heavy Industries, encouragement of the Private Sector, Nationalization, Cultural Missions and so on. Each implies the presence of certain factors which prevent orderly development within the country or in its relations with its neighbours. A Literacy Campaign, for example, shows that large sections of the population cannot read or write, and that an organized attempt has to be made to carry education to their doors. The object is to give them the benefit others have been enjoying, and to enable them to contribute their full quota to the advancement of the country as a whole. Education too can give rise to a 'problem' if its recipients find it hard to get a decent living. The 'Educated Unemployed' will then rise up and pull down the obstructive sections of the social framework in order to make a reasonable and useful place for themselves. The significance of any catchword will be badly missed, unless we clearly see the defective condition it tries to remedy through a conscious direction of popular energy into constructive channels.

Let us have a look at some aspects of modern life. Except in a few out-of-the-way villages, people mostly live in the midst of a veritable flood of 'reports', news broadcasts, advertisements, and propaganda. This is brought into everyone's house—and even poured into his ears—by numerous agencies like daily papers and radio transmissions. A small proportion of what is thus supplied deals with the progress made in science and technology and in social welfare activities in different countries. Another small fraction is related to art, literature, and cultural movements. These have great educational value for one and all. But side by side we also get descriptions, sometimes deliberately distorted and one-sided, and at other times painfully accurate, of political intrigues, pressure tactics, war preparations, or bloody revolutions resulting from selfish group loyalties, national pride, race prejudice, or religious intolerance. In ancient times too these ugly features existed and caused suffering to millions of people. Probably, owing to difficulties of communication, the affected areas remained for long beyond easy observation and the approach of relieving parties. Nowadays, we have better and faster means of communication and transport. In a way, these enable an aggressor to swoop down upon vast areas of the victim's lands in a quickly made surprise assault. But the same conveniences can be used for the spread of information and the rushing in of the necessary assistance by friends from all over the world. Natural calamities or sufferings caused by organized violence are detected, and, within a few hours at most, presented to the reading or listening public by ever-vigilant news agencies. From the information made available hour after hour, the leading men of each country can take adequate steps either to increase its wealth and internal solidarity during times of peace, or to safeguard its and its neighbours' territorial integrity and vital interests during times of danger. Terms like 'Security Council', 'Armistice Commission', 'Refugee Rehabilitation' imply that thoughtful people have studied certain pressing problems or recurring dangers, and decided to face them promptly by combining their wills and material resources. We now hear constantly of the 'freedom of the individual' or 'the right of self-determination', because in many cases, in the name of 'vital interests' or economic and industrial advancement, there is the danger of the citizens being crushed by State policies, or of the standard of life of vast masses of people being kept below decent levels by alien domination. Each term or formula is a call for efforts to see that justice is done to all and welfare enhanced.

II

All are not equally wise or fit to be leaders. It is no use saying that, the world being what it is, some of its scenes are bound to be sensational or blood-curdling, and that the ability to be perfectly balanced must be gained, and often demonstrated, by forcing one another to the edge of a precipice. Information of this and similar kinds exercises a very unhealthy influence on immature minds. The tendency to imitate older people is inherent in the young. And we know that it is easy for them to admire and copy the swagger, the defiant airs, and the clever deceptions that unscrupulous power-seekers sometimes exhibit on the well-lighted world stage. There is genuine heroism in the steady and patient labours of people on the farms, in the workshops, factories, research institutions, and centres dedicated for the promotion of peace. Prosperity and culture rest upon the work of the willing hearts and tireless hands engaged in those places. Every passerby can see them. But to what extent growing minds everywhere are positively encouraged or trained to recognize and emulate the heroism involved in their regular activities is not easy to say. If, however, such wise guidance is not given in time, younger people will become unduly impressed with the prominence given to the tours, fights, utterances, and periodic splits and feuds of the men at the top. That which is considered 'Big' or 'High' will continue to haunt them, and they will progressively leave off what they infer to be small, low, or undignified. Experienced people know that no work is ignoble. All services are interrelated. Without production and increase of wealth there will be no material for the politician and the administrator to work upon; and without the proper functioning of the latter there will be no security for anyone, or facilities for greater output. It is in this context that formulas like 'Back to Villages', 'Dignity of Labour', or 'Production Targets' attain significance. The best teaching has become Audio-visual. With suitable material, this method can succeed in creating the correct perspective in the minds of the young and the old. It can present them with unforgettable pictures of the 'heroism' involved in creative work of every kind.

In one of our school text-books there was an interesting story of a father who announced to his children that he would arrange for them a pudding made by a hundred men. The little hearers imagined that it must be enormous in quantity as such a large number of persons would be needed to prepare it and carry it to the dining hall. They were shocked to find that it was after all just what their small plates and stomachs could hold! It was then explained to them that the pudding got its final shape as a result of various processes,— ploughing to harvesting so far as the grain was concerned, and similar relevant activities connected with the other ingredients that went into its preparation. All these meant the work of men and women who were not, and could not afford to be, present to share the pleasure of eating it. It was not necessary for the story-teller to specifically mention that the same drama was responsible for the production of their dress, their home, their furniture and indeed of everything else that made living possible and profitable for them in a quiet place.

This brings us to the importance of education in its twofold function: the giving of information, and the training in the art of acquiring a correct perspective in every context. Of these, information of all types is available in abundance, though poverty may prevent many from gaining access to the higher variety which requires heavy payment in cash. To get a true perspective is difficult. For emotions distort values, and even if the truth is seen intellectually, uncontrolled emotions prevent its expression in the field of action. Each individual and community must coin its own catchwords to indicate and facilitate the controls appropriate for different contexts.

III

All desire pleasure and power, Bhoga and Aisvarya. These cannot be acquired without a certain amount of intelligence. So we seek Knowledge. But we want it to be practical and useful—belonging to the kind that promises us the enjoyment and influence which are our immediate goals. We proceed on the assumption that Knowledge has no independent value; its function is to be the willing servant of pleasure and power.

We see, however, that the frontiers of knowledge are widened by research workers whose sole object is to discover the truths related to the fields which interest them. They do not pause from their labours—often life-long and risky—to indulge, as we might, in speculations about possible personal gains. They unreservedly leave it to others to incorporate their discoveries into various devices useful to the 'consumer' and certainly profitable to the 'manufacturer' Enquiries can be brought under two main divisions according to the motives behind them: First, what is the truth? Second, How can subtle principles be made useful and profitable to the individual and to communities? While both are necessary, it is clear that if the energy that ought to go into pure research is reduced or cut off, the position of utilities would become stagnant and, in the long run, untenable. This holds good whether the truths sought belong to arts or science, economics or politics, matter or mind. Ancient Indian sages made a distinction between the search for Truth, Satya, and the hankering for results, Phala—not because truth cannot be made useful, but because craving for personal gains drains away into a totally different channel the energy that should properly be used for opening up the way to Truth embracing matter and mind, the individual and the community. Pleasure-seeking and Power-seeking being universal, the Truth-seeker can confidently close the utility tap in him and plunge whole-heartedly into the pursuit of Truth, relaxing himself periodically to teach others whenever he 'strikes' anything worth knowing. The formula has been: Know and Teach.

We do not ordinarily integrate with the rest of our programmes this awareness that the pursuit of Knowledge for its own sake is—and if we want, will be for us also—an independent and highly satisfying activity. Looking in another direction, we find that much of the misery of the world has been due to the unchecked exercise of Pleasure and Power by individuals and groups having an initial advantage over others. The remedy lies in making Knowledge the dominant factor of our lives. That knowledge has to include, among other things, such questions as: What are the most dignified ways of acquiring pleasure and power? What is the limit individuals should voluntarily impose on themselves? How are pleasure and power to be shared among all, so that all can gain from the superior talents of the fortunate few? What is this human personality which has so much creative ability locked up within it? From the creative energies that can be 'released' from it, is it not possible to move into the Supreme Source of all virtuous impulses in such a way that there can be a general intensification of intelligent activity in greater numbers of people? In other words, what is that Wisdom gaining which every item of knowledge, emotion, and action falls into its proper place in a harmonized whole? Such a Wisdom must be the most purifying agent we can possess. In accordance with the degree in which we have it, it will behave like a fire and reduce selfish action to ashes, or like a raft prevent us from sinking in the ocean of sin and sorrow. Depth and co-ordination being its very essence, it is not right to add restrictive adjectives to it and irrevocably label it, as some critics do, as 'mere contemplation', 'mere idealism' or 'mere individualism'. It has to be considered as 'Full'. Jnana or Wisdom cannot fail to grasp the scope of a process like contemplation or the furthest reaches of what constitutes an individual. We. as individuals, may be found at different levels in its pursuit, at particular times; but Wisdom, as a Goal, must be such that it cannot be transcended or exceeded. When Indian sages spoke of it (Jnana, or Vijnana), they meant it in its fulness, as the most necessary corrective to the dangerous formula of pleasure and power. Modern problems may be different and more complicated than ancient ones. But the need for this all-inclusive Wisdom to dominate our thoughts and actions remains the same—if not more urgent.

Anyone conversant with driving a vehicle knows that mastery of driving can never mean the rigid holding of the steering wheel in the same position all the time. The tilting of the vehicle owing to ups and downs on the road, however slight, will demand corresponding adjustments to the right or left to maintain the correct direction. The pursuit of Truth, both in the attempt to understand it and to express it in daily life, may be looked upon as a sort of driving in difficult areas where traffic rules are seldom observed. We know how often our good intentions are thwarted by our own faulty observation, emotional out-bursts and deep-seated prejudices. What happens in us happens in others too: and where many people rush about with clouded vision at the same time, collisions are bound to occur. The remedy lies in each one of us keeping in front a chart for ready reference. After some efforts we can learn to use it for adjusting ourselves properly to every situation confronting us internally or externally. In other words, we must cultivate the habit of quickly estimating two things: the forces playing outside our personality, and the variety of reactions we can make to them. We have to ask ourselves: Which of these alternative reactions is harmful and which helpful to us and to others—which tends to Lokopakara and which to Lokapakara? Out of the different values that can be upheld now, which is impermanent, Anitya, and worthless, Adhama, and which relatively permanent, Nitya, and worthy, Uttama? After making a thorough survey we can then decide what is to be done, Karya, and what avoided, Akarya. In the beginning, every new lesson must appear difficult, but practice will make it easy. As Patanjali points out, success is speedy to those who are intensely energetic in their application to the means of achievement, *Tīvra-samvegānām āsannaḥ (Y.S. 1.21).*

IV

When Mahatma Gandhi was shot, one prominent person remarked that the world is not yet safe for saints. In fact the conditions which caused the death of Socrates and Jesus have not materially altered in spite of our progress in many directions. But undeterred by the possibility of personal sufferings, man carries on the pursuit of Truth and of noble ideals. In each generation there arise some whose sole aim is to transform themselves into embodiments of unwavering love and goodwill for all. During the process they are sure to shed all fear, and with it, the thought of defending themselves or of retaliating, as we understand such terms. If, as scriptures say, they see nothing but the Infinite inside and outside, if they become fully identified with the creative heart that not only brings into existence millions of human beings, but also opens their inner eyes when the time is ripe—then they will not swerve even by a hair's breadth from enlightened love to worry about the preservation of their physical bodies which must perish sooner or later. Each one of them will let himself float in the midst of world forces, caring only to awaken those found sleeping yet. What does it matter to him if others learn from him or cut his body to pieces? That represents one aspect of the ideal—the man of vision who loves and teaches.

Nature does not remain unresponsive as often as someone approaches perfection. She throbs, as it were, with readiness to supply vitality to every movement to use his insight for the welfare of all. It is the duty of thoughtful people to take note of the great man's message as well as the potentialities and needs of the hour, and to create the machinery to translate his powerful 'drive' into appropriate aspirations, struggles, and achievements of the masses in general. Herein comes the importance of the administrator.

Indian writers used the term Brahma and Kshatra to denote, not particular hereditary castes, but the roles of the teacher and the ruler, both representing a single ideal—true Illumination or Wisdom. That Wisdom is surely not the monopoly of those whose inborn talent, when released from egocentricity, spontaneously expresses itself in teaching and preaching. It is possible for anyone to use his (or her) daily duties as a parent, trader, official or ruler, or as wife and mother, to attain the heights of illumination, and express it afterwards through the faithful discharge of those very duties, and through whatever taste for art, literature, or the sciences is possessed as special gifts from earlier days. Persons in all these stations of life form limbs of a vast administrative network. To supplement the parent's work and adjust it to a wider standpoint there is the officer; and to supplement, correct, and co-ordinate the officers' actions there is the King or the Head of the State. It does not mean that the spiritual preceptor's work does not have an administrative side at all, or that people in the domestic or political spheres do not instruct anyone in their respective fields. But such shares are limited. The main purpose of a comprehensive study being to see how Wisdom can be *gained* and its results *shared,* the dominant functions alone are taken into consideration,—like the storage of water in a reservoir, and the construction of the canal system in the department of irrigation.

Old Indian books extolled the Brahmarishi and the Rajarishi the preceptor-saint and the administrator-saint. Each paid due respect to the other. The work of promoting public welfare was divided between them. This could never be achieved if either of them tried to exclude or dominate the other. The only correct method was to wholeheartedly coordinate their respective functions. Through stories, narrated from the platform or presented as dramas from the stage, society managed to keep alive this tradition of a happy synthesis.

We may turn even to one of the minor scenes in the drama, *Shakuntalam,* to get a general ideal of the cordiality that existed, and should exist, between the ruler and those whose wealth consisted of their self-control alone.

Two hermit youths are introduced. They admire the radiant, but trust-inspiring, form of Dushyanta. One of them says in effect: This is what we expect in a king who is after all little different from the Rishis of the hermitage. No doubt he is in the household stage. But it is an Ashrama, like that of the retired teachers—the support and the source of benefits for all. He has his purificatory action, Tapas, too. He accumulates its virture by dedicating his energies for the protection of his subjects. Control, certainly, is the essence of Tapas. The only difference we can note is that before this one's title, Rishi there is the addition, of the term 'Royal' to mark the way in which he exerts himself for the welfare of all'.

As in duty bound, they have brought some fruits as a present to the king. He rises up from his seat, salutes them, accepts the gift, and asks for 'a command'. What they have come for is really to seek the aid of the king to drive away the disturing elements prowling about in the neighbourhood. So they start by saying that the elders have 'a request' to make. Quickly, but sweetly and indirectly, the king corrects them and asks, 'What do they command?'

Mutual respect expressed itself not only in the actual work of protection when occasions arose, but also in speech and general demeanour. And this could have become habitual only because reverence and the spirit of co-ordination must have formed parts of an integrated vision accompanying and sweetening every movement of thought while within a prayer-hall or outside it.

Brahma-Kshatra combination is a model that the modern world can profitably accept and extend to any other relationship that it considers vital for the good of all, whether individuals or communities.

7. Uplifting power behind words and acts

Learn to make the whole world your own. No one is a stranger, my child; this whole world is your own.

—Sri Sarada Devi

I

In a way, 'words' constitute the greatest 'output' of the present day. They issue out in an unbroken stream, daily and hourly, from the press, the platform, and the radio. Like oblations in ancient fire-sacrifices, they are poured into the eyes and ears of millions, young and old, all over the globe. Some portion of it deals with developments in art, literature, science, technology, and social relations. That has real educative value. A larger portion is devoted to advertisements of various sorts. Many of them are skilfully combined with tempting pictures, the object being to stimulate in unwary minds an insatiable craving for articles and satisfactions that drain away earnings without conferring any corresponding inner refinement. On the contrary, they make the 'consumer' fancy that by procuring them he is maintaining a higher standard of life and thereby ennobling himself, his family, and also his country! Lastly, there is an undue proportion of details about the ups and downs of politics, national and international.

Since events in one country cannot but affect others sooner or later, it is necessary to know what they are, so that the public can remain alert, estimate possible repercussions in their own areas, and learn to take adequate steps to meet emergencies. In economic matters, particularly, there is likely to be great confusion. Even well-meaning people may find it hard to follow the intricacies of food crops, foreign exchange earners, import licences, national development schemes, or State loans. Easy explanations of these topics must always be welcome. For, what most men feel directly all the time is that they are being taxed more and more heavily, while their demands for higher wages and salaries go unheeded, or are sternly frowned upon by those in authority. The strength of a democracy depends upon the willing cooperation of the masses in peace and in war. This can be secured more easily only when each citizen is helped to see relevant facts and the connection between them and the policies adopted by the men at the top.

But as no human arrangement is free from drawbacks, the very supply of predominantly political news, mostly ill-assorted, leads to undesirable consequences, especially in the minds of the young. Imitation comes to them, naturally and 'untaught', in their impressionable years. If they are to grow up into broadminded persons whose love of power will be subordinated to the claims of their country's and the world's welfare, they should be able to see unmistakable expressions of this supreme virtue not merely in the talks, but also in the lives, of acknowledged leaders. The spectacle of prominent men pushing their differences to the extent of forming bitterly hostile parties and struggling to overthrow one another through false propaganda or sudden armed uprisings—whether shown in films, described in novels, glorified in histories, or exhibited in actual life—can have only one result upon youngsters, to whatever race or religion they may belong. That will be the introduction into their outlook of an incurable habit of talking in one way while planning to act in a totally different way, when they think the time is opportune. It would never strike them to seek, and move into, the common ground where all available creative forces can be made to meet to exert their maximum healthy pressure. Instead, they would take delight in magnifying points of difference and harp on them till splitting and subdividing would assume dangerous proportions in society. Divergent views do indeed acquire a compelling value when their upholders succeed in giving them a concrete shape in institutions and services that change people's lives for the better, at least in a few limited fields. In such cases, words and arguments become indicators of tasks accomplished, and not weapons of offence to be brandished before opponents in the political or any other arena.

The proper scope of words may be said to be twofold: First, from the side of any 'leader', they must be charged with the mature experiences resulting from programmes undertaken for public good, in some sector or other—of errors eliminated, and of successes attained. That gives an added meaning to proposals for extending activities to fresh spheres as a next logical step. Secondly, in the case of people at the co-ordinating level, their words must be aimed at assembling and intensifying every positive element found in social movements, irrespective of party labels or affiliations, or of race, creed, or even of language. The motto has to be to collect all the good within reach and resolutely turn it to practical use.

II

This is nothing but a special application of the old saying that hatred cannot be conquered by greater hatred but only by greater love. Evils in society cannot be removed by a greater evil in the shape of a fight to a finish among different sections whose programmes for constructive work are yet mainly in the realm of promises and differ from one another only in minor matters. It will not be possible for the leader of the victorious group to have a free hand in carrying out his schemes undisturbed. For the increased output of hatred and intolerance is sure to affect his own side sooner or later. The usual form in which it breaks out is one of struggle for 'leadership,' as we see around us at the present day. All competition is not bad. But this particular form will not be at the level of actual service, to heighten its quality and widen its range, but to seize posts of command and occupy places of honour. This danger applies equally to all fields of activity—political, economic, social, and religious.

The fact is that enthusiasm and determination, which most men have in abundance, are not enough to ensure a smooth flow of peaceful and constructive work. For they are often misdirected into harmful channels owing to the slow infiltration of uncontrolled ideas and emotions. If we allow our mind to dwell exclusively on the glory of too general an 'end', like public welfare, dynamic life, or prestige of an institution, we are likely to skip over the need to examine the purity of our motives or the justification for all the steps we take. We may say to ourselves: 'We want speed. What is the use of waiting till doubters wake up to notice our immediate requirements? If they oppose us, we shall crush them into position like loose and broken metal under a road-roller. The loss of a few foolish heads does not matter since our ideal is all right. The fittest alone survive and go ahead; how else does evolution work?' Such a calculation comes because of an unconscious clothing of the ideal in a soldier's dress. We fail to discriminate and see if social-education is the field for the employment of unmixed military tactics. An engineer's insignia appear more appropriate; and they may be profitably put into two or more 'extra' arms of the deity representing the ideal. For we know that when we wish to tap sources of oil that do not become exhausted very soon, we invariably take the assistance of engineers.

They come with their special instruments and set about drilling deeper, and in all promising places. Social enthusiasm has its wells too; and the question is one of technical skill—of training available hands to reach right depths, bring up the precious contents lying there, and construct a network of canals to convey them to conversion plants. Our approaches towards problems, our reasonings, and our plans are dominated by 'figures of thought', akin to figures of speech. Discrimination is needed to estimate their moral worth and their appropriateness in different contexts. The next part of discipline is to learn to detach those which cause splits and fights and to introduce others which promote unity, co-operation, and loving service.

Democracy involves respect for the individual. The right to vote or to stand as a candidate at elections is one form in which he can enjoy equality and freedom. What is more important is recognized to be the creation of educational and other facilities, so that he can develop his inborn gifts and grow up to his full stature by using them for the benefit of society. Nowadays, there is also a greater tendency to look upon under-developed communities as units that deserve aid from richer and more advanced nations and groups. No doubt, old habits and vested interests frequently raise their heads and threaten this freedom, as they used to do before. But such attacks act as signals for the starting of counter-movements, however feeble and ineffective at the moment, to awaken the moral conscience of cultured people all over the globe. The result may be declared a failure when judged from the standpoint of immediate material gains. But every step in mobilizing higher values, through the exercise of discrimination and detachment, leaves freedom's citadel less vulnerable to future attacks.

Even in the day-to-day life of an individual, it is easy to see how discrimination and detachment play an important part. Take, for example, the business man or even a soldier. Each of them has to exercise these supreme virtues to solve the problems confronting him. What is essential and what is not; what obstacles can be overthrown, what must be bypassed; what factors are helpful and how can they be brought together? These and many more questions each one has to ask himself when making serious calculations. His success or failure depends upon the facts he manages to observe and the scale of values he keeps while fixing his plans. Imagine the case of a manufacturer who puts into the market a low-priced vehicle fitted with such conveniences that its purchaser cannot help praising it wherever he goes. To some extent the maker's success is assured. For he has more than balanced the sacrifice he makes in the selling price by gaining the services of his customer himself as a free advertiser. Most of the difficulties of argument and propaganda disappear if a person knows how to touch the strong and noble elements in the character of every individual he contacts for howsoever short a time. The magnitude of the sacrifices men can gladly make if their sense of dignity and responsibility is correctly roused is seen clearly from what happens in a battlefield. How quickly the hearts of soldiers are filled with courage and heroism when the commander tells them briefly that the country is confident that its freedom and honour are perfectly safe in their hands! To obey orders, whatever they are; to gain the objectives assigned to him; and to use in its pursuit the maximum discretion possible within the limited area where he works,—these alone occupy each man's attention henceforth. All other considerations are detached and shut out.

III

The field of battle has some unique features. There the pressures from the external world are the greatest and most dangerous. The choice before the soldier lies between a grim fight or a cowardly retreat. In the latter case, he ruins his country, his relatives, and also himself. What is there during peaceful times to compel such concentration, devotion, self-sacrifice discrimination and detachment? 'Great occasions rouse even the lowest of human beings to some kind of greatness, but he alone is the really great man whose character is great always, the same wherever he be'. 'If you really want to judge of the character of a man, look not at his great performances. Every fool may become a hero at some time or another. Watch a man do his most common actions; those are indeed the things which tell you the real character of a man'.[1]

Here we wish to record the substance of an intimate talk between a highly respected elder (for convenience referred to as A.) and some youngsters whose character became moulded through their intense love for him. They had seen A. at close quarters in various contexts. They had been profoundly impressed by the way he once recovered stolen rice during a Flood Relief work. While they fell asleep, being tired, A. kept awake. As he had suspected from the start, one of the boatmen stole half a bag of rice and jumped ashore with it soon after midnight. A. promptly gave chase till the culprit had to escape capture by throwing it into the swollen channel. By the time the young men woke up and ran up to him, A. had dived into the water and brought up the precious grains. Earlier than this, as also later, they had seen A. holding positions of authority, yet occupying a corner of the cowshed and even cutting grass for the cattle. This was remarkable since, in his youth, A. had trodden the path of violence with the hope of freeing the country from foreign yoke. So, one evening, after making him describe how he used to practise sword-play in secret, the juniors asked him:

Q: The freedom you wanted to get through violence has not yet come. When you spend much of your time looking after purchases or tending cattle, don't you feel at heart that your life has been a waste?

A: Service in any form is never a waste. I have not given up even a fraction of the desire for the country's freedom. Why should I? But that freedom is now fitted into a well-integrated ideal of service to the Lord, manifested in or as man. To get freedom and, what is more, to retain it, millions of services are needed. You know that in the case of an army, if in time food is not supplied, if transport breaks down, or if the signalling section fails to arrive, soldiers in front lines fall into danger. If any service is omitted, the total plan cracks to that extent. So, in our case too, cows, milk, stores, and food are as vital as study, preaching, money collection, accounting, or correspondence. Do you imagine that siting in a particular room and issuing orders is more honourable and important than serving guests or sick people? If any other work is assigned to me, I shall certainly do it to the best of my ability. But when I am relatively at leisure, why should I not look after these animals whose milk you and I drink? By my doing this, and your doing other things for which your education and youthful energy make you fit, are we not helping to maintain an institution doing excellent constructive work of the type required not only in the struggle for freedom, but also in the task of preserving it when got? If out of many such organizations, at some future time, a batch of large-hearted people take the final steps to win the country's freedom, do we not form essential links in that chain; and do we not have the satisfaction of playing our part in the glorious task?

The young men began to see the deeper implications of what they had gathered from books about terms like discrimination and detachment. They were shining through A'.s words and acts. There was no rejection here, no retreat, no sense of frustration. Each action was significant and immediately satisfying; every thought, hope, and plan had its proper place in a comprehensive Whole embracing oneself and others, knowledge and action, politics and religion. One more question remained to be asked.

Q: In that rice-bag incident, long ago, you risked your life for some handful of grains. The thief could have stabbed you to death, or the swollen canal could have become your watery grave!

A. Had I not risked this life many a time while following the path of violence? Surely it was more noble to risk it for the sake of serving the afflicted, wherever found. Besides, whose is such rice? Every grain belongs to the public, or to the needy, or to God who appears in all forms. When every drop of blood in this body is God's gift, or His own Self in that form—whichever way you wish to classify it philosophically—can I hesitate to shed it, if need be, to save each grain of that rice, so that it can be put to its rightful use? The same thing applies to every pie of public funds. The essence of worship consists in knowingly and reverently offering to God what is really His own, in whatever form He chooses to take it back.

Here was a perfect harmony of discrimination, detachment, and divine service. Discrimination showed the highest values to be upheld, as also what deserved to be dropped— the latter being all selfish considerations, worry, and fear. While A.'s body took up all kinds of work, his mind remained steeped in holy thoughts. He spoke very little; but his words never failed to inscribe themselves in the minds of those who wished to benefit by them.

IV

The words and arguments of one person may at most persuade another to accept an intellectual pattern for work. They do not by themselves give him any power to master the emotions that oppose his intellect. That power flows naturally from the personality of the speaker only if he has gained complete ascendancy over his mental movements. Just as the words of a man with intellectual clarity tend to cause similar clarity in the minds of his hearers, so too, the simple talks and acts of service of those who have perfect self-control become the means of helping sincere aspirants to achieve similar controls in themselves. The enormous output of 'words' at the present day can produce tangible results on a wide scale only when those who employ them grasp this principle and themselves acquire the habits they ask others to cultivate. And this means hard discipline.

Here we wish to refer to a few of the quiet utterances of Sri Sarada Devi, the Holy Mother.[2] Her external life was cast in a very limited framework, like that of any ordinary Indian woman. But wherever she was and whatever she did, there was such an outpouring of energy all around her that sincere seekers could draw freely from it and transform their lives. Her words acted more or less like the low whistle, or call, or a gentle tap with the stick, of an experienced shepherd who loves his flock as much as he loves himself. They made the hearing units respond without fail, beat a retreat from far-away grounds, and slowly start on their homeward path. Many came to Sri Sarada Devi with disorganized thoughts and harassing memories of a violent or shameful past. She led them forward, sometimes definitely like a teacher, but mostly like a mother. She roused their self-respect, and helped them to put an effective watch on their mental currents as a preparatory step to centre them round the sublime Ideal represented by Sri Ramakrishna, and ultimately direct them into spiritual perfection and acts of loving service.

To a certain disciple who was worried about the 'vision of God' and who may be taken as a representative of many others who felt like him, she replied in a few words which covered three important points. The first was a statement in unmistakable terms that the 'vision' can come only through His grace. The second explained the need for 'spiritual disciplines such as worship' to remove 'impurities of mind' and make the mind fit to receive the truth. She used just those illustrations that could easily awaken the feeling of holiness. 'As one gets the fragrance of a flower by handling it, as one gets the smell of sandalwood, by rubbing it against a stone, in the same way one gets spiritual awakening by constantly thinking of God.' Last came the correct stress on self-effort: 'But you can realize Him right now, if you become desireless'.[3]

In this self-effort, 'duty', no doubt had a very important place, 'it keeps one's mind in good condition'. 'But it is also very necessary to practise Japa, meditation and prayer'. 'Such practice is like the rudder of a boat. When one sits in the evening for prayer, he can discriminate as to whether he has done good or bad things in the course of the day. Then one should compare the mental state of that day with that of the previous one'. 'Unless you practise meditation in the morning and evening side by side with your work, how will you know whether you are doing the desirable or undesirable thing?' The hearer ran to the opposite extreme and remarked, 'Some say that one achieves nothing through work'. She was quick to move the rudder to hold the balance. 'How have they known,' she said, 'as to what will give success and what will not? Does one achieve everything by practising Japa and meditation for a few days? Didn't you notice the other day that one person's brain became deranged because he forced himself to excessive prayer and meditation?' Then she added significantly, 'The intelligence of man is very precarious. It is like the thread of a screw. If one thread is loosened, then he goes crazy'. 'But if the screw is tightened in a different direction, one follows the right path and enjoys peace and happiness. One should always recollect God and pray to him for right understanding'. 'How many are there who can meditate and practise Japa all the time?' 'My Naren (Vivekananda) thought of these things and laid the foundation of institutions where people would do disinterested work'. 'Are these' works 'in any way less spiritual than austerities?'[4]

Her method was always the same. She talked to reinforce the good thoughts of one person or to correct the wrong moods of another. Or she spoke to create self-reliance in a third who was doubting his own competency. But whatever the context, she tried to help others to establish a proper balance among their various faculties—those involved in work, detachment, and devotion. Discrimination being the most direct means to get and preserve this balance, she emphasized it in a number of ways. One example will suffice. 'What does one become by realizing God?' She asks, 'does he get two horns?' She herself answers: 'What happens is that he develops discrimination'.[5]

Her own inner harmony and poise passed into the hearers through her simple talks and motherly acts. In this sense, she 'taught' all the time, even while making betel rolls or husking paddy as much as when someone went to her to be formally instructed. Indeed, she herself answers: 'What happens is that *'mould'*, to enable 'many others' to 'make their images from it' according to their different needs.[6]

8. Scriptural aids to end 'afflictions

O Rama! Stop not your inquiry regarding the well verifed and lucid doctrines of the successive teachers of mankind till, in your own consciousness, you directly realize the Supreme Self, appearing in myriads of forms and yet absolutely pure—transcending the imperfections associated with time, space, or materiality.

As is one's knowledge so is his thought and such is the mode of his life. It is by means of ardent practice of concentration and reflection that the mind can be turned to the right direction.

In the light of what I understand, this world is the Abode of the Immortal Self, but in the sense in which you take it now it is non-existent. So the meaning of the words 'Thou' and 'I' refers only to that Supreme Reality while, according to you, it refers to the individual self and its embodied state.[1]

I

Conscious action has some definite aim. In most cases, where people are immature, it is the craving for sense enjoyment that makes them act. But as a person becomes culturally advanced, he begins to care less for the mere gratification of his senses. He remains on that level only to the extent that is needed to support his life. He may still not have a balanced view of the object of earthly life itself. He may imagine it to be the performance of various actions entitling him to subtle and lasting joys in a heaven, as popularly understood. It is here that sacred books can give him substantial help. For they tell him that the best way of utilizing our earthly sojourn is to dedicate it for the pursuit of Truth.[2]

One thing is clear. Ordinary actions, bodily or mental, being limited, their results too must be limited. How can we expect a gain out of all proportion to the energy spent? If the delights sought are of a gross material type, Nature even in her kindest mood cannot produce situations to confer values of a superior order. Inward aspiration and its outward manifestation, as a playback by Nature, must more or less tally. Thus, if our longing has been for coarse pleasures and it has not been exhausted, it must 'evolve' into an appropriate 'life-period', to give us just the joys and sorrows that can compel us to recast our aims. Indian philosophical systems have a way of putting our body and the field of its work into a single bundle. They then teach us to look upon this unit as the inevitable expression of creative forces accumulated through repeated yearnings. When not spent up through actual experience or sublimated through proper discipline, these forces behave like an unseen root. In due course, it sprouts up and grows into the tree of life. Bodily death cannot destroy this root. In this respect, it stays on like a suit pending in a court of law. The legal personnel may be transferred and the annual summer vacation may cause the court itself to be closed for a couple of months. But the suit has to be taken up for disposal by the new officers when the court reopens.

This principle is contained in an oft-quoted Sutra of Patanjali: 'If the root exists, it ripens into life-state, life-period, and life-experience'. The main idea is that anything short of spiritual illumination constitutes 'affliction'. The technical term is Klesa. We get it in its simplest form as the mental resistance put up by past loves and hatreds to any virtuous thought on which we try to fix our attention for a given time. In fact, the 'mind-wanderings' supply a clue to the residue of old longings waiting to take concrete shape. It is called Karmasaya, the vehicle of actions. Here by action is meant all our plans and struggles which, at their worst, cause pain—to be taken as a preparatory step to right thinking—and, at their best, culminate in enlightenment. One may ask: What is it that makes this vehicle or group of Samskaras move into manifestation? The reply is that it is the presence of Klesas. General ignorance of spiritual verities stands in the position of their fertile breeding ground, while egoism, love, hatred, and clinging to 'life', as we ordinarily know it, are the harmful weeds growing plentifully on it.

The relation between the Karmasaya and the Klesas is illustrated by pointing to the cultivation of paddy. 'The rice in the paddy has the power to grow only under two conditions: First, the chaff should be sticking to it; secondly, the seed-power should not be destroyed by frying etc,' 'So too, the vehicle of actions can grow into ripeness only when afflictions are attached to it and when the sprouting power has not been burnt up by the highest discrimination'.[3] But as long as insight has not reached the penetrative sweep of 'Dharma-megha', the unspent balance of false notions must fructify into 'life' in its three aspects, 'state', representing the level of evolution; 'period', meaning duration, and 'experience', characterized by pleasure and pain. The rationale of control is this: 'Pleasure and pain follow in the wake of attachment and aversion. They never exist in separation from them, indeed they cannot. Nor is it possible that if anyone is attached or averse to something, he will not feel pleasure and pain respectively when in contact with that thing. For this reason the mental plane becomes a field for the production of fruits of actions only when it is watered by the stream of afflictions'.[4] When afflictions are eliminated, the vehicle of actions and the whole of Nature may be present, but there cannot be the type of 'contact', or capacity to produce action or reaction, which we associate with ignorance or 'bondage'.

II

Systems differ in the way they frame their categories. But they all agree that by certain disciplines human awareness can function unaffected by limitations felt to be real now. The Yoga system holds that the Self, Purusha, is ever free and perfect. What prevents us from realizing this truth is the entertainment of various false notions. This is called Ignorance. It is removable by its direct opposite, right Knowledge. A difficulty may arise since one of the afflictions is stated to be egoism. This makes unwary people jump to the conclusion that the final and, therefore, the subtlest exercise must be the questionable one of knocking out the principle of 'individuality' itself. A little patient analysis will show that 'egoism', like 'experience' or 'enjoyment', is a technical term, not to be understood literally. We shall take an example. A teacher, let us say, sees his student, hears his questions, and proceeds to give him detailed answers. The senses and reasoning powers of both participants in the discussion are kept alert and actively working. Now, how does the Yoga system 'post' these movements? It says that the Selfs of the teacher and the student are distinct, but equally free at the time. They are, in fact, of the essence of Knowledge. Seeing, hearing, and thinking are movements in Nature—in the elements that have constructed, and now operate, the relevant instruments. Intelligence runs parallel, as it were, to even the minutest of these planned and controlled throbbings. It is this that makes consciousness of objects and of actions possible. The teacher's discrimination is perfect. So he 'sees' clearly that 'his act of teaching' and 'the student's process of learning' are slightly varying configurations of Sattva, stirred into 'evolution' by the mere 'presence'—not 'contact'— of the perfect Self behind each 'individual'. The student does not 'see' this, but a little more cleaning and focussing of his inner instrument will help him to do it. That there is, or can be, any 'contact' is a false notion. It disappears when disciplines are completed. When this is over, says this philosophy, let perfection as the 'result of a human effort' be 'posted' in the column of Nature in the same way as we did with ignorance, to start with! It is only the 'supposed individuality' that is 'lost'. not the real one, the ever-free Self. For this Self, being immutable, stands in a class by itself, neither to be brought in nor given up.[5] When this truth is 'seen', what happens to actions like teaching, or even simple perceptions? The reply is that all those that are consistent with wisdom will continue calmly and efficiently, but the sage will be 'habitually' aware of the fact that it is Nature that contributes the 'moving' part, and the Purusa the 'intelligent' presiding part. Words cannot carry us further than these ideas.

Let us now look into another book, the holy *Bhagavata* Here the categories of the Sankhya and the Yoga systems are beautifully subordinated to the Supreme Reality, Impersonal in one sense, but intensely Personal in another. The subtle and gross worlds are described as coming out of Him, getting their sustenance from Him and finally merging in Him. It is also shown that whenever virtue declines among mankind, He incarnates in suitable forms and restores the balance, setting a model for human conduct in various ways. The goal of our life is to receive His grace, to love Him, to direct the activities of our senses and mind to serve Him and His children, or to be one with Him. It matters little whichever concept is taken up, provided it is pushed to its farthest limit in actual practice. It is repeatedly stressed that nothing is gained by trying to go up and down to different worlds in search of petty joys. They come unsought—as pain and misery do—being natural consequences of our past acts, made available by

Time of inconceivable speed.[6] The only thing a wise man should seek to obtain is the undying bliss that consists in pure devotion to this Supreme Person. By setting eyes, speech, or thoughts on something apart from Him, we shall be only letting ourselves adrift. Our mind will then never, or nowhere, find a resting place. It will be knocked about like a vessel by boisterous winds.[7] This is the main teaching. This is presented through a number of interesting topics arranged artistically. Primary and secondary creation; duration, maintenance and withdrawal of the created worlds; 'desire for action' and 'history of the Manus' are seven of the ten subjects to be dealt with. The other three are: accounts of the Lord's glories, Liberation, and the nature of the Supreme Abode to which all beings must resort. The principle for this arrangement is thus indicated: 'Great men endowed with wisdom explain the first nine topics only to give a clear and true knowledge of the tenth. In doing this they sometimes employ direct expression and at other times bring out the purport by other means'.[8]

III

In the Supreme Reality there cannot be the distinctions of male, female, or neuter that we make in classifying insentient objects and sentient creatures. But since we have referred to a book that presents Divinity as having male characteristics, it is fitting that we should now turn to some sections of religious literature that depict Creative Power as the Mother of the Universe. Viewed through our mind and intellect, creation appears at bottom to be a change of forms permitting a progressive manifestation of the perfection which we associate with Reality. Power and Pleasure are facets of that perfection that appeal to most people even without anyone to instruct them. Experience has shown that a bare Power-Pleasure formula is capable of producing unscrupulous aggressors and injurors of humanity. It is no wonder, then, that we find religious books and teachers emphasizing the importance of Knowledge. It acts not only as an inescapable corrective, but also as their most welcome harmonizer. To a great extent names, forms, and rituals depend upon the tastes and conveniences of different worshippers. Still we may state in a general way that the three facets, Power, Pleasure, and Knowledge are symbolized pre-eminently by Kalika, Lakshmi, and Saraswati. The two latter are usually represented in their 'mild' forms—Lakshmi issuing from a giant lotus and holding smaller lotuses in her hands, and Saraswati seated near a peacock and having in her hands a stringed musical instrument, a rosary and a book. This is not 'adequate', in a sense, to assure afflicted humanity that Grace implies also a 'destruction' of the sources and instruments of wickedness. For life is a sort of fight; and without overcoming the dead weight of inerita or the storms of egocentric passions, none ever succeeds in establishing peace or stability, external or internal. To suggest this 'dynamic' side of life, meditations have been prescribed wherein Lakshmi and Saraswati are endowed with 'martial Forms, with multiple arms to wield weapons coexisting with a third eye or some other 'sign' to imply spiritual insight and the promise of Grace.

India being a vast country, we have to make

due allowance for variations in local customs and traditions. Yet in some points there is remarkable similarity, as for example in the general outlook on the creative value of mental disciplines and in the acceptance of religious stories and rituals as their surest foundation. Thus, during the period when the sun passes through the sign of the Virgin, it is the custom throughout India for devotees to conduct the worship of Divinity as the Mother of the Universe. In many parts special altars are erected or images made and installed as part of the rituals. These include, wherever possible, reading and exposition of *Devimahatmyam*—seven hundred verses dealing with the glories of the Mother as expressed during three of Her main incarnations. There are excellent hymns introduced in the midst of the narration of thrilling episodes. They provide material for philosophical reflection and loving meditation.

There are contexts where celestials are asked to choose a boon. Since their spheres and our world are closely interdependent, they exclude none from the scope of the boon they ask. They pray that if the Mother is pleased, She may so act that all the worlds derive full benefit and become objects of Her Grace.[9] What a beautiful suggestion that when we get a suitable opportunity, or even make our plans for action, we should remember not only our personal gains, but also the welfare of our fellow beings!

All, however, cannot be stepping on the same rung of the ladder of evolution at the same time. Initial equipment at birth, the problems that crop up, the reactions made, and the lessons learned must vary with different individuals. Hence no two persons are likely to agree as to what their immediate requirements are. Each will secretly wish Grace to come in the shape of the satisfactions uppermost in his mind. This is well brought out by the 'covering' story in *Devimahatmyam*. It speaks of a king and a merchant who got into the same plight. Their relatives and dependants usurped their positions and drove them out. The sage whom they approached for comfort became their common teacher. They heard the same stories, went to the same river-side, performed the same devotions, got the same vision of the Divine Mother and heard from Her the same question: 'What is it that you want?' But then came the vital difference, ignored by all who try to enforce uniformity in spiritual matters. Prompted by his unfulfilled desires, the king wanted not only to get his country back but also to enjoy undisputed sovereignty in the life to come! The merchant, on the contrary, who had had enough of the pleasures and pains of 'ownership' and whose eye of discrimination had thereby opened, asked only for the Highest Knowledge.[10] The moral is clear: each gets the blessing he really desires. It may be Enjoyment, it may be Liberation. Grace even gives the devotee the right to choose.

IV

We shall end our brief reference to *Devimahatmyam* with a glance at some of the meditations prescribed in it. The general principle is that we should not attempt to drive out from our mind the idea of any object whatever on the ground of an imaginary distinction between the secular and the spiritual. For everything is Her creation and has some characteristic property where Her Power can be seen at its purest.[11] In fact it is She Herself. It is, therefore, enough if we turn our attention reverentially to that quality which is unmistakably prominent. For example: In the house of the virtuous it is She who appears as prosperity. Likewise it is She alone who comes as affliction where people persist in wickedness. In the hearts of sincere seekers She descends as discrimination, while self-controlled sages receive Her as abiding faith. We can find Her even as the natural modesty of those whose good deeds have made them take birth in decent cultured families.[12] This is one approach that is possible.

The question may arise; Can we not discern Her presence as common factors in all creatures on whom our thoughts might alight? One beautiful hymn is devoted to give us the answer. A part of its refrain contains the expression: 'In all creatures'. The simplest noticeable phenomenon is undoubtedly the presence of life-energy everywhere. We see it as cohesion, attraction, repulsion, or as organization into complicated structures and diverse functions—as all that we mean by growth and evolution. In man it also enters into the wonderful phases of rational thinking, spiritual insight, art, compassion and the like. The common principle is Consciousness, latent or patent. Look at the strange state of deep sleep. It is as if the main switch for differentiated behaviour patterns is put off by an unseen hand. That hand is really Hers. The tiger then drops his tigerishness, the sinner his evil propensities, and the sage his successive thoughts of goodwill. Then, again, look at the compelling force of hunger. It is She who remains in all bodies as the craving for food. It is She who also digests what is eaten and converts it into relevant tissues. What better way is there to give food than to place it as an offering to the Indwelling Spirit? Or there is the expansion of heart born of parenthood, particularly of Motherhood. What is it that a mother will not sacrifice in order to protect and rear up her young ones? Acharya Sankara has written some remarkable verses pointing out that a son may turn ungrateful sometimes, but a mother loveless never. How can she stop the spontaneous outburst of love within her heart? She will remain an embodiment of patience and forgiveness as well.[13] It will not be difficult for us to find many more common factors with equal value for meditative exercises.

Lastly, all evolution must take place in Time. Units of Time are essential parts of the framework that makes our thoughts follow one another in a series—the first set for making experimental moves, the next for checking results, others for readjustments, and still more for attaining habitual certainty and calmness. Looked at from this angle, it is wrong to expect Mother's Grace to come after our spiritual disciplines. For it is really She who dances as Kala, Kashtha and other moments of Time,[14] Is it not our rare privilege to accept Her knowingly in those very forms and then proceed thankfully ever afterwards?

9. Picturesque reminders

It is the similarity of some particular property that is the essence of a comparison. A complete similarity between the two things compared destroys their difference and makes them one and the same thing.
When comparisons are properly understood, there arises the cognition of the One soul treated of in the scriptures.
Supreme Peace comes from the realization of the significance of the great scriptural statements like 'That thou art'. It is this Peace that is called Nirvana.
By proper and continuous practice, a person arrives at the point where the statements of scripture, the teacher's instructions and his own experience perfectly harmonize. By virtue of unbroken efforts to make this certainty abiding, he becomes established in the realization of the Supreme Self.[1]

We experience thoughts within ourselves and objects outside. It is the principle of consciousness that makes us aware of these. Consciousness is therefore often compared to a lamp. It helps us to get a clear view just as a lamp does in the matter of locating articles at night. It is understood that the comparison should not be stretched too far. For a lamp must have a stand or a handle; it also requires a wick and some oil. And these are not included in the comparison, unless indeed we suggest that the physical body corresponds to the stand, and the tissues that supply energy correspond to the materials for combustion. There is, however, a limit to the addition of such details. For the things compared are after all unlike each other in many respects. Ordinarily, there ought to be no need to draw pointed attention to this restricted applicability of similes and parables. Why is it, then, that certain texts and teachers make special mention of it?[2] It is because the topics discussed by them fall outside the province of the physical senses. Unless cautioned, beginners are likely to miss true relationships and assume connections where none actually exists.

Take for example the concepts we try to form about the Reality behind man and Nature. Religions have described It as God the creator and saviour. The very word 'creator' calls up familiar associations from the world of the senses. When paintings or houses are 'created', their 'creators' have to depend upon an adequate supply of materials like colours or bricks. Does God too stand in need of a fund of materials outside of Himself? What could that fund be, and who could have created it? Besides, if everything is subject to the law of causation, what must have been the condition that prevailed before the emergence of the creator himself? These are some of the questions that crop up in the course of any serious inquiry

I

That scripture does is to give us new concepts and suggestions. We are told that 'the intellect in all men is by nature competent to know the Self aright. At present, however, it is polluted by such faults as love for external objects. This has made it dull and impure, like a stained mirror or muddy water. It is unable, as it stands, to grasp the essence of the Self, though it is always near'.[3] What is required is to clarify this intellect by replacing false or sectional views by more valid ones and organizing them into a unity. One text puts aspirants into three groups, high, average, and low. Those belonging to the first have already purified their minds to such an extent that a bare word from a teacher is enough to make them open their inner eyes and see the light. The other two are not so advanced. To them mental purity can come only as a result of graded disciplines. And scripture, out of compassion, has pointed out various exercises so that they too can, by carrying them out faithfully, attain the vision of the highest Spiritual Unity.[4] Very few will have the presumption to place themselves in the first group. It is safer for most of us to join the ranks of the 'low' and climb up steadily, mastering the reactions according to the directions the sacred books have laid down.

There are people who neglect reformation of their character and give undue importance to the limited period of time that they devote for fixing their attention on holy subjects. This will not help much. For they are pulling the oars while their boat is still tied up to posts with strong ropes. The temporarily excluded or ignored fancies will not only pester them during those moments, but also lead them to crude selfish activities at other periods. These, in their turn, will sink into the sub-conscious and come back to the surface mind with added force later. The first duty, therefore, is to keep a strict eye on the character itself. Every opportunity must be taken to neutralize known defects by sedulously cultivating their direct opposites. Even this is not enough. For mental restlessness is at bottom due to an anxiety for results. In this respect the modern man stands in a bad plight. Living in an age of mass production of consumer goods, he is always driven by the desire for quick and enormous gains. He is likely to treat philosophic discipline as a sort of short cut for manipulating subtle forces as he likes. So scripture sounds a clear warning. The motive of producing effects on the material or subtler levels must go. This does not mean the effects would not follow, or that those levels would dry up for want of focussing attention directly on them. Thought itself is creative energy in its finest form, and the intention to realize Perfection acts as a mould into which that energy flows. If we do not prepare rival moulds through false values—through doubts, hatred, malice and the like—there is no reason why Nature should not manifest healthy thoughts in appropriate 'condensed' forms, according to her own law of cause and effect. If Nature is insentient, she cannot oppose us through passion or prejudice in spite of her being independent. If, on the other hand, she is subordinate to God, thoughts centred on God cannot fail to make her forces fully co-operate. Whichever way we look at it, anxiety must give way to complete trust. Technically speaking, the desire for rewards must be 'rooted out'.[5]

II

For what do we expect to get rewards? Surely, for our prayers in the religious field and for all our plans, talks and deeds in the physical, mental and other fields. It is remarkable how ancient sages used certain brief formulas to include in one sweep the entire range of causes and results. *Ābrahma-stamba-paryantam:* 'From Brahma down to a clump of grass' is one such well-known formula. We can look at its implications from two standpoints. First, from that of 'evolution' as ordinarily understood: Here we pass from the less to the more developed and refined. Grass stands for plant and vegetable life which is capable of assimilating food and organizing 'bodies' that have growth, maturity, seed-scattering arrangements and, finally, death. This group is mentioned in the formula as it marks a stage higher than earth and other elements which do not manifest such structural peculiarities. They are, nevertheless, implied, as without them, forming the basic agency to supply 'matter' or 'energy', not even a blade of grass can ever thrive. Next comes a big jump. It goes right over all reptiles, birds and animals — of which man is the one with considerably expanded powers — to the most evolved Being we can conceive of, viz, the creator, Brahma. Gods, deities, angels and other 'celestials' are superior to men, having got their status as a result of their aspirations and struggles as men. The idea is that if their inner essence is sufficiently purified, they will go higher in rank, function as cosmic controllers, and ultimately realize their oneness with the Supreme Reality that is beyond time and, therefore, perfect and unevolving. But if their purity is below a certain mark, they will — after enjoying the subtle pleasures which they desired as a reward of their efforts (which they meant to be causes initiated by themselves) — revert to the human condition to acquire further discrimination and detachment. This type of oscillation will be compelled upon them till their mental purification is complete. This is Samsara — helpless, inevitable rotation in the area of causes and results, brought on through sensual cravings and false identification. It is from these weaknesses and lower values that freedom is sought. Within this sphere of evolution, the highest result that can be obtained is shown to be the position of Brahma. In him there is the harmony of power and wisdom needed to create the bodies, physical and mental, as well as the environments whose interaction is the basis for evolution. And his own discrimination being unwavering and 'all-faced', he remains vigilant, impartial, and totally unaffected by the beauties and terrors that are found in the created fields and that tempt or frighten individuals yet on the march.

From the second standpoint, we see movements from the opposite side — from the bigger end as it were. Since it is impossible to observe all aspects of existence together, we have to assume at least one of them to be precisely as we experience it in our waking state. In this instance we shall take Time to be as it appears to us — a succession of moments, each associated with a state of Existence. First, then, is Perfection itself, non-moving, ie, neither increasing nor decreasing, and impossible to describe adequately in words. That must be the antecedent condition to any motion. Next is motion, or creation. Of what kind? One scripture very suggestively says that the Source of all created things 'increased' or became distended, being desirous to create the world. Things beyond the senses can be conveyed only through comparisons taken from objects or events of the sense world. So the commentator gives illustrations by saying: 'As a seed when sending out the sprout, or as a father gets an expansive thrill with the prospect of having a son, so the Reality, Brahman, became extended by Its omniscience, by Its never-failing knowledge and Its power of creation, preservation and withdrawal of the universe,'[6] The product of this first movement was Annam, food—what is eaten or enjoyed. This is a technical term of the ancients, meaning the Unmanifested (Avyakrtam), common to everything that is to evolve. It is not yet evolved, but is just ready to take shape. That shape, the next in order, is Prana, ie, Hiranyagarbha, the common Cosmic Entity, endowed with the power of knowledge and activity of Reality. It is the sprouting seed, as it were, of the totality of assumptions, desires, actions and of creatures. It is the Soul of the universe. In painting and sculpture, it is represented as a Deity seated on an open lotus and having faces turned in all the four directions. From it, or him, evolved that which is called 'mind', the principle whose characteristic is volition, deliberation, doubt, determination and the like. From mind were manifested, in succession, the subtle elements like Akasa (with sound as its property) and the different worlds like our earth. In these last became manifested 'actions'. This term implies actors, programmes, causes and their corresponding, inescapable results. It is clear that, in this view, the more comprehensive and powerful entities are the earlier ones and the grosser, weaker, lesser entities the later ones. If by evolution we mean progress, refinement, harmony, and stability, we do not find it in the movement from Cosmic Mind to the field of physical causes and results. We find it only in a greater approximation to the Perfection that lies beyond the field of causality — beyond the influence of Time as we now view it.

III

The Scripture helps us in our progress by contrasting the whole field of evolution with the Perfection that is its invariable background. The contrast is expected to serve a twofold purpose. First, our attachment will be removed, for we shall be made to see the pettiness and perishableness of the results we get from our labours. Secondly, we shall be impressed with the glory of the Conscious Principle that abides equally in all that we see and touch, but which we sadly miss by indulging in sense-bound fancies and trying to actualize them on the physical plane.

Often this contrast is brought home to us by representing the world of modifications as an unusually vast tree with its root above and branches spreading downwards.[7] Can we not by examining the panicle of a flower succeed in ascertaining the root of the tree on which it grows? In a similar way, we are told, we can examine select areas of this tree of the universe and find our path to its life-giving Source. The comparison to a tree is fitting also because the Sanskrit word for it, Vriksha means something that can be felled. We can fill up details using our own imagination, along the lines indicated by scriptural texts themselves or by the commentator of olden days. For example, we can picture the subtle bodies of all creatures as the trunk of this tree. We can trace 'the pride of its stature' to the sprinkling of the waters of desire. The numerous objects grasped by the sense organs and the intellect can be looked upon as its tender buds, holy texts as its protecting leaves, and virtues like the making of gifts and doing penance as its lovely flowers. We may equate living beings, from Brahma the creator downwards, to birds that have built nests on it— from which they can have access to its fruits, some of which are no doubt sweet, but the majority bitter. Naturally, it always echoes with 'the tumultuous noise arising from dancing, singing, instrumental music, joking, patting on the shoulder, laughing, pulling, crying and exclamations like 'Leave me!', 'Leave me!', caused by mirth or grief, as different situations crop up.[8]

This description is promptly followed by the instruction that we should turn away from this sapless field of modifications. We should then by a steady search gain access to the Root of this tree which is ever pure and bright, i.e. resplendent, being the intelligence of the Self. That, indeed, is Brahman—'greater than all'. That is immortal, being true. No modifications can equal It, or go beyond It, just as a pot cannot go beyond the clay out of which it is fashioned.

The main difficulty in gaining access to this Root is that It has no definite characteristics by which our senses or our concept-making faculty may grasp It as It is. One passage speaks of It, using two series of epithets. It is said to be 'That which cannot be perceived, or seized; which has no origin no properties, no ear or eye no hands or feet; and yet is eternal, diversely manifested, all-pervading, extremely subtle and undecaying; which the intelligent can cognize as the Source of every element and creature'.[9] 'It is from fear of Him,' says another passage, 'that fire burns, the sun shines', and dreaded death runs about snatching even the mightiest creatures away from the field of their work. Like one with the thunderbolt uplifted in his hand, this Supreme Reality stands as the firm controller of the competent protectors of the world. Their activities thereby become well regulated, like those of servants trembling from fear of their master. The text hastens to add that it is our duty to realize Him before the fall of our physical frames.[10] This Great Treasure must be got in this very life, with this very body and this very mind, with energies purified and properly focussed.

Some may be curious to know how this single Entity could manage to bring forth this varied creation without the aid of materials external to Himself. One text gives a few illustrations.[11] Look at the common spider, it says; does not this creature spin out its thread, and later 'withdraw' it, without depending upon an outside fund? An objection may be raised that the spider does so with the motive of catching its prey; does the Supreme Soul have any such felt need? To answer these and other doubts, two more examples are given: that of medicinal and other plants that grow from the earth which does not gain anything through their agency, and that of hairs growing upon the bodies of living men who do not suffer serious loss even if many of them fall off! The succession of illustrations is meant to facilitate easy understanding of the import and to see that we do not stray far from the right track in detecting the point of comparison.

IV

The Scriptures prescribe various meditations. They are based on the principle: As we think so we become. 'Whoever meditates on Brahman as possessed of certain attributes, himself becomes the possessor of such attributes'.[12] The essence of meditation is the guided repetition of a desired mental wave. It is well known that a repeated idea gradually enters the habit level and exerts its pulling power from there even when there is no further attempt to repeat it as part of a daily exercise. Nay, it operates without a break even during sleep— and after death, unless suitably neutralized earlier.

We usually proceed by making a distinction between ourselves and 'others'. In the latter term we include not only other creatures, but also the store of elements and forces out of which all bodies, physical and mental, are produced and sustained. In the language of the sages, we draw a line between the 'Self' and the 'Not-Self'. Without this demarcation, our talk will become unintelligible and daily activities almost impossible. But, unless we take steps to cross this as well as other conceptual barriers, the creative powers inherent in our thinking cannot flow freely and evenly everywhere. Meditation, wisely performed, can help us to skip over assumed divisions, for the personality, with its Conscious Principle and its obediently turning instruments, is the happy meeting ground of the Self and the 'apparent' Not-Self.

Thus, if an aspirant finds himself struggling on the physical level, he is advised to put his own body and all other bodies into one big mental bundle and improvise a formula for cultivating an equal attitude towards it in its entirety. In an 'identifying' way, he can train his emotions to feel: 'I am all this'. or 'This is all mine'. Alternatively, in a 'detaching' way, he can develop the idea: 'I am none of these; I am the Pure Self'. A devotee can enrich the feeling by introducing the note of self-surrender to the Lord, and say to himself: 'I am His child, dependent upon His grace, not upon this bundle of matter.' This same principle is to be adopted when the aspirant is no more obsessed with the compelling force of 'matter', but is yet caught up in the whirlpool of vital energies. He will, then, identity himself with, or detach himself from, the whole fund of energy of which his personality is an infinitesimal part.

Next, in accordance with his competency and the instruction of his teacher, he will take up an appropriate meditation starting with his own mental field, till the related barrier of individuality is transcended. One text suggests that he should picture the head, arms and trunk of this extended mental body to be composed of different sections of scripture itself. What does scripture, mean in this context? The commentator says, in effect: Any section of scripture, say Yajus, is the name for that product of mind arrived at through the senses, ear etc., and through thinking on the organ of utterance, on sounds, letters, words and sentences. All hymns represent knowledge of the Self; and Mantra or the formula to be chanted and whose meaning is to be thought of 'is a name for a function of the mind' and, therefore, capable of being repeated. If this meditation is properly done, our basic idea of any living being must be radically altered. We must become fully aware of Reality as an Ocean of Self-knowledge, spreading its waves in all directions in the forms of scriptural texts, examples, ideas and values. All creatures on whom our eyes or thoughts alight must appear to be floating on these brilliant waves—the wise ones consciously identified with them and drawing inspiration from them, and the rest woefully unaware of their glory, nay, often indulging in totally false notions and suffering in consequence, like persons under the influence of a terrible nightmare.

No wonder one text exhorts: 'Awake, Arise!'

III. REFLECTION

10. Synthesis through deeper reflection

It is useful to watch the course of knowledge within ourselves. For the sake of convenience, we may restrict our observation to a limited period, say, ten years, already over. Probably, some of us have gained experience in two or three fields of activity within this time. A fairly versatile person may even be able to sum up his progress thus : first, by utilizing spare moments, he cultivated art for which there was an inborn taste ; secondly, he entered the University and took a degree in science; lastly, he secured a post in the Administrative Service and was quickly promoted for his tact and thoroughness. Whatever the details may be, it is clear that the 'power' to understand and master subjects is capable of considerable extension, provided the conditions necessary for the continuance of formal learning can be fulfilled.. As a matter of fact, however, beyond a certain stage most people do not try to increase the number of subjects for detailed study. In the first place, none can, or need, waste his time to become proficient in many matters. In a world of varied talents, it is more economic to seek the services of experts, wherever available, than to rely upon one's own stock of information picked up at random. There may be also other factors that prevent a serious penetration into new fields. For instance, there may be a natural distaste for or fear of certain subjects. Or there may be a conviction that settling down to some quiet business, with a steady income, has become very urgent. The 'power' of knowledge is then employed for making a survey of the forces in the midst of which we happen to live. This leads to a co-ordination of all acquired knowledge, related to the home, academic training, art, social obligations, and possible careers. We mentally hang them up in front, like coloured threads for weaving, and combine them according to desired patterns to fashion the unique fabric that constitutes our life. Insufficient observation or faulty calculation may result in our omitting or wrongly combining some of them. This may cause losses or defeats, or our progress may be held up for a time. The remedy lies in learning to direct the 'power' of knowledge to various new aspects of the forces playing in and around the personality and in attaining greater depths of comprehension. Surprises and shocks will then be minimized; and in the handling of every situation higher values will be preserved.

Let us go back to the example of the versatile person. It may, at first sight, appear that art and science on which much effort was bestowed may be of no further use to him. But his inner progress really lies in recognizing the danger of shutting out any aspect of the personality from the active concerns of life. Excluded aspects create an undercurrent of disappointment, a feeling of something secretly gnawing at the heart at all times. He can avoid it only by widening his outlook and by assigning a proper place to his love of science and art. If he has the will, it will not be difficult to find out ways to infuse their essence, namely, aesthetic refinement and devotion to truth, into all his relationships, domestic, social, and official. He can also use his spare moments to get into circles engaged in scientific and artistic pursuits. But whatever adjustment he makes, its soundness can be tested only when fortune's wheel turns in its usual course and he finds himself caught in an environment, unyielding and definitely hostile. That is really Nature's signal to him to regroup his energies round an Ideal that transcends the claims of his limited self,—an Ideal that embraces the best and the noblest virtues, not only gathered from the text-books of his student days, but also heard of from traditional accounts and directly witnessed in the lives of contemporary men and women acknowledged as truly great. Each one of us has to create an intellectual picture of such an Ideal, and continue to hold fast to it till perceptions, memories, plans, loyalties, and personal prospects revolve round it and ultimately stand transformed into its vital organs and extended limbs.

II

Tastes and temperament have a great share in regulating the initial approach to the Ideal and in its clarification and expanding application in the light of growing experience. But whatever course the refinement may take, certain characteristics are sure, and ought, to be present in it in an increasing measure. They would be accommodated in such a way that the perfection of one blends imperceptibly into those of the rest. The total feeling awakened would be one of certainty that its attainment includes everything worth gaining,[1] and that in it lies the fulfilment of all duties,[2] towards oneself and others. The achievement of ordinary aims depends on external factors, like the situation of wished for objects in particular settings and the proximity of people favourably disposed. They act as causes. The desired condition is their result. But the Ideal cannot be dependent upon something else and at the same time be 'perfect'. It must stand in its own independent fulness, unaffected by human failings, yet silently impelling all towards maximum development by its luminous presence. It must be such that each human heart can function as a reliable instrument to be tuned to it—especially when the intellect is convinced about its uniform existence everywhere and in all beings,[3] and sincere steps are taken to 'pick up' and 'amplify' those elements in thoughts and emotions that are consistent with its supreme poise and grace. Its vision implies the complete transformation of the personality into a clean and promptly responsive medium for its manifestation in daily life. In its all-encompassing truth, the movements that mark the birth, growth, and illumination of beings would fit in like innumerable triangles drawn with sides of varying lengths within any given circle—in this case, the sacred Circle of Wisdom and Glory. The thoughts, words, and actions of one who realizes such an Ideal cannot but be conducive to the welfare of all without distinction. People will not shrink away from him through tear of ill-treatment; nor would he think of avoiding them[4] due to considerations of self-defence or dread of physical pain. In the drama of life enacted in the benign light of this Ideal he would play his allotted part with zeal and satisfaction. He would do his best unaffected by praise or censure. Nothing that enters into the Ideal can be unworthy or discordant.

There is no hard and fast rule as to how these different values can be fused into a single harmonious unit. We know that when the proper materials are supplied and left undisturbed for a time, Nature, by using her own technique, produces many-sided crystals capable of responding to light in special ways. Something similar takes place in the case of anyone who presents to his mind the requisite values through appealing symbols and maintains a steady level of faith and devotion. The values so presented blend spontaneously, purifying the personality, filling it with an inward light and permitting the unhampered flow of creative energies through it. The cultivator manures the plant and pulls out the weeds around it. In a way his duty ends there. It is the function of the power inherent in the plant to combine the food materials in the correct proportions, arrange its own growth, and put forth flowers when the right season arrives. Mental discipline follows more or less the same law. What is within our conscious control is to make a selection of thoughts, memories, arguments, and affirmations which can aid in keeping up the feeling of holiness at as high a level as possible and in replacing the usual doubts and anxieties by quiet trust and unwavering thankfulness. Time acts like an invisible slope. With the rise in momentum of controlled energies running along it, the stage is set for the coalescence of values into an immutable, many-sided awareness. The last 'movement' which marks this 'welding' is not a voluntary act like the introduction of different thought-patterns to reinforce devotion or effect self-surrender. It takes place by itself when voluntary efforts remain at the peak of intensity, with no place in it for uneasy flutters or impatient peeps.

III

The one prominent object that helps us to distinguish ourselves from others is our physical body. How we came to possess it and when the process of 'assembling' it into its present shape will end, cannot ordinarily be understood. Nor is such knowledge of any great importance in leading a noble life. It is enough if we remember that as long as it stays, it is the most faithful instrument to enable us to go forward. When we speak or act, it functions like a willing tool; and when our talks or deeds create reactions, favourable or unfavourable, it records them, often receiveing a good portion of them directly on itself. As one poet wrote,[5] the tip of the tongue is the abode of the Goddess of Prosperity. On it, of course, depend also friends and relatives. But the trouble is that, in its liberality, it gives equal accommodation to the agencies that cause imprisonment and even death! But whether the result of our behaviour recoil on our own bodies, or become distributed widely in the external world—the domestic sphere or the country at large—we learn from them unforgettable lessons that go to strengthen our virtues and eliminate our faults. In thus preparing the ground for the attainment of wisdom, the body constitutes the main 'field of action', Karma-bhumi. The 'world' (Loka) of the aspirant is, in this sense, not an extensive area filled with creatures, but the commencement and continuation of bodily connection. It is, technically, 'birth', Janma,—the basis for observing and comparing actions and their consequences in the broadest sense.[6] The view taken is that life is an opportunity for a series of experiments culminating in wisdom, and its expression in loving service. If the programme is not completed before the bodily structure breaks down, kind Nature will surely erect another for us. But why should any sensible person put forth half-hearted efforts and find himself badly in 'arrears' while the rest of the world has been marching on diligently? 'That which naturally takes a long time to accomplish can be shortened by the intensity of the action'. 'Given rapid growth, the time will be reduced' and perfection got 'in this very life',[7] 'before the fall of the body', as one scripture puts it'.[8]

The body is, indeed, a portable laboratory, housing the experimenter, an assortment of probes, sensitive meters, calculating frames, and special sections for co-ordination of results and modification of plans. By good fortune, it is so constructed that it can withstand a variety of shocks, and repair minor damages caused by rash ventures. What junstification is there for injuring it in the name of spiritual pursuit? It is a tragedy we sometimes look upon different parts of this establishment as stumbling blocks and break them down by self-inflicted tortures! Exercises should be only 'purificatory' measures—not punitive expeditions. Tapas has sometimes been translated as 'asceticism' or 'austerity', implying cruel vows of self-denial. It is refreshing to see that one saintly writer explained it as 'the taking of food (surely, not only physical) that is pure, sufficient, and conducive to welfare', *Hita-mita-medhyasanam tapah.*[9] Another raised the question: 'Is it not possible that certain practices, although undertaken with the idea of aiding purification, can be actually such as to upset the harmony of the fluids and tissues of the body ? How can such practices be considered aids ?' He himself answered it by indicating the general principle: 'So much, or. that type, of purifying action (Tapas) alone is to be carried out as does not cause disorder to the vital functions of the body'.[10] Put it in positive terms, we may say 'all those steps are to be taken that ensure a steady supply of energy of the requisite kind, at all times'

Scientists and medical men have their own special approach to the study of the physical body. They observe its various parts and tissues, and find out the laws governing their growth and their treatment during disease. The approach of the spiritual aspirant is different, but there is no need for him to come into clash with those laws. Rather he stands to gain by following them. They are included in the wisdom that he seeks. In fact the pattern of reflections does not require any modification even if a hundred more details are discovered about the formation of cells or the nature of glandular secretions. For they all come under the subheading, 'body'. They cannot affect the basic position taken in reflection, namely, that the body itself is produced out of 'food' (Anna) meaning by that term the entire world of 'matter' found in the 'external' world. It may consist of many kinds—elements like water, or organic substances like leaves, grains, fruits, or the flesh of animals that live on them. In imagination we may even picture the theoretical possibility—provided time and circumstances could be so strangely propitious—of all the matter in the world outside being 'cooked' piecemeal for our food, transformed into our body for a while, and sent out again, in due course, to build up the bodies of others ! But a little cross-section of this movement, the 'circulation of matter' taking place in a single day, is quite enough to give a healthy turn to our thoughts. It can remove some of the barriers that seem to separate us from our surroundings. For, in so far as the external world is made up of 'matter' (Anna), it may be regarded as the 'raw material' of our body, and our body itself as a highly 'refined' form of it, rendered capable of being carried about with us for making our experiments, whenever we like. We identify ourselves with our limbs and say, 'This is my head, these are my arms and trunk'.[11] Day to day life will be impossible without such identification. But when we put this valuation into a wider setting, we see these limbs as temporary formations of cosmic material, continuously running 'into' limited areas like our body, and whirling itself 'out of it' when its time expires. Do we utilize properly these incoming 'units' from the space surrounding us? This is a question worth asking. Often we are troubled by our failures which we attribute, not to our mistaken policies, but to the machinations of 'others'. During such moments we give vent to our worst passions which strike, not our supposed enemies as we imagine, but these very serviceable 'units' that stand arranged as our own body and are meant solely to enable us to make our life noble. It is not the sign of wisdom, while getting an endless stream of helpers, to misuse their precious energies for keeping up a sad chorus chant that 'none really comes to help' and that 'the world is bad'! There is nothing creative in an attitude of complaint or lamentation; hence the instruction to avoid it[12] and put forth every effort to cultivate positive virtues like faith and devotion.

Matter as such is not perceived by our senses which work only within definite ranges. What they perceive are its manifold forms. But this very analysis shows us something that is beyond their reach, namely, the truth that there is a twofold movement in, or of, matter : first, the change from the formless into forms ; secondly, the rearrangement, through our power of digestion and assimilation, of independently growing substances, like fruits on distant trees, into complicated structures like our vocal cords which can send forth exquisite music. Desirable results are obtained also by controls unconnected with the building up tissues on our own body. Even if we do not know the art of singing, we 'encourage' our children to become proficient in it. So too does the head of a State, through political, military, economic and cultural 'organization', extend his influence and enhance the welfare of millions who come under his sway. If 'forms' of matter can be innumerable, equally innumerable can be the 'forms' of control and direction which alter the groupings of matter and help the attainment and the manifestation of the highest Ideal of human life. What is described as 'bondage' in religious books is not caused by matter as such, but by the harmful framework in which we make it work. We can overhaul the framework through reflection, backed by a passionate love for the Ideal.

IV

'Internal' and 'external' are distinctions observed when the limits of our physical body are kept as a rigid demarcation line. In a smaller view and for certain purposes these distinctions hold good. But if we take a bigger view, we shall find that 'matter' in its totality remains undiminished even while we witness the birth, growth, and death of individuals all around us. It stands as a Whole, our experiences notwithstanding. Who does not remember the little experiment in the school laboratory, designed to show us that 'when a candle burns, nothing is really lost'? There was a time when this indestructible 'matter' was thought to be at bottom different from 'energy', its mover. Science has now found out that matter itself is a form of condensed energy. The discovery is having far-reaching consequences in many fields like industry and economics, as also, unfortunately, in the manufacture of weapons of mass destruction! But in the path chalked out by the ancients for spiritual reflection it does not create any serious repercussion. Far from disturbing the indicated pattern of thought, it tends in a way to make our intellectual grasp of certain points much more easy.

For instance, it helps us to pass, without delay or confusion, from our previous concept of the invisible fund of matter, taking shape as our body, to the more comprehensive concept of an equally invisible flow of energy, depositing itself as cells and tissues for a time. While it is true that the body is made up of matter, Anna, it is much more true that it is an expression of energy or Prana. It was not in ancient philosophy, but only in old science that matter and energy were kept in a manner which gave room for mutual exclusion. Principles of spiritual practice have always accepted both of them as products of evolution from a common Source. There is, thus, no danger of reflection ordinarily making us ignore or sacrifice the physical aspect when the more inclusive value of energy comes to be upheld. The very purpose of reflection, Manana, or Tapas, is to approach each problem from all possible angles till every shade of significance becomes clearly impressed on our mind and our earlier valid conclusions become fully integrated with subsequent extensions of knowledge. To a person who does not belong to the rational type, this process may appear long and tedious. But to those with the right temperament, it is sure to be interesting and highly beneficial.

We may, for convenience, plot a few points suggestive of the majesty of energy's sweep across space. We may contemplate it sucessively in the heat of the sunbeams ; the clouds rising up from the sea ; rainfall on land surfaces ; growth of vegetation and food crops ; formation of the bodies of generations of creatures ; in man, particularly, gain of experience through thought and action ; break-down of tissues as a result of work ; and escape of waste products till at last the 'circuit' of energy is complete. What we call the inanimate and the animate represent only a small fraction of this invisible whirlpool of energy embracing the earth and the heavens.

We may imagine our physical body in its various stages to be a kind of 'mould' into which energy is being poured, with special arrangements to drain it out, the net result being that it is kept fresh and full[13] during our life-time. We may also picture to ourselves different 'limbs' standing for its head, sides, and trunk. For example, the energy functioning as and through our mouth or nose can be counted as its head.[14] Similarly, we may assign the position of the trunk to the currents that supply nourishment equally to all other parts. With additions and alterations we may get ready other symbolic pictures to make us intensely aware of the creative activities going on everywhere in the universe. Here too there is identification : first with the forces regulating our own personality, and then in due order with the forces behind our relatives and others. Identification alters the outlook and leads to a greater power of control over the environment. As the grip over the subtle becomes effective, the sense of dependence on the physical side of life disappears. Fear and anxiety connected with such dependence also progressively vanishes; and these are gains worth having.

We know that when the Head of a State loves *all* his subjects, he does not, and cannot, literally go about cultivating the acquaintance of everyone of them individually. What he does is to develop in himself an attitude of equal love, an equal readines to help one and all without distinction. That shines in his heart like a steady light; and when he meets anyone or discusses any problem, that inner radiance enters into his conduct and his decisions. There is complete detachment in his outlook, in the sense that he refrains from thinking of himself in 'isolation', or as an entity competing with his people or having claims against them. Their welfare forms so wide and pervasive an Ideal that, while engaged in striving to achieve it, he finds himself nearing his own perfection as an individual.

Thus, when by reflection we 'identify' ourselves with the fund of energy taking shape as the universe, we shall awaken in us an unwavering love and goodwill for all. Even while gazing at the beauty of natural scenery or watching butterflies with multi-coloured wings flitting in the sunlight or among the flowers, we sometimes imperceptibly lean over the edge of the superficial and merely physical aspect of things, and get a glimpse of the grandeur lying beyond the field of the senses. That itself is sufficient to cause a glow, though passing, of wonder and awe. What, then, must be the feeling of reverence and adoration when, by systematic discipline, we 'live, move, and have our being', consciously, in the Power that sustains not only our little personality, but all manifestations in the universe, by a 'fraction'[15] of Its inconceivable might!

There, in reflection's depths, the distinctions with which we commence our discipline, namely, physical and vital; ego and non-ego; ourselves and others; detachment and identification; thought and action; attainment and expression; wisdom and service—all these become gradually transformed into an illumined awareness,—'crystal-clear', many-sided, and abiding.

11. Reflection and control of reactions

I

Verification is an essential element in scientific pursuit. Certain kinds of verification can be done by many persons at a time. For example, while one student turns the handle of a simple electric machine, the sparks produced can be witnessed by everyone in the class-room. But in other cases, like the identification of bacilli invisible to the naked eye, it is only the student who looks through the microscope that succeeds in detecting them. What bystanders see is merely the fact of his handling an instrument. To get the enlarged view they must do exactly as he does. Every item of knowledge which alters the outlook comes under the same category, verifiable directly by the learner alone. His teachers and others can judge his mastery only indirectly, by putting some problems before him and by marking how he tackles them. If this is true with regard to subjects like mathematics or engineering, we can imagine the difficulty of our neighbours attempting to verify the effect of our controlled thoughts on ourselves. The extent to which such thoughts penetrate the personality, the type of resistance they encounter there, and the chain reactions till equilibrium is established are no doubt verifiable, but only by ourselves, the experimenters. What is wanted is the ability to keep the power of observation steady and unwavering. It is well known that when the interest flags, the mind 'winks', as it were; and during those intervals, irrelevant thought-forms appear, make unexpected turns, and run into strange corners! Reflection, which involves connected thinking within a definite framework, is one of the most effective methods to prevent these awkward 'jumps', When properly undertaken, it speeds up 'mental purification'.

Even substances of daily use, like water, can become the starting point for useful reflection. Electrolysis shows that water is made up of two gases. But even when they stand together, we do not see water as such. We see it only in the company of heat, technically called 'fire' in scriptural texts. So far as our sense organs are concerned, we may say that the invisible union of the two gases takes three widely different shapes according to the degree of heat added to it. In a way they are its 'reincarnations'—first, as ice over whose surface non-swimming creatures can safely crawl, next as water whose tendency to flow into lower levels can be utilized for irrigation purposes, and lastly, as steam whose pressure can make engines run and drive the wheels of industry. Our mind not only traces the movement of this 'element' from anyone of its 'halting stations' to the others, but also grasps the relations between its formless aspect and its controllable manifestations.

Familiarity often blunts our power of observation, or prevents us from learning useful lessons. Take the example of any tree standing in front. The power latent in the seed selected the necessary materials from the environment and gradually organized them into the forms of its gigantic trunk, and its own special type of leaves, flowers, and fruits. It is remarkable how the same field and the same extra manure become the support for trees of many varieties. Each one of them retains its individuality while passing from the state of the minute seed into its fully developed form. Animal bodies too present the same feature. An elephant and a man may live on the same food-stuffs for a month, but there will be no violation of the manner in which the tissues of their respective bodies are built up. The movements involved are twofold: from the formless into forms, and from an unmanifested state, with individuality latent in it, into the manifested state. By the practice of reflection, we learn to shift attention quickly, first from the external appearance of any creature to the imperceptible rearrangements constantly taking place in its bodily cells, and secondly, from every individual formation to the non-differentiated aspect of the entire universe. It is from the unmanifested fund of matter that creatures evolve their bodies, and it is into it that all bodies become dissolved when the force that 'organized' them is exhausted. The next step in reflection is to introduce the wider concept of energy into all gross formations and habituate ourselves to look upon the birth, growth, and final disintegration of physical bodies as expressions of an invisible fund of energy pervading both the inanimate and animate worlds.

II

The special characteristic of the human 'mould' is that the energy flowing into it takes the shape of thought which, under training, can be used for a conscious intensification of virtues and extension of goodwill. Mind and thought can be viewed from different angles. To begin with, we may call mind a sixth sense whose range is much greater than those of the other five. The eye, for example, sees only the object to which we can direct it at the time. It does not directly operate when we listen to a radio broadcast and come to the conclusion, 'This is the voice of the person whom we saw in the library yesterday'. Co-ordination implies not only the existence of a store where records are kept, but also an agency to pick them up and weave them into patterns which can even run counter to the events taking place in front. The General who sees the battle going against him and who quickly regroups his men to outmanouvre the enemy uses something far surpassing the records of his eyes and ears. If we accept only five senses, his creative thinking transcends them. If, on the other hand, we regard mind as the sixth sense, all thinking processes fall within its special field; and its user, the thinker, remains, technically, distinct and independent.

Often we put body and mind in opposing categories and try to estimate the influence of the one over the other. What is needed for a trial of strength is that there should be 'two' parts to be moved. They can as well be taken wholly from the physical side. For example, we can press one palm against the other, or drag the head down by both hands while using the muscles of the neck to resist the pull. In a similar way, when the body is tired after a full day's work, we can goad it into further exertions by presenting to the mind the urgency of some important business beneficial to ourselves and others. When imterest is sufficiently aroused, it has a way of penetrating the body and releasing abundant energy for physical activities. If we can learn the art of shifting the point of interest by turns, we shall seldom be overpowered by dullness. And when we decide to let go all interest, we shall drop off into sound sleep almost at will, leaving it to Nature's delicate hands to rebuild our wasted tissues and fill them with fresh vigour. Reflection itself can lead to an unceasing flow of energy, provided we approach every topic from its most attractive and creative aspects. What is essential is to see that the mental horizon is actually widened so as to include and harmonize the sectional views given by piecemeal analysis based on body, mind, chemistry, physics, or psychology. Reflection must be considered incomplete if gaps persist.

Influence works the other way too; for, as is well known, weakness of the body reduces mental efficiency. When curd is churned, its subtle portion comes together and rises to the top as butter. Likewise, of grains and other items taken in as food, and 'churned as it were by gastric fire' and other processes within the stomach, the subtle part rises up and becomes transformed into mental energy. Following traditional ways of calculation, one ancient teacher explained to the student, his own son, that 'this strength of mind, increased by food, is divided 'into sixteen parts', which may be called the sixteen parts of the human being. It is only when this strength exists that the man can see or hear, think or understand, do or know.[1] On its waning, his faculties slip away from him. To convince his son of the truth of this assertion, the father made him go without solid food for fifteen days and then asked him to repeat familiar scriptural texts. The young man could not remember them. But when he began to take food he got his memory back. If out of a well-lighted fire everything except a single coal of the size of a fire-fly is gone out, it would not be possible by means of that surviving ember to burn anything more than what its size warrants. So it was that when fasting had brought down his bodily strength to a bare one-sixteenth, his mental ability proportionately dwindled. Eating revived it, as the careful addition of dry grasses and faggots can revive the fire in the remaining piece of coal and make it blaze forth as before.[2] The basic energy is one alone. Under certain conditions it operates in and as the world of the five senses. Under others it functions in and as the sphere of the sixth. Each influences the other since they form parts of the same 'organized' unit, the personality. Both move in perfect agreement if controlled from a level higher than either.

III

For our present purpose mental movements may be divided into two main kinds: conscious, and those that fall outside the conscious. One scripture gives a 'specimen' list of the conscious thus: 'Desire, deliberation, doubt, faith, want of faith, steadiness, impatience, modesty, intelligence, and fear'.[3] It says that 'all these are but mind', in other words, 'forms' taken or presented by the internal organ. Psychology may have a more exhaustive list, with facts and relationships arranged in different ways. The requirements of reflection do not come into clash with them.

What the man of reflection finds particularly useful to him is the capacity of thought to disconnect itself from sense reports and shake off its slavish subservience to them. When properly trained, it can come back to resume control of bodily limbs and senses with a greater light and power developed in the course of its independent flight. Thought is in some respects like an aeroplane. We know that the plane uses its own power to cover the runway and to maintain its position in the air during a survey flight. So too does thought rely on its own inherent energy to speed along the sense contacts before and after everyone of its creative sweeps. It matters little whether the runway and the take-off points for its upward movement are supplied by objects that appear attractive or repulsive at first sight. There is no direct causal connection between them as such and the moral or spiritual worth of the return 'dive' when survey is complete. No one willingly agrees, ordinarily, to forgo his night's rest or ask his limbs or life. And yet, when greater loves are involved, people keep night-long vigils near a sick-bed or rush into the field of battle to defend their native land. All acts of self-sacrifice or heroism are the result of a rearrangement of values, slow or rapid, stimulated no doubt by external events, but planned. refined, and resolutely upheld by an inner drive, a passion and a sense of dedication waiting to blossom forth in the individuals concerned. Had the mere presence or perception of pains or dangers been the invariable compelling force for broad-minded reactions, fellow-feeling and compassion would have been universal, and murders and plunders absolutely impossible.

It looks as if reactions in an ascending order of good will and sublimity are arranged in our personality, like a series of cylinders, one inside the other, each capable of rotating in the same direction as the one outside it, or of pausing for a while and moving thenceforth in the opposite direction. Thus a king, seeing a prosperous country beyond his frontiers — exactly as its ruler or subjects see it, so far as sense records go — may consciously rotate within himself the 'cylinder' suggesting the glory of selfish possession and annex it after a ruthless massacre of its valiant defenders. But when he marches in triumph into its capital, the death and destruction wrought by him might penetrate into his heart, as nothing could do before, and set the 'cylinder' of compassion whirling in the reverse direction, carrying along with it higher 'cylinders' lying in deeper levels.

How strong even a temporary revulsion can be after the destruction of an enemy, who had once been an object of love and respect, is brought out vividly in Valmiki's *Ramayana*. The context is Vali's death and the piteous lamentation of his wife, son, and a host of faithful followers. Smarting under his brother's continued persecution, Sugriva had been eagerly waiting for this very moment of total vengeance. But he was not prepared for the final picture as it took shape after the hero's fall. It literally swept him off his feet and the memory of all the good Vali had done came rushing into his mind all together. The poet says that Sugriva then slowly approached Rama and, in effect, said to him with tears choking his voice : 'You have been pleased to carry out to the very letter what you promised to do for my sake. But I see now that I have committed a crime whose enormity is beyond description. Many a time in my previous encounters with my brother, he almost stunned me with severe blows, often using branches of trees which he wielded with his prodigious strength. Each time, however, he took pity on me, consoled me and let me off with the remark,

'Go, go; but do not do this again!' Such words expressed the magnanimity natural to him. His large heart could not seriously entertain the idea of endangering my life. He stuck to brotherly love, nobility, and virtue, while I gave full vent to anger, lust and monkey-nature. For as soon as an opportunity presented itself I took his very life, dictated by the crookedness that has been mine all along! I seek your permission to enter the flames and join my high-souled brother'. The poet adds that on witnessing this sudden turn of events, Rama stood dejected for a time, his heart overflowing with sympathy and his eyes with tears![4]

Readers of *Adhyatma Ramayana* are familiar with the description of how Valmiki's life was transformed by his contact with the seven great sages. He was then leading a robber's life. On seeing the reverend ones, his first reaction was to try to rob them of whatever they had—even their wearing apparel—so that he could maintain his wife and children therewith. It was easy for the sages to see that the man before them was proceeding on the false assumption that those whom he looked after would surely take a share of whatever sins he committed for their sake. So they asked him to go home and ascertain for himself how far each member was prepared to join him in facing the consequences of his cruel deeds. The sages assured him that they would not leave the place till he returned. That appeared to be a fair proposal and the man hurried to his wife and children. Their replies acted as a partial eye-opener. For they told him bluntly that if there was any gain it would be theirs by right, while if punishments were due, they would go to none but himself! The rest of the story is simple. The merciful sages instructed him, and by faithfully carrying out the discipline they precribed for him, he developed supreme insight and became the well-known saint Valmiki—so called because of the Valmịka, ant-hill, that grew, around him during his prolonged meditations.[5]

So far as the study of reactions is concerned, this story is highly significant. What Valmiki's eyes recorded before and after his conversion did not alter in the least, for that was the physical appearance of the sages. Their faces always indicated fearlessness and kindness. The revolution that took place was solely in his own thought world. His programme had been built on three notions: a fancied identity of interests, in every respect, between himself and his family; a supposed unalterable responsibility to maintain them at all costs; and as the direct means to it, the snatching of material goods from those whom he chose to regard as his legitimate 'victims'. It is interesting to see what the sages found at the same time. What their eyes recorded was naturally the fact of the robber rushing towards them shouting. 'Stop, stop!' But since their perceptions moved unobstructed in the subtle world, they were able to understand the inner worth of the man in front. Behind the threatening attitude and murderous intention which were indisputable psychological facts at the time, they noticed that the 'cylinder of wisdom and service stood ready to begin spinning in the opposite direction for ever. What was needed was a little help from outside to pull back the only obstacle that stood in its way, namely, his misplaced trust in the people whom he blindly loved. When that help was given in a manner which fitted well into his dominant ideas, two things happened. First, his original programme was found to be untenable, so it disintergrated. Secondly, its essential element, the desire to gain something useful from others, passed quickly from the first lesson in discrimination, already completed with proper verification, to other lessons, more valuable, that the venerable ones might surely be willing to teach, if properly approached. We may sum up the change by saying that the profit motive inherent in the very first movement of thought, became disentangled from some of the false assumptions he had made and the base attachments he had built up on them. It survived as the yearning for illumination—that being the only form in which it could stand when divested of the extraneous factors which may manage to cling to it and lead it astray, if one is not vigilant.

Re-shuffling of values can come either through the disillusionment caused by shocks from the external world, or through calm and quiet reflection, deliberately undertaken when there is nothing paricularly unpleasant in the environment to upset the mind. It goes without telling that the second alternative is the nobler one.

IV

Where, however, baser emotions have become well entrenched in the personality, peaceful methods like those which the sages tried on Valmiki, may be of no avail. It is possible for an individual sometimes to count upon his physical strength, social influence, or financial resources and utilize them to exploit and oppress the weak. When his inequities increase, the machinery of the government is put into action against him. The law courts, the police, and the army 'mend or end' him and his accomplices. But there can arise a situation when the offender is the ruler of a State, who contrived through foul means to seize the administration and keep every limb of it tightly in his own hands. The very army which, normally, ought to serve as an effective instrument for enforcing justice and promoting virtue, becomes in his hands an unfailing tool to enslave neighbouring States and indeed all humanity. This possibility was clearly seen by ancient Indian story-writers. The greatest tragedies of life, according to them, were not caused by the murderous instincts of those who had no occasion to step into cultural fields. They were — and they are still mostly — due to the endless scope for exploitation and persecution which any shrewd and unscrupulous person could get by doggedly disciplining himself in certain ways. Those writers have depicted their villains as men who saw the necessity to push aside their wicked intentions to the extent that was required to enable them to pick up from the surface flow of mental energy just the elements signifying 'powers', as distinguished from universal compassion. They then relied upon the sheer force of repetition to step up this 'power' till it assumed almost irresistible proportions. The psychological drama enacted to facilitate the execution of the project to build up a 'position of strength' involved the invocation of favourite deities representing Power, until they appeared in a vision and granted the desired 'boons'. When this stage was reached, there was no further obligation, they felt, to hold back their schemes for aggrandizement. They found that they could thenceforth make their own mental movements produce corresponding combinations in the fields of energy and of matter whenever and wherever they chose. It was a tragedy, in a personal sense, when anyone took the trouble to climb up all the steps leading to the highest wisdom and contented himself with merely snatching the power lying scattered along the route. Many a small-minded man goes to a place of pilgrimage, prompted by the profit motive and comes back delighted with the wealth gained by clever speculations in the shopping areas found near by! But tragedy transcended personal limits and spread steadily in every direction, like a wild fire, when armed with the boons — which meant, in their case, a fusion of wickedness and military might — the villains started on a career of conquest and extended their sway not only over the whole of the earth but even beyond its limits.

There was only one way to pull down such an oppressor; each sufferer had to, and could, push his virtues up. His body might be held in chains and his mouth shut. But there was one dimension where his movements could never be obstructed. That was his own mind. His hot sighs or tears could not be expected to give a direct hit to the tyrant. But every mental heaving for freedom could do it, whether accompanied or not by language in the form of a complaint or of a fervent prayer addressed to the Supreme Dispenser of Justice. If the aggressor could pick up 'power' from the stream of thought flowing through him, amplify it, and employ it to injure others, his victims too could follow the same procedure, though guided simply by faith, till the total forces sucked up and converted by their individual heavings, in their inevitable evolution, led up to a Cosmic Stress, too strong for earthly schemers to withstand. Its visible effect would be the appearance of a Hero, a Man of the Hour, a Liberator, a Royal Sage, or what Hindus call an Incarnation. His, or Her programme would be twofold: promotion of virtue, and the elimination of wickedness — even through the utter destruction of the physical prowess and military superiority on which alone tyrants usually count.

The *Chandi* gives us two striking examples of incurably perverse reactions. Of its three main stories, one deals with Mahisha and another with two brothers, Sumbha and Nisumbha. The pattern of events is the same: They enslaved the celestials, tormented religious people, and made spiritual pursuit well nigh impossible. In answer to the appeals of the afflicted, Divinity descended to the earth as the Divine Mother to take the field against the oppressors. She came as the embodiment of matchless valour and boundless compassion. Sages left off their silent meditation to fall at Her feet and sing Her praises. Dwellers in heaven were filled with delight, for they saw their day of deliverance fast approaching. At the sight of Her calm and trust-inspiring face, lit with a half-smile, charming like the full moon, and glowing like burnished gold, they too made repeated obeisance to Her and chanted Her glories. But that same face evoked altogether different reactions in the minds of the demons to whom sense pleasure was the highest goal. To Sumbha and Nisumbha, ever on the special look out for gems of all kinds, this 'gem' of a woman seemed to be an ideal mistress to be brought over by persuasion, or captured and dragged by the hair if She resisted. The only concession they were willing to give Her was the right to stay with either of them, as She chose! They were left with no other alternative than to fight to the death, since She not only taunted them, but also went on striking down the armed men sent against Her in larger and larger numbers. As for Mahisha, Her challenging roars from the start excited his ire and compelled him to resort to arms, This left him little room to dwell longingly on Her exquiste beauty. When the celestials hymned Her after She had slain him, they particularly mentioned that it was a wonder how he—or anyone with even common notions of physical charms—could respond to Her only by rushing in anger to strike Her captivating face[6] which unmistakably showed the protection and grace She was ready to bestow on those who wanted them!

If a person is sincerely desirous of lifting himself above the passing attractions of the sense world, he can find plenty of take-off grounds for reflective flights, all around him. Wherever there is uncommon progress, greatness, or splendour, it is She, the Mother, the Divine Saviour, who exists there, assuming that particular form to bless Her struggling children. It is again She who functions as Art and Learning, as Prosperity in the abodes of the good, as Faith in the hearts of the devout, and as the very Womanhood among all human beings.[7] Where is it that the reflective mind cannot perceive Her gracious presence?

IV. VISION

12. Spiritual ascent through art and worship

> There is an Infinite, Omniscient Spirit behind, that can do everything, break every bond, and that Spirit we are; and we get that power through love.[1]
>
> 'The Bhakta (follower of the path of devotion) wishes to realize the one generalized abstract Person, loving whom he loves the whole universe. 'Everything is His and He is my Lover,' says the Bhakta. In this way everthing becomes sacred to the Bhakta, because all things are His. All are His children, His body, His manifestation... With the love of God will come, as a sure effect, the love of everyone in the universe'.[2]

The story of Rama and Sita has inspired Indian art in all its branches. Poets, particularly, have loved to dwell on different scenes showing Rama's personal graces, his numerous virtues like truthfulness, and his strict observance of the duties of an ideal king. One imaginative poet composed a stanza in the form of a short dialogue to indicate Rama's agony during his wanderings in search of his missing wife. Lakshmana, his faithful brother, was ever by his side, trying every possible means to rouse him into heroic effort. Rama's all-comsuming grief, however, had its own way of quickly jerking his attention back into itself whatever suggestions were made to divert his thoughts into new channels. His mind had come to a stage when burning sorrow appeared to him as intense physical heat in the surrounding atmosphere. So he said to his brother, 'Let us move into the shade of yonder tree to save us from this noon-day sun'. Lakshmana thought that this was a chance to alter Rama's internal condition by a pointed reference to actual facts of the external world. So he said, 'Brother, how does the question of the sun arise at this time of the night ? It is the moon that is high up in the sky !' 'How did you find this out, my dear one ?' said Rama, making a feeble attempt to get rid of the heavy load of pain that was oppressing him. 'Because it bears the mark of the deer,' answered Lakshmana, hoping probably that this proof would be convincing, and that reason might now get a firm foothold in his distracted mind. But to his amazement the law of association took a turn totally different from what he expected. The mention of deer reminded Rama of the similarity between the eyes of the deer and of his wife, and he fell headlong into the ocean of grief once again, exclaiming piteously, 'Alas ! Where art thou, my beloved, doe-eyed, moon-faced daughter of Janaka ?'[3]

Apart from being an example of a subtle poetic device, this stanza is valuable to us as it shows some of the forces normally operating in our own mind. Even when we are not seriously interested in directing the course of our thinking, our ideas do not flit haphazardly, as we might be tempted to assume. For a little observation will reveal that between every two thoughts there is some kind of similarity, if not a striking dissimilarity, which makes a jump from one to the other possible. It is not necessary that the notion connecting the two should correspond to objective facts or relationships, which people standing near at the time can also perceive. It is enough if the notion is in keeping with our temporary emotion, or our habitual outlook. Thus, if we were painters or hunters who overheard the dialogue, as presented by the poet, and had no acquaintance with the speakers, the mention of the moon and the deer would probably call up in our mind only ideas like that of painting a moon-lit landscape or of hunting wild animals! As our emotions and deeper convictions can be centred round various persons, objects, and satisfactions, the turns in our thought-patterns can be practically endless. We can see this for ourselves from the difficulties experienced in concentrating our mind on any chosen subject. By regrouping attention and the power of visualization we may leave off the farthest point of wandering and trace our way back to the starting place in the thought world—only to find, to our chagrin, that often within a few seconds, the law of association weaves an absolutely novel web and leads us astray to a considerable distance before we detect it! If this is the nature of the thought-stream in what we take to be its normal condition, what can we say about the trouble of controlling it when our entire outlook is dominated by grief, as in the case of Rama, or by fear, anger, or greed? The mind would then act like an invisible whirlpool. In most original ways it would quickly and forcibly suck into itself, and alter, every thought that our friends, and we ourselves taking the cue from them, may put within its area to reduce its violence.

This very law of jumping, however, becomes a positive advantage when the ruling emotion happens to be one of sacredness or love of God. For, then, whatever may be the nature of the hindrances our body or the environment may thrust upon our notice from outside, the jumps would be regulated by the yearning within the heart, and made to take lines leading progressively to the heights of faith and spiritual awareness. Thought would then function at levels where creative energies operate freely without being distorted by the medium of baser emotions. Even an intellectual conviction of the possibility of this transformation can help us considerably in improvising easy mental exercises, irrespective of what our neighbours may be doing or experiencing at the time. When once this skill is acquired all daily activities can be used as take-off grounds for spiritual flights, thereby eliminating the dependence on conventional 'runways' in the shape of a sacred place or religious-minded companions.

To illustrate this, a story is often narrated of an incident that took place at a big competition in scripture-chanting. It was the custom for thousands of able men to gather on such occasions. The most daring among them would by turns act as the challengers. That is to say, they would agree to chant any sacred hymn, rearranging its words in different well-known patterns, without minding all the disturbances the others might deliberately create to distract their attention. People were permitted to shout, make faces, crack jokes, or even suggest wrong word combinations in their ears; the only restriction was that none should touch the challengers' bodies! What must be the mental mastery involved in completing the chants with ease and grace, setting at naught the combined ingenuity of determined fun-makers! Once, without even casting a glance at all this struggle and noise— which had nevertheless reverence for scripture behind it— a certain invitee sat busying himself with a pack of playing cards! He was naturally caught by some and produced before the king who was the organizer of the function. When he was asked to name his associates in this sacrilegious act, he said to their amazement that he knew how to play alone! By way of demonstration he kept an ace before him and said that it acted as a good springboard for his mind to begin an excellent meditation on 'The One Lord, dwelling invisibly in the heart of all creatures, pervading all and abiding as the inner Ruler of all.'[4] He added that after having his full satisfaction of seeing himself filled with the love of the Lord, he would place before him the card with two marks and start an appropriate reflection based on the duality of the Seer and the Seen. In this way, he said, he would go on varying the philosophic framework for his meditative climb according to the markings on the faces of the cards. All were highly benefited by the explanations given by this calm-minded scholar, who showed not merely the freedom of his memory from the control of external factors—which the challengers too were showing—but also the possibility for everone to utilize any object, available in any context, as a basement for planting a reliable ladder to climb to spiritual heights. The gold chain that the king gave him as the scheduled reward for the best performance in the competition was but a poor token of the heart-felt gratitude of all for the free lesson he gave them on the art of using even most unpromising objects as symbols for mental control.

II

It is the artist who, more than anyone else, first sees, and then applies the right technique for manifesting higher values in common objects. How often do we throw away a piece of wood or stone on the ground that it is too small or irregular to be of any service to us! The experienced eye of the artist sees its worth in no time. He quietly takes it home, eliminates the unwanted portions with the help of a few simple instruments and gives it back to us as a little figure — a permanent reminder of the noble ideas welling up within him. In India there was a time when religious emotion expressed itself in an exuberance of art. The heights that it attained in the fields of architecture and sculpture can be seen from he magnificent temples that were erected in olden days. In some of them even nooks and corners contain carvings that elevate our thoughts. The beauty, that filled the heart of the artist to overflowing found its way also to those few square inches of stone available there after adequate provision had been made for bigger images. And the result was the creation of a line of miniature lotus flowers or heads of sages, to symbolize meditation and spiritual perfection. People must have felt that in a place set apart for the worship of the Lord of creation and of beauty, it was not proper to leave even the least bit of stone unaltered but that a loving effort ought to be made to help it reflect celestial glory in howsoever small a measure. For that would be a standing object lesson to all thinking men. If even insentient matter contained within it such exquisite possibilities, waiting only for the delicate touch of an expert's hand for bringing them out, can any worshipper fail to see the extent of the power and the serenity that can come to him through systematic discipline ? In the case of a sincere aspirant, whether he cares to know it or not, every devotional act, physical or mental, acts like a chisel stroke, detaching without pain all undesirable aspects of his personality, and filling in the needed virtuous aspects to make it a living temple of God.

Painting gives the same stimulus to mental embellishment. The canvas or wall on which the work is done has no doubt to content itself with one dimension less than what sculpture gets. But the loss can more than be balanced by the use of a well planned perspective and from the wide range of shades got through a skilful mixing of colours. If a painter is unable to rise above the level of sensual beauty, his productions will be restricted to an exact representation of muscular limbs or the smoothness of skin and silken dress. But there are artists who seek heavenly guidance and thankfully receive the light granted by the Most High. Theirs becomes a steady hand and with a few touches of their brush they produce the maximum effect. In fact, they make those who look at their pictures feel that earthly life, under proper care, fulfils its important function as the preparatory stage for the human soul to develop the wings of virtue required for its divine flight. To him, however, who can regard the Indwelling Lord Himself as the Supreme Painter, there comes the unique experience that transforms his very personal existence and fills it with the highest spiritual art.

While sculpture and painting are characterized by some kind of fixity, music has the merit of being able to give a 'running' thrill without losing the capacity, which they have, of leaving a lasting impression. Here too, in composition and in execution, it is possible to aim at a mere reinforcement of the ordinary craving for sense pleasures. But the greatest outpourings in music have come from the human heart, either in its passionate longing to get the Lord's grace, or after being blessed with the vision revealing life and thought to be sportive movements in His infinite being.

In India, from ancient days, the value of devotional music has been fully recognized. It is worth observing what happens even in remote villages at the present day. Even people of the labouring classes gather together in a convenient place at nightfall and spend an hour or two of their hard-earned rest in singing familiar pieces to the accompaniment of simple instruments. If they have kept up this tradition in spite of difficulties and discouragements, what will they not do if they are given suitable accommodation, better instruments, and systematic training? Available songs fall into different categories. Some the women sing even while rocking the cradle. They are so nicely composed that they apply to the baby that may be sinking into, or waking from, peaceful slumber, and can also be used as an appeal to the Divine Power lying dormant in everyone to wake up and manifest Its glory. What philosophy calls Liberation, devotion looks upon as the Music of the Soul.

We may, in this connection, take a useful hint from Shakespeare's description of how Hamlet dealt with Rosencrantz and Guildenstern who tried to ascertain his intentions. Hamlet handed a pipe to Guildenstern and asked him to play upon it. He repeatedly declined, saying he knew 'no touch of it'. Hamlet then showed him the stops and said: 'Govern these ventages with your finger and thumb, give it breath with your mouth, and it will discourse most eloquent music'. 'I have not the skill,' the friend once again pleaded. 'Why, look you now,' retorted the prince, 'how unworthy a thing you make of me!. You would play upon me; you would seem to know the stops. You would pluck out the heart of my mystery; you would sound me from the lowest note to the top of my compass; and there is music, excellent voice, in this little organ; yet cannot you make it speak. Do you think I am easier to be played on than a pipe?' By 'music' in that context, Hamlet meant his secrets, which spies like Guildenstern had little chance of detecting. It needs no special effort to see that this music reaches its highest significance only when it is applied to the spiritual field. It is fully expressed when, as a result of suitable discipline, our thoughts are regulated, emotions purified, intellect made steady, and harmony established with the Cosmic Will. To treat our personality as a musical instrument, the practice of virtue as the process of tuning it, and prayer itself as a fervent request to the Lord to take it in His hands and to play on it to His heart's delight—what more ennobling thought can we entertain! If our personality is a flute, let Krishna play on it, if it is a Vina, let the Goddess of Art and Learning move Her delicate fingers across its strings!

III

This brings us, naturally, to the vast field of mythology and religious traditions. Every cultural group has had them. Taking Greek stories, by way of example, we find one of their underlying ideas to be that gods gladly come down to the earth and take active interest in the affairs of men. Many of the Greek heroes are literally the children of the gods, and they carry out their exploits because of the divine power infused into them. Ancients, whether in (what we in a narrow sense now call) the West or the East, did not like to retain any thought barriers between the worlds of men and of gods.

From the Indian standpoint, the main moral of the stories is clear. If even in matters like the satisfaction of daily needs, protection from enemies and the achievement of martial greatness, man's efforts are not only aided, but also in many cases prompted by the celestials, is it not reasonable to expect the full grace of the Almighty to descend on anyone who sincerely struggles to get it ? The Lord in His mercy is ever ready to make us sharers in His immortality, it is our childishness that prevents us from seeing this. What a pity we remain preoccupied with earthly trifles, and think of approaching Him only to get some of them 'released' to answer our fancied needs ! This idea is often repeated. The *Bhagavata* puts it very forcibly when it accounts for Dhruva's dejection. There was good justification, in one sense, for being specially delighted ; for by a discipline lasting only about six months he was able to get a vision of the Lord, for which great sages had meditated for years in vain. But in another sense he had committed a folly. He had failed to eliminate from his mind the initial bitterness which made him run to the Lord for redress. What he, therefore, got in the shape of boons were merely power and pleasures of the ordinary type, enormously prolonged and extended through divine will ! Having contacted the very Source of self-mastery and undying bliss, he had in effect — so he felt — begged for and accepted the cause of greater pride and bondage. In this he had acted as foolishly as a pauper askig for mere chaff — ***phalikaran-ivadhanah*** —when granted an interview by an all-powerful king![5]

Looked at in this way, mythological stories contain lessons useful for spiritual practice. In the first place, they stress the importance of ceaseless exertion. Not one of the heroes mentioned in them was at any time passive or lazy. Many of them certainly decided not to retaliate or strike the striker. It was because they saw the wisdom and the glory of grouping all their energies on the superior plane, which we loosely call 'moral', but which the hero or the heroine realized as the plane of the creative principle operating behind man and nature. Non-resistance to evil, in their case, meant not merely a refusal to hit back on the material level, but a total employment of the powers of protection and goodwill in an enveloping movement in which conceptual differences of attacker, defender, and the Almighty Saviour became fused into a single sublime experience. Its worth was convincing, unquestionable. All other values faded before it. That was their God. He was not in their eyes an extra-cosmic being. They saw Him rather as the Inner Ruler of all, having His eyes, ears, and limbs everywhere. They also saw that by serving Him, by dedicating all their activities to Him, all that could or need be done for the welfare of 'others' would be accomplisihed as surely and naturally as nourishment for the branches and leaves of a tree would be supplied by depositing the manure round its roots. Thus, in a sense, although without realizing it, the same path of dedication is taken by all those who gladly risk their precious lives for the sake of others, as for example, the young nurse who smilingly works in an area of serious epidemics, or the sole earning member of a family who rushes into the field of battle to save his country from foreign aggression. The nurse, the soldier and, indeed, every other worker can carry out their respective tasks with efficiency even with the ordinary idea of serving man as man. But there is a more ennobling way of doing them. That involves the introduction of spiritual values, the widening of their outlook and the undertaking of the same activities as a form of worship of the Lord abiding in man, or appearing as man. There is not the least danger of efficiency going down by the change in attitude. On the contrary, there is sure to be the added gain of seeing devotion and thankfulness rising steadily in the heart.

Printing and other facilities, like that of translating books from one language into others, have now made almost all mythologies and written religious traditions available to us. They contain the world's inspired thoughts, clothed in attractive literary form. The fact that they abound in stories and anecdotes makes even children enjoy them and imbibe their spirit without formal teaching. The narrow sectarian grooves in which our minds ordinarily run, are sure to be broken down by a reverent study of these records. Far from diluting our loyalty to our particular creed, it strengthens our conviction that the voice of God has spoken to men of one-pointed devotion in all countries and in all ages. It also shows us that every revelation has led to the laying out of fresh paths along which people of varying tastes and capacities could easily make their pilgrimage to the highest Truth. This very discovery puts us into close mental contact with the hopes and joys of the great ones who climbed up earlier. It helps us to evolve invisible feelers to discern their course and to make suitable adjustments in our own approach to the goal.

IV

Stories thus become a reliable foundation for self-improvement. The effort we make to enter emotionally into the higher levels of awareness experienced by saints and sages helps our creative imagination to become habituated to effect similar movements within ourselves. This gradually opens up our power of finer perception and gives us access to a store-house of suggestions about the technique of keeping our thoughts and feelings properly tuned. Well has it been said that the more the mind is cleansed by listening to and reciting sacred tales, the more it sees the subtle Reality, like eyes through the application of medicinal pastes.[6]

Every system that has provision for God in His personal aspect lays down rules for adoration or worship of some kind. The underlying idea is that worship is the direct means for strengthening virtues and preparing the devotee's mind for the descent of divine grace. In India, worship takes many forms. While the ultimate aim is to realize the Lord as all-pervading, the first practical step is taken with the object of making the mind steady on some symbol, and learning to attain a harmony of the maximum discrimination, consecration, and certainty through it. Once this mastery is achieved, attention could be swung over to other symbols arranged on the philosophic framework that the aspirant considers to be most satisfactory. After mentioning a few objects suitable for securing this basic stability, Patanjali states the guiding principle in such matters by saying, 'Or by meditating according to one's predilection'. Vyasa explains that by becoming steady in that one instance, the devotee's mind reaches the position of steadiness in other matters also.[7] The Bhagavata refers to this freedom of choice, as applied to worship, by saying that offerings can be made 'with sincerity and love, by means of various presents, to an image, or in the sacrificial ground, or fire, or the sun, or water, or one's own heart'.[8] Of course, the procedure varies in accordance with the symbol used. For example, one is to meditate that the various deities are present in the sacrificial ground; place oblations mixed with melted butter in the fire; address prayers to the power behind the sun; or take water in both palms and pour it back into the tank or river after chanting appropriate hymns with faith.

The most widely prevalent form of worship, however, is that done in temples, where quite often there are two images, one fixed on a pedestal, and another small enough to be carried about in processions. It is not uncommon for cultured people to set apart a room in their own house as a chapel, and after completing their prayers in a public temple, enter into it and conduct a service along with the members of the family. Wherever an image is used, the ritual proceeds more or less on the same lines. The thought of God is the only purifying agent, and it is applied in various artistic ways, first to purify the worshiper and the articles used in the worship. Identifying himself with the form of his chosen Deity, he imagines it as pervading his own body. He then mentally worships it; and being one with that, he invokes it into the image.[9] If funds permit, he may bathe the image with scented water, dress it in silk clothes, decorate it with garlands and ornaments, place before it various dishes, and wave incense and lighted lamps before it — all the while meditating on the Lord's spiritual presence in and around him. The intelligent worshipper learns within a short time to keep the flow of his devotion steady and coordinated to the movements of his body. If funds do not permit, and even materials like flowers are lacking, the entire procedure is gone through mentally, the vital gain being the deepening of the feeling of intimate relation with the Lord, neutralizing automatically the common notions of His being remote and of man being separate from Him. In the course of worship, the devotee may in his overflowing love remain rapt for some time in singing to and praising the Lord. Or he may listen to or himself narrate His exploits, enact His deeds, or dance in ecstasy.[10] Here is a total blending of art and worship, leading smoothly to the transformation of the whole personality and to perfect spiritual awareness.

13. Intention s penetrative power

'There is only one thing which we see as many'. 'God is neither outside nature nor inside nature, but God and nature and soul and universe are all convertible terms. You never see two things ; it is your metaphysical worlds that have deluded you'.

'Whomsover you hurt, you hurt yourself; they are all you. Whether you know it or not, through all hands you work, through all feet you move. You are the king enjoying in the palace, you are the beggar leading that miserable existence in the street ; you are in the ignorant as well as in the learned ; you are in the man who is weak and you are in the strong ; know this and be sympathetic'.

—Swami Vivekananda*

I

It is interesting to stand back, as it were, and watch

the drama of what we call 'attention'. In a way it is difficult, as the object of our observation seems to slip out before we can take a good 'look' at it. It is formless and we get only various 'forms' where we expect to find it. These forms consist of our thoughts or concepts. They may also be described as a continuous registration of sensations and emotions, pleasant or unpleasant. What we can sum up after a study of a few minutes is that we witnessed a flux, a succession of internal 'waves' sometimes coinciding with external events. How can we express its implications to ourselves? In two ways to begin with: We can look upon attention as a point of awareness running along, or being directed to, a number of objects, gross or subtle; or we may look upon it as a highly sensitive point remaining steady while, by a strange process involving the use of special instruments, phenomena are unrolled before it. Often we say we want to draw the attention of others to important facts, and our hearers act in accordance with that concept of 'motion'. At other times we say, 'I suddenly remembered a song I learned as a boy; it thrust itself upon my attention'. In the latter case we speak as if attention was steady, and ideas or memories flitted before it. Whether we imagine it to be steady or moving — two simple, ordinary categories — we can learn useful lessons by taking further 'looks' at it from different angles. The very oscillation of thought between two (similar or opposing) concepts implies a distinction between a 'field' and its 'observer' Even this recognition means a heaving or swinging between concepts!

Though attention by itself is beyond direct observation, its sensitive character is indisputable. When we see this quality, we also notice the presence of a 'field' and the possibility of various motions within that field. Such is the main design of our internal structure. It does not become the cause of pain any more than the external arrangement that makes our leg bend at the knee joint or places the eye-ball within a bony framework. Pain comes only when we employ our limbs, external or internal, for some purpose for which they were not originally meant, and which, therefore, puts undue strain on them or actually damages them. Wisdom comes by a twofold process: by an intellectual understanding of the benefits we can derive from proper use of our limbs, and by learning to carry out in actual practice all the adjustments needed to make those benefits flow into daily life.

II

There are some who hastily read a few printed books and form incorrect opinions about the scope of mental discipline. They argue as follows: The methods advocated in these books want us to stop all mental 'waves' all movements, even tremors. The aim seems to be to create a thoroughly homogeneous condition, eliminate the 'field' altogether, and imagine that the observing principle is thereby 'isolated,' kept 'unrelated,' and made 'pure' and 'free'. It is hoped that the very possibility of pain (or joy) which exists only in the field, can thus be ended once for all. Surely, this is an attempt to upset the internal arrangement that nature has given us. What else is this but sheer pessimism and a misguided retreat from life? It shows utter irreverence to the All-wise Creator of the human personality!

We have put the position of the critics as briefly and clearly as possible. It is not necessary for our present purpose to go into a detailed examination of what is meant by the control of 'modifications' of the mindstuff mentioned by Patanjali. A few facts, however, stand beyond dispute. Every system current in India lays down that its technical portions—concerning theory and practice— must be learned from a competent teacher. The student was, and is, in a way even now expected to 'stay' with the teacher and duly 'serve' him. Insistence on service is not a condition imposed by the teacher for his personal convenience. It is meant to create favourable opportunities for the student to increase his alertness and receptivity. We are living immersed, as it were, in an ocean of higher meanings and values. Our inability to perceive them and adequately respond to them is because our attention is centred on unworthy objects of the sensual world. These objects and, indeed, the entire department of the ego dealing with them, can be tuned out by the heightened feeling of sacredness associated with the service of the teacher. The first positive gain is the development of the faculty to pass easily from the teacher's looks, words, and movements to the principles that guide his thoughts and judgements.

By making his own attention run along these principles and their appropriate expressions in his teacher in different contexts, the student gradually implants in himself an ever-ready standard of reference for understanding the real significance of the philosophical terms employed in formal teaching and of the mental exercises prescribed to him in a graded series.

We can look at it in this way ; The teacher is a perfect person. He eats and sleeps, talks and discusses, chants and meditates. He is sweet and compassionate. If there is a need, he does not hesitate to correct or admonish.

But whatever he does, his whole personality swings into action at a moment's notice. Ease and poise mark his concentration as well as his detachment. We ask him to tell us his theory. He says that the Self is only the observer and that all movements are in the 'field''. What is the goal of disciplines? He answers that they lead to the unique experience showing that the Self was not 'related' to nature. It did not 'evolve' as a result of the changes occurring in her. Just the opposite was true; she evolved because of the perfection of the Self. Thus the question of any action to detach the Self or to be free does not arise. We question him again: 'When we see you eating, talking, meditating and sleeping by turns, is not your consciousness modified? Does it not 'move' from one object or activity to another? And you have been speaking of the control of modifications!' His answer is a smile, or an attempt to translate his indescribable inward illumination into bare words such as: 'Consciousness does not go from object to object. It does not really move. Therein is its uniqueness. Experiences are shown to it. It is ever pure and infinite. Realize this within yourself'.[1]

What remains is the need on our part to learn the art of rotating our concept-coils in our 'own field' in such a manner that the spark of illumination may appear and harmonize our values and emotions once for all.

We do not ordinarily run out to stop the moving branch of a tree on a windy day. For we are convinced that we are not the branch. Likewise, the teacher too is convinced that the little area of nature which we mark out as his trained personality is in reality *not* he. It has been stamped by the perfection of the Self, and we may use it as we like. If we wish to learn from it, it will make a spontaneous movement to teach us the truth. If we strike it down 'on a bed of arrows' and again go to it for instruction, it will discourse to us, as Bhishma did. Or if we nail it to the cross, it will forgive us and bless us from that cross and even from beyond, like the Son of Man. Consciousness is immutable, and the teacher has seen that he is That.

Without a living teacher as a standard of reference, we are likely to miss the true implications of the technical terms of the different systems, and move our internal limbs in most unprofitable if not harmful ways.

III

When one object occupies the centre of attention, others automatically go out of focus. Nature arranges some form of 'forgetting' when a shift takes place. What we can achieve by conscious effort is to learn to observe more things in quick succession within a given time, or to keep the same thing within the field of observation for a longer time But whether the contact of attention with the chosen object is brief or sustained one alone stands in full view at a time; others have to wait for their own turn. What nature thus keeps aside, or 'hides' from view, we can, however, bring back before the power of attention by memory. Whereas in reading or listening we gather records and send them 'in', in meditation we acquire the skill of remembering the selected idea before it can fade away, or natures make it disappear.

Forgetting can cause serious troubles. A military man who forgets the orders issued to him ruins himself and often his country too. But the principle of forgetting, in its higher reaches, confers remarkable benefits. When a mental process, like the one connected with the study of mathematics or music, is sufficiently repeated with quiet determination, we form a 'habit' in due course. In other words. we acquire a habitual clarity in those departments of knowledge. The forces that delayed mastery are then shut out once for all. The detailed records of the daily anxieties, struggles, and little gains, which marked the period of preparation of our Sadhana, are as it were, bundled and stowed away in nature's 'hold' as luggage not needed for daily use in life's cabin. The mental 'waves' related to them may be said to have 'fulfilled their duty'. They have become *charitadhikara* in yogic terminology. Controlled waves have achieved the task intended for them; they have removed the coverings to knowledge. They can never rise up again with that purpose; and we are released from the compulsion to depend upon them. The 'knower' is to this extent isolated and established in his own immutable glory. What has disappeared is not nature as such, but that aspect of hers which we previously could experience only as *klesa,* resistance, or as Avidya, relative ignorance. Nature hereafter does not add anything further to that knowledge, but faithfully manifests it wherever other forces require her to do so. We know our own name and place of birth; we repeat them not to add to our knowledge, but only because someone else wants to know them. Nature, in such a condition, becomes a second violin-player—playing the song of knowledge suited to different contexts. If we insist on counting, she certainly forms a second 'unit', but in respect of the notes, played there is only harmony and probably an increase in gross volume, not the gap and divergence which duality involves.

It is when nature drops the 'hiding' curtain that we experience deep sleep. While in the waking state, objects of the external and internal worlds could get into the focus of attention, although only in strict succession, one after another, that order and the very possibility of the entrance of anyone seem to be suspended altogether during deep sleep. But the power of attention must have remained intact even then; for on waking, everyone invariably feels that he slept well and that nothing disturbed him. If attention and its field were really inseparable, deep sleep would have been an impossibility, and the disappearance of the familiar duality of subject and object should have caused trouble like the absence of an important limb. Experience, however, shows just the opposite. While hiding the world of duality, nature evidently kept herself busy doing us some positive good; for on waking, we always feel fully refreshed in body and mind.

In dream, the essential facts of the sensual world continue to be hidden, as in deep sleep. What is new is an extra mind-made drama, carrying with it the sense of reality and certainty ordinarily associated with the conscious movement of physical limbs. It seems to be a matter of indifference to attention if the objects presented to it are drawn solely from what the waking ego calls an exclusively mental field, or even if they too are dropped and none sent to replace them. During the arrival season, anyone from anywhere is free to enter, but only one at a time, the rest being ever forced to go behind the screen. Since, thus, there is a constant disappearance of all except the single object presented to view, nothing unusual happens, from the standpoint of attention, if even that bare one is eliminated, and further interviews end. Such is attention, apparently 'related' to anything that may come to bask in its steady rays, but perfectly detached, immutable, and peaceful even if—as waking concepts go—duality vanishes, leaving it 'alone' and 'isolated'! And this attention is the most valuable characteristic of our personal existence. It is the witness of our sense of smallness and of our struggles. It is bound to shed on us its assuring light when we reach our Goal, or Grace descends.

IV

Air, as we know it, acts as a carrier. It brings to us a certain degree of heat or varying amounts of water vapour. It can convey to us smells and sounds too from a great distance if there is a favourable wind. Out of the two views regarding attention, if we accept the 'moving' concept, and grant that it is a force that can be 'directed', we have to concede also that it can carry our meanings and intentions with it. If, on the other hand, we attribute 'steadiness' to it, we have to imagine that meanings or intentions can be 'presented' to it till, by the strength of repetition, a habit is formed, and they are shunted out of focus, as already stated. As habits, again, they continue to influence the mental field, altering its movements into the 'expressive', instead of the 'adding' pattern — as the mastery of mathematics, music or any other subject shows.

Religions teach us that if we habitually 'seek' righteousness, other things will be added unto us. This means that if our intentions are pure and unwavering, nature (or God's grace) so arranges matters that we shall get not only bare food and drink to support our life, but also a proper teacher and other aids for our spiritual pursuit as occasions arise. Aspiration matures into the realization of the Divine Hand behind the movements of heavenly bodies and even in the fall of a sparrow on earth. With this all 'resistances' cease, and the personality becomes a fit vehicle for the transmission of perfection. Whatever thoughts arise in the mind afterwards can only be for 'the good of the many, for the happiness of the many'. There is nothing to prevent them from penetrating into the plane of matter if someone with faith requires it for his further progress. A centurion's faith may thus very well create a condition for a mere word from Jesus, standing in one place, to cure a servant lying far away and out of sight.

It was this same penetrative power of habitual holiness and faith built on direct vision that Sri Ramakrishna meant when he said that bees come of their own accord as soon as the flower opens. In his own case, when his yearning reached its peak during his days of Sadhana, adepts in different disciplines came to him without his going in search of them, and without even his cherishing a desire to get help from anyone. It is recorded in his 'Life' that once he wished to put up a fence round the Panchavati since 'the plants planted by him were cropped by cattle'. Shorly afterwards, says the biographer, 'there was a high tide in the Ganga and all the articles necessary to make that fence—some mangrove posts, coir-rope, with even a chopper came floating and ran aground just near the spot, and he put up the fencing with the help of the gardener of the Kali temple'. This is probably an extreme case, but it shows how the principle acts. In the case of his disciples, however, he actually 'yearned' and 'called them' till they came and he recognized and received them.[2]

Our thoughts are mere feeble ticklings of the mental field. They are not well directed or sustained. So they lack penetrating power. But when they do penetrate, they are often ill conceived and harmful, without our being aware of it. The hiding introduced by nature into our internal set-up is needed for the forward movement of thought. But when we resort to hiding, we deliberately intend to put others on a wrong track. The entire world of movement is a single unit at its bottom. A hiding pull started in any area must have its continuation in other areas related to it. Just imagine the consequences of not only our enemies but also our friends and children too imitating us, and, for what appears to them an immediate personal advantage, pulling down nature's hiding curtain at the ends within their easy reach! Sooner or later, there is bound to be a total hiding of the truth, causing severe suffering till the very shocks each receives makes him pray for light and try to get the curtain lifted up! We know that the terror of a nightmare marks the limit of straying from the waking reality. On the breaking of the dream, we find ourselves back in the 'assuring' condition that was all along there, hidden in the midst of unchecked imagination. This principle of falling back on a more stable position holds good also when excessive pain compels us to drop the hiding formula, and makes us, at least for a time, push up our virtues which we ignored till then. Cultivated virtues act as the solid ground on which we can safely stand when the evil wave passes off.

V

Students of the *Mahabharata* will remember how the virtuous king. Yudhishthira, had to suffer the consequences of the little hiding, *Alpam jihmam,* he practised on his teacher, Drona, in the battelfield. Finding it impossible to overthrow this redoubtable commander of the Kaurava forces, it was decided that his self-control should be shaken by telling him that his son had been slain. Since Yudhishthira was the only person whose words in such a context would carry conviction to Drona, the king had to tell him this falsehood — which, of course, as expected, made Drona lay down his arms and meet his doom. Because of this intentional straying from the truth, Yudhishthira experienced 'hell' from which arose cries for help from his brothers, wife and friends who had led noble lives on earth. When thus his sin was expiated, the lord of the celestials greeted him and explained to him how this was the result of his having cheated his teacher who wanted to know what had really happened to his son,[3]

Even popular dramas like *Sakuntalam* convey the same lessons although without a direct statement of the connecting links. Readers of *Sakuntalam* will easily see the chain of hidings it portrays.

King Dushyanta started the game by hiding the truth from Madhavya, the jester, by telling him: 'I have no particular fancy for the hermit's daughter. I am going to the hermitage solely out of respect for the ascetics. Please do not take seriously what I have told in jest'. Behind this outer expression was the cold calculation: 'This Brahmin youth is a chatterbox. He will probably betray my loving approach to Sakuntala and spread confusion among the ladies of the seraglio. Therefore I will speak to him thus'.[4]

In their own little ways Sakuntala and her friends too hid the truth. The king joined them. When they first stared at him in surprise after seeing his name on the ring he held out playfully as 'fee' on Sakuntala's account, he tried to throw them off the scent by the remark: 'Don't suspect me; it is a royal gift'. No wonder, in due course, this very ring went into hiding to set the chain of sorrows moving! Later, when Gautami, the elderly lady, approached the bower where the lovers were staying, the truth was hidden from her by the friends who shouted a warning: 'O bride of the cakravaka bird,! Night is come, bid farewell to your companion!' Sakuntala too, taking the hint, made the king hide himself behind the branches of neighbouring trees.[5] Durvasa's curse was only a cosmic stress in advance, indicating the coming of total darkness, in which it would be difficult for anyone to find out the truth. A few gentle pulls more completed the fall of the hiding curtain. Out of various considerations, the girl companions hid the story of Durvasa's curse from sage Kanva as well as Sakuntala, and from Gautami who joined the escorting party. No doubt, they cautioned Sakuntala a little by saying: 'If perchance the royal sage be slow to recognize you, then show him this ring marked with his own name'. Sakuntala shuddered at their misgivings. But instead of explaining everything and thereby making everyone keep the ring safe at all times, they explained away their caution with the words: 'Excessive affection is apt to suspect evil'![6] All these little hidings culminated, as every student knows, in the loss of the ring and all repudiation of Sakuntala by the king whose mind remained in a cloud of forgetfulness till the ring was put into his hands by the police officer. By that time she had left!

Such is Intention's 'creative' role.

14. Vision that supplements and balances

Sustained effort, backed by a desire to get a clear understanding, leads to the truth of any matter. We know that all development in science and technology have resulted from long-continued thought. The thought of a man of research does not stop with mere ideas. When he sees certain possibilities, his thought moves to the next logical step ; it suggests to him a series of experiments to put them to the test. Very often he has to strike out a line for himself and invent even the instruments for conducting those tests. Behind every one of his activities, there is the constant pressure of a generalized thought or attitude which may be expressed in the form : 'I am determined to find out the truth, whatever obstacles stand in my way'. That very pressure contains within it the germs of his plans and processes, his persistence and resourcefulness. From the very commencement, it is a drama of action and reaction between these germs on one side and levels of the environment on the other. The first scene shows a hypothesis and the last the vision of the truth.

Scientific thought, thus, is never divorced from 'work', especially of the type involved in testing and verification. In fact, it is in the nature of all thought to lead to some suitable action, the gain of new experience, and an appropriate change in the existing pattern of behaviour. Why is it, then, that no man jumps into commerce or politics when the idea of wealth or the country's progress comes to him for the first time? It is because other ideas dominate his mind, and there must be sufficient time and opportunity for the new idea to run alongside the old ones in such a way as to make his intellect accept it as a basis for an experiment in a fairly safe context to begin with. Till it gets such strength, there is bound to be a gap between its first appearance in his mind and its eventual entry into his programmes for daily work.

The subtler the field, the greater the gaps must be. And what can be more subtle and difficult to control than the forces operating within the personality and in those aspects of Nature connected with it? Their study and mastery fall within the province of religion and philosophy. They teach that at bottom these forces partake of the character of the Divine and that they are therefore capable of being completely transformed. The disciplines laid down for the aspirant can be brought under three broad heads. The first consists of information gathered from scriptures and teachers. As the material with which to start work, this has to be classed as hearsay evidence. To make it effective, the hearer or student has to apply his reasoning to it and relate its details to one another and to his own life. The utmost the intellect can do is to arrange essential facts and values in graded layers and fit them into an Ideal, 'gaining which, there would be nothing greater to be gained later'. Being 'infinite' and 'unlimited', Ultimate Truth must ever remain beyond the reach of such products of the intellect as 'definitions' and 'formulas', however useful they may be in building up understanding and certainty. All these processes come under the second group. Lastly, there is the most important task of refining the emotions and keeping them always in harmony with the Ideal. It is only when the inner apparatus is thoroughly purified and delicately 'poised' — that it can get the spark of illumination, — that Grace can descend into the personality and make it fully creative. Among the paths open to aspirants, that of devotion has this advantage that 'love is its own fruition, its own means, and its own end'. When mental energies are centred on a Personal God, 'a love-body is created, with eyes and ears of love; and with them' the devotee 'can see and hear Him'.[1] When this stage is reached, the information gathered from external sources becomes directly verified, though not through ordinary sense perception; and the intellect gets a certainty from an experience that transcends and includes it at the same time.

II

It is not possible to estimate beforehand how a man of illumination is likely to behave in different situations. Still a few general statements may be made. For example, we may say that although his vision remains all-comprehensive, the creative aspects of his personality will have a preponderance of the elements which he stressed while picturing his Ideal to himself. Thus, if he had been invoking it as 'the protector and friend of all' his own speech and conduct will continue to be cast effortlessly in a protecting and friendly 'mould'. Or, if he had been regarding it as 'the unseen awakener' of its sleeping children, he will turn out to be a person who avoids the limelight, but yet will pour out his energies unceasingly to remove the ignorance of the people around him. He will spare no pains to make them open their eyes and march forward by their own efforts. He will do so without giving them the least direct hint that he is the immediate cause of their strength and mental clarity. Such have been many of the greatest benefactors of humanity down the ages. They lived the ideal life, loved and served, but left no record of their personal lives. Or, again, the sage may have looked upon the Infinite as 'the inexhaustible'. In that case, there cannot but be something novel or original in whatever he thinks or does later—something that does not fade away soon—is no mere duplicate of what happened previously, but has the capacity to sprout up and show unexpected qualities at other places and times. The *Bhagavatam* illustrates the working of this principle. Its numerous stories have this one point in common: Two devotees are not blessed in the same way; nor does the same devotee receive grace in the identical form twice. Look at Parikshit. The Lord saved his life from Asvatthaman's weapon at one stage, but did not prevent him from being killed by snake-bite at the end! Instead, He so arranged that Sri Suka should stay with him during his last days, explain to him the glories of the Lord, and help him to keep his mind immersed in them while the body fell. In this respect there is close similarity between the Lord and the free souls who identify themselves wholly with Him. Their 'ways' become as difficult to forecast or detect as the track of birds that fly across the sky.

Terms like 'desirelessness' and 'inaction', used in describing men of insight, have often led to great confusion. We shall take a commonly ignored example,[2] in order to see what alterations in outlook are meant by these technical expressions. A certain devotee commences an elaborate ritual, say, lasting for about forty-five days. He has implicit faith that its successful performance will entitle him to two rewards, a son to continue his line, and a seat in heaven after his death. To be sure, the rules laid down would require him to restrict his food and personal enjoyments during the period. He would also have to spend most of his wealth not only to pay his priests, but also to feed large numbers of people, invited and uninvited, and to provide entertainments like music for their minds, and spiritual discourses for their souls. One object behind these stipulations is clear. They put him through a series of activities entailing self-sacrifice and devoted service of others, the combined pressure of which can make him receptive to higher truths. One day, for instance, while listening to the chanting of scriptural passages he may see, as never before, that it is no use trying to go to heaven since its enjoyments must end when his merits are exhausted. Another day, when with this increased clarity of mind, he looks at the happy faces of hundreds of people deriving benefits because of his ceremonies, the absurdity of longing for a son to call his own may strike him with an irresistible force. He may then see everyone around him as his sons—rather as God's sons, and therefore 'sacred'—whom it must henceforth be a privilege to serve with all the means at his command. With this, the personal desires with which he started the functions vanish for ever. But if the ritual is only half-finished and normally he should conduct it for about twenty days more, will he now abruptly terminate it on the ground that he has nothing to gain from it for himself? The fact that he does gain much more than what he originally hoped to get will surely make him continue it, probably with greater fervour, and when it is over, start many others for serving those sons—or brothers or sisters—though such actions may put him to the trouble of acquiring wealth, and managing the details of cooking, feeding, and educating. The continued activities technically constitute 'inaction', because the sense of being the 'actor' no more operates in his mind. If his mental purity becomes greater still, he may see the Lord alone everywhere, and not simply 'His children'. Then, on whatever object his attention alights—earner, wealth, and items of expenditure, or cooker of food, and eater—he will have only an unbroken consciousness of the Lord's presence. The feeling of sacredness, natural to the worshipper, would never leave him.

From a purely psychological standpoint we may ask: While feeding and educating others does he not 'desire' that the persons served should be benefited? Similarly, from the purely physical standpoint we may ask: Is he not moving about and 'acting' while doing the service? Yes, we say, as he too would doubtless say. There will also be the desire to produce the best 'results', viz. the best service. But here we are dealing with a situation where totally new and all-embracing values are involved. Ordinary 'action' is prompted by the motive of removing one's sense of smallness by snatching something from the external world and adding it to oneself. A person who feels such smallness is the 'actor' in the technical sense. His attempts to snatch something is the 'action', and what he imagines to be an addition to his personal possessions is the 'result'. Service and worship, as in the case of the man who attains wisdom in the course of the ritual described above, do not and cannot fall within the category of 'actor-action-result', which was certainly applicable to his efforts when he began the ceremonies.

Even in daily life, we are not right in calling a messenger an 'actor', in the sense of one who 'begins a piece of work of his own accord'. He is only a 'carrier', a channel for conveying the intentions of others. When an executioner hangs a criminal on the orders of the Judge, we have to say, from this standpoint, that the criminal is the real 'actor'. It is his 'action' in the shape of a cold-blooded murder that sets the machinery of the law rolling against him and gives him the 'results' which he deserves but may not have expected in that form. The executioner and the Judge are themselves 'acted upon' by that law and are 'actors' and 'desirers' only in a narrow, or grammatical sense, as when we say, 'The Judge acted quickly'. The same reasoning holds good in the case of a person who realizes 'with his whole being *(sarvabhāvena)*', and not merely on the intellectual level, that his body, thoughts, self-control, and opportunities for service are all equally 'holy' manifestations of the Lord's Will and Grace. He does not literally 'lose' the differences of himself and others, or of giver and receiver. What has happened is that they are all harmonized in a wider experience which, qualitatively, neither increases nor decreases with what others may do to him as an individual. No single term can fully express the all-inclusiveness of the spiritual awareness that reinforces reasoning and service-mindedness after freeing them from egoistic associations.

III

The *Gita* itself furnishes the best example of how such a 'free' awareness functions in day to day life. It shows Krishna remaining unarmed and driving Arjuna's war-chariot. All that he did by way of 'military' service fell outside the category of 'action' caused by any 'desire' on his part to 'add' anything to 'his own' earthly or heavenly advantage. The perfection he enjoyed was unaffected by what he did or what others did to him. Since he identified himself wholly with the supreme creative Principle behind man and Nature, his thoughts, words, and deeds were no more than different modes in which that Principle operated among the peculiar political, moral, and spiritual forces of his day. They were free from the limitations of the ordinary 'actor-action-result' complex, and so came technically under 'inaction'. He did not mind the physical pains or dangers in which his activities landed him. No hero or wise man is ever subject to fear.

It is not difficult to see why Krishna's adult life was spent mostly in politics and military adventures. The purpose of God's descent to the earth is declared to be twofold: to protect the virtuous and to eliminate wickedness or the wicked. Wherever it was found specially necessary, Krishna himself played the part of a preceptor. But as a rule, he left the work of teaching to qualified people who were already in the field. Has there been any generation that did not have them in sufficient numbers to meet the requirements of those who stood in real need? No genuine lover of society indulges in wasteful competition. He only supplements and balances. So Krishna bent his energies to carry out the one great task that none else was competent to undertake, viz. the removal of the serious obstacles to the free pursuit of virtue. Unfortunately then—as now also—the reins of political control in many places were in the hands of unscrupulous men who counted on their military prowess and violated moral and spiritual laws whenever it suited their nefarious schemes. A person who stuck only to peaceful methods, and who could only love and bless all without distinction, was powerless against them. The times needed the appearance of a new individual who was firmly entrenched in virtue and possessed, in addition, the same military strength as the unrighteous—someone who had the skill to strike them down if they failed to mend their ways after marking his personal example and receiving repeated warnings from him. Even if we drop the idea of the Incarnation, the picture of Krishna remains for all time as that of an ideal man of illumination who used his inborn military gifts for the promotion of virtue. His whole life is a model of 'disinterested action'—of 'inaction', as he himself chose to call it in a technical sense. There was none whose legitimate desire he did not struggle hard to satisfy. If we analyse his motives, we shall find that he did not make a distinction between wisdom and unattached work, and deliberately combined them into a spiritual discipline for himself. His wisdom itself took the shape of the right actions in each context. We may call it 'disinterested action', or 'inaction', or the spontaneous expression of 'illumination', as we like.

Dedication being an attitude of the mind, it is within the reach of people in any walk of life. Parents looking after children, farmers producing food crops, artisans engaged in their craft, all can learn to carry out their programmes in a dedicated spirit. What they have to do is to regard, whole-heartedly, their talents and the related environment as tangible forms of the Lord's own Power and Grace. As the new value penetrates into their personality, its natural opposites, viz. ignoble and injurious habits become neutralized and finally uprooted. Human relationships and business policies then stand freed from duplicity and greed. Worship is not inconsistent with the feeling of holiness. So the need to stop daily occupations in their purified state, as worship, does not arise. What is transcended is their earlier restricted use as means to inner refinement. They now remain as eminently satisfying and ever-open channels for manifesting higher values. We cannot rightly attribute the position of an 'actor' to such a devotee. He will himself repudiate it. For in his mature experience he sees only 'One actor', the Lord Himself, and not any individual, however strong and majestic he may appear to his contemporaries.

Does spiritual eminence give access to strange powers, as a result of which the sage becomes able to do whatever he likes with his personality and his environment? Vyasa, in his commentary on Yoga Sutra III. 44, takes care to point out that no illumined soul will 'interfere to set the objects of the world topsyturvy. For his desire with reference to them will be in harmony with that of a prior Perfect Being. In other words, he will not act against the Will of God'.[3] The maximum we can say is that he can grasp the truth of any matter on which he chooses to fix his attention long enough. But he will not do so at all unless there is any special reason for such conduct. From his side, that reason may be an inborn tendency to search for truth. We know that all intelligent students do not become scientists or engineers. Usually, a student selects the subject for which he has an inborn taste, and he attains proficiency in it. So too even among those who struggle for insight, the competency to discover the truths about different levels of existence may be found only in a very limited number. Mere curiosity does not mean competency. Tradition says that Patanjali was a genius who mastered three subjects. An oft-quoted stanza salutes him as the great sage who helped humanity to remove its three main afflictions, commonly called impurities (Malas). He expounded Yoga to remove the impurity of the Mind; the use and scope of Words to remove the impurity of Speech; and finally, the principles and practice of Medicine to remove the impurity of the Body.[4]

Multiple talents can also be accounted for from the side of cosmic needs. When a sage meditates on them, 'he brings down' or 'God sends down through him', just those powers of understanding and action that the world requires at the time. Those powers never lead to aggrandizement and exploitation. They appear only to stimulate, supplement, and balance the efforts of high-minded men to lift up cultural values. The sage who receives them becomes 'the man of the hour'. Humanity's highest aspirations take shape through his disciplines, self-sacrifice, insight, plans, thoughts, and words. Devotees call him a Prophet or an Incarnation. The reach of his mind, or his 'meditations', will extend from the smallest atom to the supreme Reality—like the musician's mastery over his instrument extending from the lowest note to the highest.

IV

One of the best illustrations of such an effective and worthy employment of 'meditation' in modern days can be found in what Swami Vivekananda did after he finished worship at the shrine of the Divine Mother at Kanyakumari. Sitting on a rock, a little away from the shore, on that 'last stone of India', as the biographer says, the Swami entered into a very deep meditation. Outside, the ocean 'tossed and stormed, but in his mind there was even a greater tempest.' His mind dwelt long on 'the present and future of his country. He sought for the root of her downfall, and with the vision of a seer he understood why India had been thrown from the pinnacle of glory to the depths of degradation. The simple monk was transformed into a great reformer, a great organizer, and a great master-builder.' In the silence of meditation 'the purpose and fruition of the Indian world' flashed across his mind. 'He thought not of Bengal, or of Maharashtra, or of the Punjab, but of India' in her entirety. 'All the centuries were arranged before him, and he perceived the realities and potentialities of Indian culture.' He saw quite vividly that 'India shall rise only through a renewal and restoration of that highest spiritual consciousness' which has made her at all times the cradle of the nations and the cradle of the Faith.' In that comprehensive vision he saw not only her greatness but her weaknesses too. It was clear to him that religion was not the cause of her downfall, but the fact that true religion was nowhere followed; for religion, when dynamic, was the most potent of all powers.'

With great tenderness and anguish he brooded over the country's poverty. 'What use is the Dharma, he thought, without the masses? 'Everywhere, and at all times, he saw that the poor and the lowly had been oppressed and down-trodden for hundreds of years by every Power that had come in the changes of fortune to rule them.' 'His heart throbbed with the great masses; he seemed to have entered, in some supreme mode of feeling, that world of India's outcasts and poverty-stricken millions.' How could all this be remedied? Through Renunciation and Service, his Inner Voice said. If these could be intensified, national vigour would be revived and every problem would automatically be solved. Renunciation had always been a great dynamo of strength in this land from ancient times. 'We have to give back to the nation', he said to himself, 'its lost individuality and raise the masses.' Religion was not 'an isolated province of human endeavour; it embraced the whole scheme of things,— not only Dharma, the Vedas, the Upanishads, the meditation of the sages, the asceticism of great monks, the vision of the Most High, but the heart of the people, their lives, their hopes, their misery, their poverty, their degradation, their sorrows, their woes.' 'Verily, at Kanyakumari the Swami was the patriot and prophet in one!'

The student of the Swami's life can easily see, among other things, how his vision, in its actual expressed form, was like a many-sided crystal, some of its unique facets being the exchange of services between the East and the West, and the harmonization of science and religion, or of meditation and work for social advancement. Its main keynote was 'to guide individuals and nations to the conquest of their inner kingdom by their own ways which are best suited to them, by means corresponding best to the needs from which they suffer most.'

To those who value his teaching that Freedom is the basic condition for anyone's growth, even his progressive withdrawal from all active concerns, when once he saw that 'his machine' was in 'strong working order'—that 'no power' could drive back the lever he had 'inserted' in the massive block of India' 'for the good of humanity'—must appear highly significant. Says Sister Nivedita in her chapter on the 'Passing of the Swami.'[5] 'Strangely enough, in his first conversation after coming home from Banaras, his theme was the necessity of withdrawing himself for a time, in order to leave those that were about him a free hand. How often, he said, does a man ruin his disciples. by remaining always with them! When men are once trained, it is essential that their leader leave them, for without his absence they cannot develop themselves!'

That was, indeed, the right leadership— as fully detached, as it was truly creative! It did not dominate or forge personal bonds, but awakened, supplemented, balanced, and quietly slipped out, leaving others free!

---

15. Refinement of reactions

Pure reasoning, like a strong lion, tears to pieces the elephants of great error that ravage the lotus beds of the mind.

He in whose mind, resembling a clear lake, reasoning faculties shine like a cluster of lotuses, holds his head aloft and stands exalted like the snow-capped mountain, Himalayas.

The mind that is fixed on the unshakable foundation of virtue and whose foremost characteristic is the courageous pursuit of Truth, is not shaken by afflictions, but stands steady like a painted creeper which outside winds can never move.

The mind rendered pure through good company and the cultivation of contentment, self-control and proper reasoning meets with prosperity and success like the king who has wise ministers to guide him.[1]

I

Life compels us to react. It throws us into various situations mainly unexpected and often painful. If we choose to remain indifferent, we only make matters more difficult. In the first place, refusal to act is itself a kind of reaction—a most dangerous one when repeated and turned into a habit. Secondly, if we refuse to make a wise move, the problem does not end with our missing a chance to go ahead. For others may act wrongly, injuring not only themselves, but also ourselves and the rest of society as well. All progress, thus, whether individual or collective, depends upon our learning to react promptly and in ways that draw out and coordinate the virtues present in every context. Religion and philosophy, at their best, offer disciplines to help us learn this supreme art.

There is deep significance in the comparison of the human personality to a car.[2] Its sense organs are made to stand for impetuous steeds, the mind for the reins, and the power of judgement for the charioteer. The implication is that unless the driver combines in himself a variety of talents, the owner of the car and every other factor involved would be wrecked owing to the unchecked behaviour of the horses. He must be thoroughly conversant with the nature of the road, and he must be proficient in releasing and directing the energy of his pulling team. It is necessary to bear in mind that the students who were given the example of the car were familiar not merely with the slow-moving conveyances of the civilians of those days, but also with the fast vehicles used with deadly efficacy in the field of battle. They knew that a careless turn of a military car meant the death of the hero occupying it, and probably defeat in the war and subjection to the conqueror.

Another example used was connected with the sea. It was not even hinted that wisdom consisted in avoiding the sea altogether, so that one could be safe not only from drowning but even from beatings by a few rough waves.

The example, on the contrary, implied a bold and purposeful crossing of the deep. Naturally, it suggested the need to employ one's resources to prepare a suitable vessel for doing it. What is more, it stressed the importance of preliminary training in seamanship. Even children knew in those days that successful navigation depended upon the ability to manipulate the sails and the rudder—to take advantage of favourable winds and to withstand the onslaughts of storms and boisterous waves. Thus, whatever examples were used, the lessons conveyed were always of a positive kind. They emphasized the value of fearlessness, of untiring efforts, of accurate gauging of prevalent forces, of quick judgements, and of timely manoeuvres. The refrain of every song that inculcated discipline invariably ran along some of these essential keys. It said, in short: 'We ought to rely on our own personal exertions, attain clarity of understanding by studying scriptures and by keeping the company of the virtuous and thus fully equipped, cross the ocean of worldliness'[3] When Truth is realized, 'the journey of this world becomes delightful' indeed.[4]

II

All people, however, do not react in the same way to any given situation. In fact, they cannot; for tastes, temperaments, and capacities differ from man to man. In a way this diversity is good. For where one is weak, another can help him with the requisite strength and support. Besides, where all are endowed with skills of different kinds, society itself stands to gain enormously by a judicious pooling of their resources.

How a well planned coordination makes for speedy progress can be seen by examining any cross section of social life, taken at random. For the sake of simplification, let us take the example of a tract of land whose physical features can be registered more or less alike by the eyes of everyone who looks at it. Let us specify further that it has a running stream on one side and that it gradually rises to high wooded hills, with rocks and boulders overlooking the entire scene. As it stands, no tourist will take the trouble to visit it ; but one who knows agriculture will. For his trained mind will show him that he can have there enough land for himself, with not many competitors to purchase it. He will also mark that there is sufficient good water for man and beast as well as for cultivation of foodcrops. He can thus confidently shift his family and animals there. The construction of dwelling house and barn will not present any serious problem. For the main materials, stone and wood, are in plenty and near at hand. What is needed is the sheer labour to cut and remove them to the chosen site. If one man takes the initial risk and does something profitable, we can rest assured, others of the same bent of mind will hasten to copy his example. Thus, within a short time, that land would become a colony of enterprising farmers occupying its most fertile parts.

At this stage other and more far-reaching changes would begin. How can people with an eye for making profits through trade fail to notice the heaps of cereals and other edible products available there for sale ? The coming of merchants means the construction of better types of houses, with special godowns and offices for transacting business. This, in its turn, means the arrival and settling down of various specialists like carpenters, masons, smiths, tailors, washermen and so on. Every added facility is bound to attract someone who has been on the look out for it and who will be prepared to take a little risk himself to open up a new line with his own talent. As reactions follow one another in this fashion, we can expect a prosperous town to come up there as years roll by. The clear perception of a genuine need ordinarily provides the mental background for a series of reactions, each later one correcting and supplementing its predecessor, till finally the need is adequately met. With the increase of population, there would be a proportionate multiplication of requirements. And by and by, social responses would condense into visible form as educational and medical institutions, meeting halls, markets, banks, transport services and the like. We may call this the beautiful pattern of reactions.

An ugly pattern will not be slow to raise its head as well. Human nature being what it is, the sight of wealth and luxury enjoyed by a few is likely to awaken jealousy and malice in some. Why this should happen we can never easily decide. What we can safely say is this : The desire to experience sensual delights is equally spontaneous and insistent in everyone. The method of securing them, however, is bound to vary according to the cultural level and the working capacities of the people concerned. As these qualities admit of numerous permutations and combinations, the differences in reactions are practically endless. Let us take a few examples. Who is not familiar with the sensitive type of person who has been living in comfort, but whom adversity deprives of his accustomed pleasures all on a sudden ? He may probably try his best to keep up an air of being unruffled by his loss. But it may rankle in his heart all the same. In the resulting clash of thoughts, it will not be surprising if baser emotions appear in his mind now and then, making him more miserable than otherwise. As against men of refinement like him, there can be many whose longing for pleasures is as powerful but who are too badly equipped from the start to compete in honest work and to procure them through normal payment. Most antisocial activities and even crimes are developed forms of little perverse reactions to painful pressures. There can be a combination of poverty, absence of educational opportunities, compelling desires, and the existence of tempting fields, often unguarded, right in front. It is such settings that give the earliest suggestions to attempt short cuts to enjoyment through thefts, robbery, organized dacoity and the like. A more subtle form of enjoyment consists in the continuous exercise of power, of social or political authority — of what religious people call 'name and fame'. It is well known that in the scramble for it, the usual pattern of reaction includes misrepresentations, intrigues, and the deliberate creation of factions to overthrow actual or possible rivals. There is no guarantee that the little town of our example will be safe from these troubles. There too, as prosperity increases, some immature minds will be found to leave enough doors ajar for mischief-makers to enter and start pernicious movements. Society as a whole will then have to react by setting up the police, law courts, and even an armed force.

History shows how tourists in the past often visited wealthy lands to reconnoitre and prepare the ground for the quiet entry of astute schemers a little later. We also know how in medieval days every wooded hill with big rocks and boulders attracted the attention of military adventurers. What more convenient place could be got than such an eminence for erecting a fort? From it the surrounding territory for miles in all directions could be dominated with ease. Though in matters of theorizing about 'one world', moderners have made spectacular advances, yet in actual practice the old pattern of reaction, viz. to seize, exploit and domineer wherever a foothold on any pretext is got, continues unchanged. In fact, the progress of science has shown that there is inexhaustible wealth almost anywhere — in the sands on the seashore, under the snow-cap at the pole, and in the limitless 'outer space'. Where there is wealth quarrels may follow! Knowledge, as it stands, thus offers two equal chances: to react in a beautiful way or in an ugly, destructive way. We can either enrich human life and lift it to sublime heights, or debase it or even annihilate it by clinging perversely to narrow sectional views and fighting for them. Race, religion, language, economics, and politics have their legitimate places in constructive work. It cannot be a sign of knowledge or of evolution to put wrong values on them and employ them consciously to cause splits instead of unity, or hatred in place of love.

III

The remedy for sectional views is a type of education that leads to more and more inclusive views. In this matter, religious and philosophic disciplines can give us utmost help. What is required is that their explanations should not be designed for winning polemical victories and swelling the ranks of formal 'converts'. The idea of spiritual 'liberation' is not an enemy of individual and collective benefits that social, economic, or political measures can ordinarily confer. What spiritual men have condemned is the rigid attitude that fails to see anything beyond the apparently disconnected creatures and objects of the sense world. What they have pointed out is that there is a vast area of Existence beyond the range of the senses, that it is not exclusive of the perceived fields, but that it contains within it a supreme creative principle harmonizing everything. How are we justified in assuming that we have an independent power to deal with problems and to solve them satisfactorily? To complete the picture, we have also to understand that there is a most reliable Principle regulating every movement of the environment within which we live and work. It is that Principle which makes us recognize problems, stimulates us to act, receives our effort and manifests the result as a reaction from Its side, according to Its own laws of Being. A unified outlook demands that we should intelligently connect our birth, growth, perceptions, hopes, judgements, endeavours, and achievements with that all-embracing Principle. We may look upon It as a Person; in that case the steps we take to unify our outlook will be accompanied by a feeling of reverent adoration which will be eminently satisfying in itself. If we prefer to regard It as an Eternal Principle, the element of worship may be lacking, but not that of certainty or of abiding trust.

By whichever methods the unification is achieved, the impact on the field of work is bound to be considerable. Other factors being equal, the man who plans and acts with the constant awareness of the creative Background for all evolution must succeed in evoking surer and mightier responses from every level he contacts. This will not be possible for one who believes that he has to wrest his gains from a grudging, if not hostile, material environment. Every conceptual barrier causes a diversion of the energy that should go into confident forward movement. The assumption that improvements can come only as the final result of a prolonged fight with the environment is a formidable barrier. It not only creates an undercurrent of doubt and fear, but also alters the structure of the worker's personality into that of an engine of destruction. When it enters any field, its performance will be limited to threats and challenges, or smashings and levellings. It will be without the delicate limbs that can heal wounds or give an assuring touch. It will be unable, for want of proper instruments, to revive hopes, rouse self-reliance. or release the energy of virtuous endeavour in the persons whom it faces. If such limbs are to develop, there must be the pressure of the right attitude and aspiration from the start. In other words, conceptual barriers must be eliminated. Philosophy has to be learned and applied in such a way as to accomplish this. The last barrier will disappear only when misguided men and apparently insentient Nature are realized as nothing but temporary sense readings of what is, in truth, an eternally Perfect Being—the constant Witness of the very readings themselves. With this realization, the last inhibitions will vanish. Work then becomes spontaneous and attains the refinement ordinarily associated with worship in a shrine.

IV

So far Indian philosophical ideas are concerned, we find that they were not meant to be put into practice only by those who led a retired life and restricted their activities to simple teaching. An impartial study of available literature shows that these ideas were exemplified also in the lives of people who commanded armies and governed kingdoms. It was understood that spiritual insight infuses a rare type of vigour,[5] surpassing the one derived from the intellect that bases its judgements exclusively on sense data. Unless an administrator knew, by direct experience, what illumination meant, how could he enable his subjects to canalize their efforts to attain it through graded steps ? If society as a whole is to be trained to drop sectional views and adopt a more and more unified outlook, from where can it draw the necessary inspiration ? It has to come primarily from those persons who are so stationed as to be able to mould the thoughts and emotions of the masses—i.e. from the rulers and others who occupy key positions in social, political and similar fields.

Some of the stories that deal with spiritual disciplines are highly suggestive. For example, there is the story of Nachiketas. It shows that even children before puberty,[6] can take an irrevocable decision to pursue Truth and shake off everything standing between them and the final goal. The teacher's words of appreciation when Nachiketas refused to yield to temptation are worthy of recall. For they show what inner qualifications must be acquired before higher perceptions can arise. He said, in effect: 'O Nachiketas, how intelligent you are! I have tried my best to tempt you into accepting various objects of desire such as children, and charming attendants like celestial nymphs. But you have sternly rejected them, being fully convinced of their ephemeral and sapless nature. You have carefully avoided the contemptible path of wealth which is trodden by the ignorant and in which the thoughtless come to grief.' What the boy insisted on knowing, when framed in its final form, stood thus: Apart from what is commonly called virtue and its opposite, vice; apart from visible results and their subtle causes; apart also from things conditioned by time in its three modes, past, present, and future—apart from these and other limiting factors, if you see or know anything, please tell me That'. The main discourse which forms the answer deals with the eternally Perfect Principle, which can and should be realized by all. At the close of the teaching, we get the statement that not only Nachiketas, but everyone else who transforms his outlook as that boy did will surely attain the insight with which he was so early blest. Referring to the technical term 'Atman', the commentator says: Its derivative meaning is 'what pervades, what absorbs, what enjoys objects here, and what makes the continuous existence of the universe possible'.[7] Insight, unified outlook, and realization of the Atman cover the same ground and mean the same 'goal'.

Turning to another valuable text, we find a classification of virtuous people themselves into four types.[8] It is natural that it must include 'the wise man who, as knowing the Truth already, is ever steadfast and fully devoted to the One all-embracing Principle'. He will find no other object of worship whichever way he turns. The list must also surely include the enquirer who vaguely feels the existence of this One, and struggles for a direct experience of it. It is remarkable that the text in question gives the other two places in the list to 'the distressed' and 'the seeker of wealth'. The commentator explains that the distressed man is he who is attacked by a robber, a tiger, illness and the like! In other words, it matters little what the immediate cause is that makes a person turn in the direction of the Supreme Force that responds to his heart-felt call. It may be the need to escape pain; or it may be even the idea of owning and enjoying objects of the senses.

All desires are not bad. The mental movements that seek to gain an object or to produce a better situation, as also the running thrill that is felt when any movement succeeds, become harmful only when they go against virtue, i.e. when they block the way to a unified outlook. In fact, a step in the right direction is to understand that the fruits of actions are ordained by the Omniscient Lord Himself. Whatever the form of the deity worshipped and whatever the relief prayed for by a simple-hearted devotee, the All-merciful One responds to him to the extent that is needed to strengthen his faltering faith. It will enable him gradually to look upon "desire' itself—consistent with scriptural demands—as a manifestation of the Lord's presence in the mental field. The next step will be to weave it intelligently into an attractive pattern along with various other manifestations, like that of strength in anyone, free from passion or prejudice. In that list will come discrimination and self-control of spiritual people, 'human-ness' among mankind, life itself in all creatures, and the special properties of different elements, like physical brilliance in the sun. The harmonization and refinement of thoughts can be complete only when they lead to the realization, intellectually first, emotionally later, of the One outside whom no entity can exist, and in whom the whole universe is woven as a cloth in the warp or clusters of pearls on a string.

16. Towards Fuller Vision

He sees rightly who sees clearly within himself that the Omnipotent and Infinite Spirit, Non-dual and of the nature of Consciousness, is present in all the states and conditions of all beings.

He sees rightly who sees clearly within himself that the individual soul and the world appearing to be different from it are ever non-different from the Supreme Self and that everything is a spark of the Supreme Intelligence.

He sees rightly who sees clearly within himself: 'What is called the "three worlds" is verily like the limbs of my body—as waves stand in relation to the abode of waters'.

He sees rightly who sees clearly within himself: The three worlds are like a younger sister to me—tender and deserving compassion and protection at my hands'.[1]

I

Much of our present knowledge is due to 'specialization'. The items on which thoughtful men are conducting research is almost endless. 'Food' may be taken as one of them. But that itself is as vast as an empire. Vegetables, fruits, nuts or edible oils form just a small subdivision within it. We know that successful production of these depends upon a number of steps like classification of soils and their enrichment, or improvement of the quality of seeds through grafting and allied processes. As we make further observations along these lines, we shall get a mental picture of a huge world of enquirers, each original in his or her own way, but all eager to grasp subtle truths and eliminate obstacles that stand in their path. One prominent feature of modern discoveries is the realization that there is amazing power locked up in the subtle as contrasted with the gross aspects of the universe. To take a simple example : Let us remove more and more heat from the human body ; a stage must come when physical death will be the result. But deal with certain metals or chemicals in a similar way ; when cold or 'pressures' are stepped up as far as technically possible, what do we find ? It is not anything 'akin' to death that takes place, but the emergence of hitherto unexpected qualities like ability to defy gravity or penetrativeness of an incredible type ! It is the glory of science that it enters different fields, 'unpromising' in the beginning, devises experiments to evoke reponses from deeper levels, and arrives at a better understanding of the creative forces that lie embedded in them. This is with regard to the world of the senses.

Compared with this, the world of religion and philosophy may be called 'internal'. But it is not strictly or exclusively so. Most of us may be so obsessed with our own problems that we may often imagine the goal of spiritual disciplines to be the end of personal sorrows and entry into a realm of personal security and happiness. Our individual limitations, however, should not be used to lower the ideal as it is presented in sacred texts. Disciplines, according to them, are meant primarily to aid mental purification. If practised properly, they can help us to shed selfish values and the complexes developed through faulty reactions to the environment. Does this accomplish anything more than the acquisition of a noble and admirable character? What the books claim is that the faculty of 'attention,' when thoroughly disentangled from wrong associations and emotions, also becomes capable of registering the subtle principles underlying every aspect of the universe on which we may choose to focus it later. The scientist can take advantage of the resultant clarity and use it for the discovery of the 'truths' related to the field of his investigations. The social worker, the economist, and the politician too can likewise depend upon it to gain successes in their own spheres. It does not matter what the area to be covered is; what matters is the clarity—single-mindedness of the aim, the passion for truth.

What, then is the department in which the spiritual aspirant is expected to specialize? Is there one such at all? If there is, how is it related to the other kinds of enquiries? One text, by way of an answer, so to speak, makes a sweeping movement in which it brings together three items: [2] the universe before its manifestation, the functioning of life in the bodies of creatures like man, and the Supreme Self in which all knowledge is unified. What is the basis for the selection of these three?

II

Ancient books are highly suggestive. Their object is to take us to the realm of the Immutable, the Immortal, as distinct from the realm of the changing and the perishable. Reaching It, the wise man, they say, will 'see' himself abiding in perfection even when his body is engaged in its own day-to-day activities. He will be intensely conscious of 'himself' as free awareness presiding, as it were, in a general way over all that evolution means and, in a particular way, on those sections which cosmic pressures bring before him from time to time. The field of evolution is not blotted out, ignored or rejected, but estimated, outgrown, and seen reverently in the glorious light of the Supreme Self, apart from Whom it cannot be conceived of. Ordinary 'specialization' consists in cutting off a small unit from a vast area and in digging into it for getting detailed information. Naturally, as a result of such specialization, discoveries mount up, and increasing need arises to fill up gaps and to co-ordinate the numerous laws that happen to be framed. In the case of the spiritual seeker, there is no cutting off, except in a figurative sense. He puts the world of change, of efforts and gains, into one big bundle and tries to attach himself to the Totality which alone can account for all rise, growth, and development. There cannot be a Totality in addition to the 'parts' which are observed moving from an inferior to a superior state. If a causal relation is to introduced, the Perfect Entity itself must be accepted as the Prime Cause leading to individual 'perfections' as 'results'. But is it not possible, at a certain stage of mental purity, to rise above the causal complex? One text insists that we should. It says that as long as we allow ourselves to be 'possessed' by the ghost of belief in causal connection, so long our rotation in Samsara or relative experience is bound to continue unabated. It adds that if, on the other hand, we outgrow the tendency to view events only in terms of cause and effect, the oppressive delays and frictions of a compulsory relative experience will cease to operate in our case.[3]

We may explain it thus: A man may think, 'I am the agent. These virtuous and vicious deeds belong to me; and I shall reap their consequences in the present or in a future state'. In other words, he attributes causality to the Atman and devotes his mind to foster this conviction.[4] He does not understand that thought is cosmic creative power; or that its repetition can give it the momentum needed to transform it into 'expected' or 'dreaded' forms on the material plane. That thought takes visible shapes is clearly referred to in many places. One passage points out the fact that even little worms have the ability to make their own cortices or coatings. It then applies this principle to human beings and says that it is the 'mind' that has, by its own inherent power, produced the body for its abode, though normally we are unable to detect the subtle processes by which this is accomplished. The physical, vital, intellectual and other layers of the personality are also declared to be only fitting expressions of condensed aspiration—right or wrong, knowingly or unknowingly entertained. In fact, 'there is nothing that the mind cannot get or build out of its unique field of throbbing imagination, however difficult or unattainable it may at first appear to be'.[5] As a person thinks repeatedly, so he becomes and so he experiences.

But is this the highest level that man can reach—run after various objects of sense pleasure and fritter away valuable energy to secure perishable stuffs that only fan the flame of desire in him? Instead of using that energy to aim at a future satisfaction and to struggle day and night, full of doubt and anxiety till it is got, is it not wiser to employ that same energy in the present to reach its inexhaustible Source and to abide in Its plenitude with unshakable assurance and profound gratefulness ? We unquestioningly accept that the hope of getting something is an essential ingredient of the aspiration that produces favourable changes later. In other words, we believe in the efficacy of mental formulas like this: 'I feel myself small: I hope to fill up this want, this blank, by gaining that object. I fear I may have to strive hard for a long time. But I am determined to succeed'. It is not difficult to see that the really creative 'pull' in this mental operation comes from the focussing of 'attention' on a specific desirable condition. The rest, viz. the assumption of present smallness balanced by future fulness, or the present feelings of fear and anxious waiting, balanced by the determination to enjoy, are all parts of a psychological drama which the aspirant finds helpful in keeping up his interest and in releasing his energy without a break. Now the question is whether there is any absolute value in the details of this drama and whether it could not more profitably be replaced by another in which the belief in causality is pushed away from the centre of 'attention'. A formula, for example, like this: 'This seeming imperfection is like a dream or reverie, sure to break, and fit only to excite a smile when full waking takes place. Nay, it is the Supreme Perfection alone that is shining through this space-time set up. It is fully awake and free even now. Whatever is registered through the senses and the mind as imperfect bits is indeed the Infinite, the Immutable, which in Its Totality can never be caught in thoughts and concepts'. A little reflection will show that the 'pull' exerted by this conviction leaves nothing to be 'desired'. On the contrary, it has the exceptional advantage of eliminating doubts and anxieties from the mind of the person who arrives at it by valid means, and corresponding delays and resistances from the fields he contacts in the course of his daily work.

III

Among the valid means, scripture occupies a dominant place. Without it to light up our truth with its illuminating words, guiding corrective illustrations or poetic suggestions, we would at every turn reduce the Supreme Reality to the position of a rigid concept and afterwards, become perplexed at seeing it stand as a rival or supplement to other concepts equally limited. Scripture knows, so to speak, our inability to grasp subtle principles without the use of the causal relation. So in different ways it 'delineates the projection of the universe, the entrance of the Self into it, as also the continuance and dissoultion of what is thus projected'. These descriptions are not given with the idea that we should unduly discuss or, in a strictly laboratory sense, try to verify the steps involved in the manifestation of the visible world from its unmanifested condition. These descriptions are meant only as aids to the realization of the Self, declared again and again to be 'the highest end of man'. As the commentary puts it, 'the entrance of the Self into the universe is but a metaphorical way of saying that it is perceived in the midst of the latter'. 'For the all-pervading Self, which is without parts, can never be supposed to enter in the sense of leaving a certain quarter, place or time and being joined to new ones'. And wherever conscious activities like seeing or thinking occur, there cannot be any 'seer' 'other than the Supreme Self', as is testified by such scriptural passages as, 'There is no other witness but This, no other hearer but This', or 'It knew only Itself' 'Therefore It became all'

As in other instances, scripture facilitates realization by drawing pointed attention to the personality itself, where the intelligence of the Self is perceived up to the 'very tips of the nails'. In what way has It entered or does It exist there ? Two simple examples are cited. 'As in the world a razor may be put in its case' or 'perceived as being within it', 'in one part' ; or 'as fire lies in wood, pervading it' and may be brought out through proper rubbing, 'so does the Self reside in the body', pervading it in a 'general way' as 'living', and in 'particular ways' as 'hearing', 'seeing', and so on. But this is not enough ; 'people do not see It' yet as It really is. 'For It is incomplete' when known only so far. In what way ? The text explains. When It does the function of living, It is called the vital force ; similarly, when It speaks, the organ of speech ; when It sees, the eye ; and so on. In other words, we are observing only single functions indicating either Its powers of action or Its powers of knowledge. 'He who meditates upon each of this totality of aspects', 'without combining the other aspects' or functions, misses the Truth. 'As long as the man knows the Self as possessed of all the natural functions and thinks that It sees, hears or touches, he does not perceive the Whole Truth'. Then by what kind of vision can he fully know It ? It is replied that he must realize It as the Unity in which 'all these differences due to the limiting adjuncts such as the vital force and denoted by names arising from the functions of living etc. become one with the unconditioned Self—as the different reflections of the sun in water become one in the sun'. This is the significance of the term *alone* in the direction : 'Of all these, the Self alone is to be realized'.

One may ask: If this is the intention, why is there the mention of 'all these', viz. movements in time and space—all that is implied not only in the life and spiritual exercises of the aspirant, but also in the compassionate behaviour and the formal acts of teaching of the illumined sage ? Are these to be neglected or shut out altogether ? The reply is : 'Not so ; although they are to be known, they do not require a separate knowledge over and above that of the Self. For one knows all these things other than the Self through It when the Self is known'.

Most people will like to ask whether a distinction should not be made between 'knowledge' and 'attainment'. In reply it is said that 'the non-attainment of the Self is nothing but the ignorance of It'. In the case of every other thing, there is a difference between the attainer and the object attained. A person who assumes that there is something else to attain, considers his individual 'self' to be the attainer and the 'not-self' the thing to be got. And 'this, not being attained, is separated by acts like producing', themselves dependent upon the presence of various factors like the agent, his instruments and the like. The results too, when they appear, will be found to be perishable, since things procured under specific conditions cannot remain intact when those conditions change. But the case of the Self, dealt with in scriptures, is quite different. It is being perceived all the time, but wrongly apprehended. What is needed is the removal of the mental obstructions that prevent Its being 'seen' as the grand Unity, outside of which there is no second to be seen, heard or thought about. As this 'seeing' implies a radical alteration in the outlook, scripture insists rightly that It should first be heard of from a teacher and from holy texts, then reflected on through reasoning, and then meditated upon, i.e. dwelt upon reverently in the mind till conceptual distinctions of Self and 'not-Self' or of agents, action and goal, or of aspiration, waiting and achievement, are all harmonized and smoothly outgrown.[6]

IV

There are, however, many concepts that positively assist in the widening of awareness till total harmony is achieved. Each religion supplies a number of them. Each individual who is sincerely interested in actual practices can easily pick up some suitable to his taste and temperament. If attention is made to play upon chosen particulars — 'forms' of God, as devotees call them — the mind of its own accord gradually lifts up their barriers and accommodates them in the 'general' knowledge which, at each stage, is relatively 'infinite'. Thus disputes about the superiority of the initial concepts or 'forms' serve no useful purpose, What is essential is, in the words of Sri Ramakrishna, to 'hold' fast to some form of God or some mood, whichever you like; it is then only that there will be steadfastness. For, 'He is realizable by spiritual moods (Bhava) alone'. And this consists in 'establishing a realationship with God and keeping it bright before our eyes at all times — at the time of eating, drinking, sitting, sleeping. etc'.[7] When the principle is understood, it will not be difficult to cultivate the right type of feeling conveyed in the *Saundaryalahari* hymn: 'Whatever actions I do may be taken as intended for Thy worship — my prattle as prayer to Thee; the manifold forms of my manual work as Mudras, pious hand-movements employed in Thy worship; my loiterings as circumambulations round Thee; my taking nourishment as the offering of oblations to Thee; my lying down as prostrations to Thee; and my attending to all other comforts as the dedication of my entire self to Thee'.[8] Of course, in the case of the aspirant the feeling would be one roused by special effort, while in the case of the sage it would come like a spontaneous downpour from his steady illumination.

This brings us to some of the conversations of Sri Sarada Devi about various other details of Sadhana. Once a disciple wanted to know why the name of God should be repeated 'using the fingers'; could it not be done solely in the mind? In her own quiet way she answered: 'God has given the fingers that they may be blessed by repeating His name with them'.[9] Is there any limb that cannot become purified by being actively associated with devotional acts? Her own life was an object lesson in this respect. One never found her 'idle'; at least her hands would be busy doing something or other connected with the shrine, say preparing betel rolls for regular offering. When spiritual vision dawns, men and material objects appear transformed, thereby introducing a special element of sweetness and sacredness into daily activities. This was revealed in a most natural way when one day, by sheer accident, the disciple's elbow touched the Holy Mother's feet while he was carrying some Prasada for the devotees. 'Ah!' said the Mother, and saluted him with folded hands. Ignoring the young man's protest, she even bowed down to him and expressed her feeling in other suitable ways. 'Thus', says the record, 'she used to respect her disciples as the manifestations of God, and at the same time show her affection to them as a mother does to her children'.[10] The intensity of genuine compassion, found in all great souls, can be easily gauged from a little anecdote casually given by the Mother herself. 'Once Balaram's wife was ill' and the Master asked her to go to Calcutta and visit her. But the Mother hesitated as she could not 'see any carriage or other vehicle' there. The Master, who was always considerate in his talks with her, 'replied now in an excited voice: "What! Balaram's family is in such trouble and you hesitate to go! You will walk to Calcutta. Go on foot"....

'Where, indeed, will man be if God will not protect him in his trouble?'[11] Her ability to infuse courage and confidence was superb. Once she referred to the exclamation of Naren: 'Let me have millions of births, what do I fear?' Commenting on it, she quiety added: 'It is true. Does a man of knowledge ever fear rebirth? He does not commit any sin. It is the ignorant person who is always seized with fear'.[12] Herself absoultely pure, she yet fervently 'prayed',—'with tears in her eyes', says the record—in the temple of Radharamana: 'Lord, remove from me the habit of finding fault with others. May I never find fault with anybody!' The disciple tells us that 'her prayer seems to have been answered literally'; and she herself speaks about it and observes: 'It is the nature of man only to see defects. One should learn to appreciate others' virtues'.[13] How significant is her rejoinder to Golap-Ma who once exclaimed in a pique: 'Mother, what is the good of telling you? You cannot see the defects of others!' The Mother told her these unforgettable words—which can serve as an excellent motto for us as well—'Well Golap, there is no want of people to see the faults of others. The world will not come to a standstill if I am otherwise'.[14]

Indeed, how can one who 'sees' the Self alone be ever moved by emotions opposed to reverence and the spirit of loving service? 'He who sees everything in his Atman and his Atman in everything' can never perceive any 'object' to excite the feeling of revulsion in him.[15] His unified outlook will make him an embodiment of love, goodwill, and peace.

V. GUIDANCE

17. Creation of Interest and Certainty

> As the dawn heralds the rising sun, so sincerity, unselfishness, purity, and righteousness precede the advent of the Lord.
>
> —Sri Ramakrishna

Excellence in any field of activity depends on hard work along right lines. Spiritual endeavour improves all fields. For it aims at the realization, in full, of the harmony and the glory which, from the plane of the sense, we can experience only in refracted forms, as life, thought, multiplicity, compassion, or evolution. Any slackening of effort in its pursuit means serious loss. First, as is well known, time misspent cannot be recovered; secondly, inertia that suggests the idea of seeking relief from the struggle, for howsoever short a period, is sure to carry its own momentum and reappear variously disguised.

Even in executing a work of art, say, a painting, there are many factors involved. To start with, the painter must himself feel satisfied that the beauty captured by his mind is adequately expressed on his canvas through the arrangement of figures and the combination of colours. Next, his finished product must be able to awaken in the minds of the viewers at least a glimpse of the idea abiding within him. Lastly, this idea must be more or less in keeping with the cultural refinements of previous generations, with the highest aspirations of contemporaries, and with the likely expectations of posterity. When we apply these standards to the field of spiritual achievement, we see the magnitude of the task as well as the ennobling character of every sincere step taken to carry it out.

If Cosmic Energy be roughly compared to a vast reservoir, remaining full at all times, each section of Nature manifesting life corresponds to one of the canals conveying its waters. Every community, then, becomes an important branch of it, and every individual a sort of pipe or fountain functioning at some point along its course. In the uncontrolled state of the individual, his wild emotions, low tastes, selfish decisions, and aggressive actions work like alternating jets, dangerous to himself and to others. The purpose of discipline is to make him see the total picture, change his values, lift up his level, catch the maximum pressure, and evlove the greatest possible harmony, beauty, and utility out of the energy flowing through him.

Such a thorough overhauling of the inner set-up of the personality cannot be done quickly. Our common weakness is to associate happiness with an unbroken chain of enjoyments, supposed to come as the recurring interest from the fund of previous exertions. We imagine the ideal condition to be one in which we can safely retire from all active life and fall back on the rewards we think we deserve. Such a condition, even if it arises, cannot remain steady for long. For, whatever energy we spend—'invest', as we fancy—being limited, the results we get out of it must also be limited. They are bound to end sooner or later. Material objects have some stability. A house, once built, can be used for a long time. But circumstances other than those that brought the wealth for its construction may confront us and compel us to mortgage or sell it. The security on which we counted may thus be lost unexpectedly. If this is true regarding material possessions which retain their shape and identity for some time, what need is there to speak of the uncertainty in the field of thought control? Thought is the creative power coursing through our personality. It is essentially free. Therein lies its supreme value. But unluckily for us, it exhibits its freedom in a specially disconcerting way by eluding our attempts to hold it down. If, through carelessness, we leave them to themselves, new units of thought that come along the orbit of time form strange associations and awaken our dormant passions. Then the usual drama is enacted. They distort our vision, dictate unwise decisions, and throw us into activities causing needless pain. As freedom implies the possibility of jumping in any direction, the only way of preventing a gliding down is to turn vigilance into a second nature. Acharya Sankara devotes nine stanzas of his *Vivekachudamani* to show how ruin may overtake even advanced seekers if they leave a loophole for carelessness to creep into their minds. He compares the resulting downfall to the bouncing, with increasing speed and force, of a ball inadvertently dropped by a player standing on the top of a staircase. He winds up his warning by saying that to the person engaged in harmonizing his mental powers, there is nothing so fatal as the failure to be vigilant.[1]

II

The safest way is to accept spiritual pursuit as a life-long affair. Practice, says Patanjali, becomes firmly rooted when it is well attended to for a long time, without interruption, and with devotion.[2] Someone may embark upon it hoping to make himself receptive to the highest truth within a few days or months. To remove the possibility of any student making such false estimates, one commentator compares an aspirant of that kind to an ignorant man, who wonders why the boy who went to study the Vedas, which are only four in number, has not returned home even after the expiry of five full days. To induce, the correct attitude the writer says that we must be prepared to continue disciplines not only for years but, if necessary, even for a number of lives.[3] If we are sure that the steps taken are right, why should we become anxious to put a time limit, and waste precious energy to have a periodic look at the clock?

We may become reconciled to the necessity of carrying on exercises throughout our life. Still there is the danger of creating periodic breaks in them and turning them into a seasonal adventure. In this alternating arrangement, every uncontrolled state neutralizes the gains made during the periods of control. This would result in a sort of painful stagnancy, if not a serious setback. It is to prevent this that there is the stipulation, 'without interruption'. The question arises whether interruption is not inevitable owing to the need to look after the body and to fulfil the responsibilities of our station in life. The reply is that practice is not exhausted by the repetition of certain prayers or the visualization of connected holy scenes. So far as they are concerned, they must be done daily, at a fixed time. What is more important is the general feeling of sacredness, of being in the presence of the Supreme Spirit, or of entrusting oneself into His protecting hands—it matters little what formula we adopt. Rituals or chants, supplications or affirmations are ways of creating controlled waves in the surface mind, so that, in due course, the right feelings may be awakened and sustained. They correspond—if one may be permitted make such comparisons to devices like 'turning the handle' when the 'self-starter' of an engine fails to work efficiently under certain conditions. They are like attempts to play with a child to make it love us. We know that when the engine starts functioning, it carries loads in any direction; and when love enters the child's mind, it may do many little things without further coaxing. So too, when higher values dawn on us, a continuous current is kept up long after the ending of formal exercises during scheduled hours. The attitude then remains serene even when we enter upon our daily duties, domestic, social, or official. When this control is achieved, the earlier dependence on particular times, places, and formulas to raise up and maintain the proper emotion is no more felt. On the contrary, spiritual disciplines as well as activities ordinarily called 'secular' become charged by the sublimity of the inner current and become spontaneous manifestations of higher moods.

This is more easily said than done. All disciplines are difficult in the beginning. A physical limb can be pushed into a desired position by using another limb against it. But where is the instrument to push the mind away from the familiar fields of love and even hatred (do we not sometimes feel upset if told to stop describing how we would chastise our enemies ?) into a strange area where visibility is poor ? Our first attempt is to use the will, meaning by it a kind of stubborn determination to crash through all obstacles. We imagine it to be the one internal agency capable of permitting the chosen thought to remain on the mental platform undisturbed by adverse elements. It does not take long to discover that roughness and violence are powerless against the irrepressible creative exuberance of thought. By persisting in the fighting attitude, we only tire ourselves out and run into clouds of dullness and uncertainty. They are Nature's earliest warnings that our methods are wrong. We love nobility, self-sacrifice, helpfulness or meditative calmness when we see it in others. We believe that these qualities overflow from their hearts as a result of the spiritual vision that they enjoy We wish to acquire that vision for ourselves; that is why we commence our disciplines. The thought that we are moving towards that ideal ought to give us greater enthusiasm than when we merely see it manifested in others. The first necessity, therefore, is to approach the exercises with a feeling of welcome. The period devoted to them must be repeatedly presented to our mind as the most precious and enjoyable part of the day. It is here that those who believe in a Personal Deity have a decided advantage. As a first step, they can easily rouse up the love and reverence that are ordinarily shown to their parents. teachers, and even honoured guests. By further efforts, they can then direct these satisfying emotions in a heightened form towards the Supreme Creator and Saviour. It is certainly a piece of 'imagination' to picture to ourselves that we are standing in the presence of the Heavenly Father, or that, seated within our hearts, He is watching and regulating our thoughts, words, and actions. But the resultant welling up of devotion, and the replacement of our crookedness by straightness, self-seeking by self-sacrifice, or dullness by interest, become psychological 'facts' with a more elevating content than before. As we repeat this process, along with the self-presented and deliberately guided imagination, the reaction in the form of newly associated emotions also becomes repeated, till in due course it changes our habits and lifts up our values. The principle of economy teaches us to make use of every available type of mental energy in the construction of a ladder giving us access to higher and vaster regions favouring the realization of truth, goodness, and beauty. Reasoning within a positive framework can lead us from doubt to certainty, and a faithful use of scripture can confirm the conclusions arrived at by reasoning. By the wise employment of imagination we can complete the process by infusing love and reverence into every effort we put forth. Without the spirit of welcome, which it alone can easily introduce, practice is bound to be dull and progress slow and even doubtful.

Every teacher or lecturer knows the importance of keeping up the interest of his hearers. When the speaker fails to hold their attention, the energy that appeared as their initial willingness to listen and learn demands a suitable outlet. If he is not competent to direct it himself into profitable activities, it is sure to make its own arrangements which may be unpleasant for all. For, in its attempt to find the line of least resistance, what can the stream of each individual's energy do except to issue out through the half-open gates of his follies and weaknesses ? It will not be a wonder if often the streams combine and flow into organized mischief or revolt ! Our mind, with its hundreds of plans and voices, is more or less like a group of people called up for work. The common factor behind these divergent plans is the desire for love, peace, and harmony. The work assigned must be such that this desire can be satisfied to some extent while executing it. If the ideal is divine bliss, every step taken must be accompanied by joy and serenity. For we are entitled only to the inner content of the means adopted. If every sitting for practice ends in dullness, repeated sitting can never produce joy. If wrong handling does not lead to dull stupor, it may lead to persistent wandering of thoughts, which is equally bad. The commentator, therefore, takes care to point out that in the absence of the spirit of welcome, the mind will be afflicted by evils in the shape of slumber, or wild distractions—the seed of ignorance putting forth its usual sprouts all the time ![4]

III

It is in creating this feeling of welcome that art in all its branches plays a decisive part. Even those who do not believe in God with form construct 'imposing' prayer halls, if possible, on hill tops, or river banks, or overlooking valleys—in short, in places noted for natural grandeur. The idea behind the selection of such sites and the adoption of such structural forms is that the beauty and majesty picked up through the senses can easily combine with the initial aspiration with which the devotee comes for prayer, and help him to create and maintain higher spiritual moods than those he gets while sitting at home. Many religious sects encourage the free use of paintings, statues, rituals, and music in their places of worship. This arrangement has a great psychological value. For, it considerably increases the number of avenues for the entry of influences which a willing seeker can joyfully transform into higher receptive states within himself.

Rituals serve many purposes, if we can use them wisely. We are so consitituted that we can, within certain limits, stress bodily or mental movements as we like, proportionately reducing the one we wish to check at the time. As spiritual exercises involve purification of thoughts and emotions, it is necessary to prevent the physical body from causing any kind of distraction. The usual method is to ignore the body after taking a fairly comfortable seat, and to direct all available energy for internal control. This throws unwary people into some danger. This peculiar quietness of the limbs is to a man of active habits akin to the preparation for actual sleep, and unless he takes extra precautions, he may unconsciously glide into a dream condition, in which vigilance and creative effort are both lost! The remedy lies in improvising bodily movements expressive of the holy emotion to be kept up. Hindu rituals make ample provision for a delightful co-ordination of body and mind. The Hindu does not believe that worship means only the particular actions done after formally occupying the seat for it. There is a good deal of preliminary work to be done, like cleaning the place and utensils and arranging lights, flowers, and other materials in their proper places. It is unreasonable to do these in a light-hearted mood. Any serious-minded devotee would consider his total personality purified by each one of them. They give not merely his mind, but also his physical body the privilege of being actively associated with what is recognized from the start as divine service. This recognition stands steady as the flame of an internal lamp, corresponding to the one kept lighted externally for the period of the worship. It also looks on like a silent witness, under whose supervision the different faculties are focussed on the Ideal and at the same time allowed the freedom to move and remain lively. This is a work which requires special skill. The rising waves of thought and feeling must be sifted; waves of inferior content must not be allowed to go forward in their original forms; even a fraction of a second should not be wasted in standing back embarrassed; instead, spiritual associations must be added to them in rapid succession till their values are altered; so that all mingle into a single orderly column dancing towards and round a centre of divinely illumined awareness. Rhythmic movement of bodily limbs constitutes ordinary dance; rhythmic movement of sounds characterizes music, vocal or instrumental; rhythmic dance of thoughts and sacred sentiments transforms the devotee's heart and fills it with 'Truth-bearing' clouds of virtue.[5]

Every religious tradition finds a place for some rituals or sacrifices symbolic of self-surrender. Whether it is an animal, or a cake, or a flower that we offer, there is a feeling of ownership at the back of it. We think that we part with something to which we have a right. The habit of giving it away in the name of God surely helps to neutralize the ego, the clinging to things for our own satisfaction. It is possible to knock down the ego further by a searching analysis. For instance, we can ask ourselves how we, and not someone else, managed to possess the things we now propose to sacrifice. If we are honest, our answer must be that we used God-given talents in a society that lacked them, and therefore, got our possessions at the expense of those less favourably placed. In offering anything at an altar, after we feel satisfied with this answer, we only gratefully give back to God what is really His own. Thus, as our perceptions become finer, we drop the idea of rituals as devices to propitiate a reluctant Deity, and accept them as most natural ways in which we can satisfy the inner urge to express our thankfulness. It does not take long to extend this idea of sacrifice to non-material offerings, like prayers or chants. What are they but special patterns in which we weave time, energy, and intelligence which are also God's gifts ? They are like flowers laid at the altar with the full realization that the garden, the plant, the manure and the gardener were supplied by Him alone. From this standpoint, every act connected with spiritual discipline, like reading, discussion, devotional singing, dancing or meditation can be looked upon as different forms of sacrifices. The attainment of final illumination includes the virtues of all of them, and may rightly be called the supreme sacrifice.[6] Whatever the enlightened person does for the welfare of others continues to bear the stamp of the sacrificial spirit. Sacredness, once acquired, remains unshaken and enters effortlessly into every thought, word, and act.

IV

Nature has endowed us with the ability to stand back and estimate the changes that take place in our personality from time to time. Even a man who does not believe in God often says, with pride, about various affairs of his daily life, that he has outgrown the stage of being tempted or frightened by them. He is certain that he has progressed, for by looking within, he directly notes the contrast in his values and reactions. His friends too are convinced about it; for they are able to mark big differences in his actual behaviour. Most men of education and culture consider strength of character and moral excellence as goals worthy of being attained by them. Sincere struggle in that direction can take them quite far, especially if they are determined to push any single principle of conduct to its perfection, as for example, to take a vow to uphold truth and justice, if need be, against overwhelming odds, or as the *Gita* puts it, 'unshaken even by heavy sorrows'.[7] Whatever ideal a man regards as noble has the power of altering and enriching his personality beyond his expectations. Nature's laws are such that by the time his mind becomes fully focussed on it, virtues not consciously aimed at while embarking on his disciplines begin to move into his heart of their own accord. The wonders of creation, the very mystery of the phenomenon called life, the transforming influences radiated by genuine love and compassion—contact with any of these, though probably for the hundredth time and so not new, can all of a sudden give a surprisingly novel direction to his thought current, and open the sluice gates for the rushing in of holiness and a host of allied qualities, till they fill his whole being and overflow into those who get into touch with him.

One advantage of studying scripture and of comparing notes with advanced souls is that we can know ahead what is likely to follow the acquisition of virtue. Sri Ramakrishna declares most unmistakably that 'There is no delay for him in attaining unto God, within whom the glories of affection are becoming manifest'. He himself raises the question as to what these glories are, and enumerates a few of them by saying: 'Discrimination, dispassion, tenderness to all life, service to the good, and love for their company, recounting of God's name and glory, truthfulness—all these'.[8] He explains the same truth in a different way in another context: 'As a master, before going to visit a servant, sends to his dependant from his own stores the necessary requisites, seats, and food, in order that he may worthily receive him, so before the Lord comes, He sends yearning, love, reverence, and faith into the heart of the devotee whom He is about to honour'.[9]

Here is Sri Ramakrishna's description of the behaviour of one who is so 'honoured': 'He indeed is blessed in whom all the qualities of head and heart are fully developed and evently balanced. He bears himself well in whatever position be may be placed. He is full of guileless faith and love for God, and yet his dealings with others leave nothing to be desired. When he engages in worldly affairs, he is a thorough man of business; in the assemblage of the learned, he establishes his claims as a man of learning, and in debates he shows great powers of reasoning. To his parents he is obedient and affectionate; to his brethren and friends he is loving and sweet; to his neighbours he is kind and sympathetic, always ready to do them good; and to his wife he is the lord of love. Such a man is indeed perfect'.[10]

18. Awakening and Grouping of Talents

'Whatever is glorious, prosperous, or strong, know that to be a manifestation of my splendour'.[1]

'There is nothing to obstruct you. For, if there is one common doctrine that runs through all our apparently fighting and contradictory sects, it is that all glory, power, and purity are within the soul already... potential or manifest, it is there.. Stand up and express the Divinity within you'.[2]

'As we come to know each other, love comes, must come, for are we not one? Thus we find solidarity coming in spite of itself. Even in politics and sociology, problems that were only national twenty years ago can no more be solved on national grounds only ... They can only be solved when looked at in the broader light of international grounds'.[3]

I

Creative imagination, untiring research, inventive skill—these are some of the special virtues of great scientists. There is nothing insignificant in their eyes. Sands on the seashore, mud, rocks, moss, plants, worms, poisons, light, gases—all these are approached, not certainly by all scientists alike, but by individuals among them and by teams, in accordance with the bent of mind natural to each of them. Theoretically no material need be wasted or utterly thrown away. For by suitable additions and by rearrangement of the elements into which it can disintegrate, it must be possible to manufacture various articles of daily use. What is wanted is knowledge, more of what is termed the 'know-how'.

Nature is full of possibilities. It is only a small fraction of these that are turned into actualities by man's efforts. Enormous changes are taking place outside this limited field. Taking a wider view we find that man's life and movements themselves are no more than one type of change, slightly more complicated, no doubt, than those involved in the lives of plants and animals. The scientist proceeds on the assumption that, by proper and persistent inquiry, the principles underlying these change can be discovered. Every discovery leads to the acquisition of power. With the aid of relevant techniques, we can utilize the discovery to make some of the principles operate more at one place, and to that extent shut out others or facilitate the entry of new ones. For example, we can pump out air and use the same principle of suction to bring up water or oil from deep wells, neutralizing the force of gravity that had kept the liquids beyond our reach before. Or we may transform the energy of a waterfall into electricity, convey it to far away places, and make it carry messages or turn the wheels of industry. It is remarkable how with the increase in knowledge there have been revolutionary changes in the tapping of power—actual burning of wood or coal, petrol and the internal combustion engine, and now the atom!

It is useful to examine a little more closely some of the factors that have brought about these important developments. First, the best scientists have been men of striking originality. Their vision has embraced new fields. They have confidently stepped into those fields in search of subtle and mighty forces, while people of inferior abilities have remained content with what has been achieved in the past. Secondly, every pioneer has had to improvise a series of novel experiments to detect those forces, with nothing to guide him except his own creative imagination. The combination of mental qualities that led to the discovery of radium may be taken as fairly representative of the outlook needed for success in any research. Lastly, as in the case of atomic power, there has been the exceedingly complex problem of perfecting the machinery to 'tame' the energy, and harness it to 'peaceful' uses. Every forward step has been taken by men who were passionately devoted to truth, who had an unshakable faith that steady pursuit must end in the discovery of Nature's laws, who did not hesitate to handle materials that might affect their health and even life, and who, above all, had the capacity to infuse their enthusiasm into others and to coordinate their efforts.

II

With slight modifications and additions these very qualities lead to greatness in every walk of life. We can see them in action in a gymnasium. Weak-bodied young people, with more than average longing to become strong and vigorous, brush aside their shyness and diffidence and enrol themselves as regular students. The 'fusion' of the quiet assurance of the teacher with their dormant wills releases tremendous energies. Standing before big mirrors which show them only their actual leanness at the time, they faithfully go through the prescribed simple exercises, taking care to fill their minds with hundreds of pictures of well-formed muscles, capable of functioning like iron bands at a moment's notice. In an atmosphere of confidence that eliminates all opposing forces, these pictures enter Nature's invisible, 'assimilating' regions and emerge as the power of rearranging available food material into the patterns cherished in the world of thought. The same principles are at work in the sustained efforts, often unnoticed by others, that ultimately produce the foremost men in sports, in running, jumping, weightlifting, boxing, or wrestling. When we cross over to the field of social relations, we find heroes there as well. What matters there is not wealth or scholarship but warmth and broadness of the heart. Defects can be found in plenty in every society. Many a well-meaning but misguided enthusiast wasted precious years in making frontal attacks on them, thereby turning his own mind into a capacious vessel for assembling and boiling them! But someone who is an embodiment of unwavering love moves quietly in their midst and, through constant example and whole-hearted service, makes increasing numbers see the value of positive thoughts and deeds. His love acts as an unseen cement binding his and their personalities into a single unit, while his humility leaves them free to mobilize all their noble traits and employ them — of their own accord, as they feel — for creating new and better conditions at every turn. In spiritual pursuit, the scope for such effort is infinitely extended. In it the environment is made to include the entire field of thoughts, emotions, and values. The aspirant learns to trace to their very foundation the limited forms and qualities appearing before him. We may, for convenience, classify them also as the ego and the non-ego. His aim is to become intensely aware of the inexhaustible Source of the stream of life and consciousness, one little branch of which he feels his individual existence to be. Instead of remaining ego-centric, he wishes to be fully identified with this Source and to be 'free' and 'perfect' like It. If the steady love of the social worker silently penetrates the complexes of the people around him and makes them take up constructive work suited to their capacities, what need to speak about the transformations which can be brought about by the much more subtle and all-embracing love of the spiritually perfect person? Buddha and Jesus—to mention only two—have shown how the currents set in motion by illumined souls can mould the lives of more and more millions with the passing of centuries.

All these examples of greatness can be taken as starting points for useful reflection. For one thing, they are present in some form or other almost everywhere; and they strike the imagination powerfully and at once. What is to be guarded against is the likelihood of dejection or jealousy creeping into our minds at the sight of greatness in others. These wrong reactions arise from a morbid brooding on the difficulties of developing all good qualities in ourselves. The remedy lies in altering our general outlook. Delight comes from a kind of mental identification. This need not be restricted to personal acquisition, as in owning private property, or to blood relationships, as in making our own children more educated than ourselves. Identification with noble causes and their advancement confer superior delights and inner expansiveness, as every unselfish person who has organized institutions of public utility knows by direct experience.

The most effective way of avoiding and even uprooting baser emotions is to awaken the feeling of sacredness. This can be done by diligently cultivating the habit of looking upon every form of greatness as a manifestation of the power and glory of God. For certain conveniences in managing daily activities, we have to make a distinction between man and Nature, between man and man, and between ourselves and everything else. By taking note of greatness, wherever found, and by inwardly adoring it as an aspect of the Supreme Being, we gain a unified outlook, carrying holiness with it and neutralizing the evils springing from compartmental views. In carrying out a programme of this kind, we shall find that the sources from which we can draw inspiration are almost endless. Glancing at the sky we see the sun and the moon; the Lord alone is there as splendour. In the earth on which we live He exists as fertility and wealth. Among tracts of water, His greatness appears as the ocean. Likewise, we have a glimpse of His strength in creatures like the shark, or the whale abounding in the seas, or the lion roaming in the forests. He, again, is consciousness; as mind He rules over the organs of sense.

In administrators He functions as the ability to protect, while in other gifted individuals it is He alone who descends as poetry, revelation, knowledge of the Self, or even as beauty, fame, constancy, and forbearance. From the standpoint of an earnest seeker, 'there is no end to the manifoldness' of His manifestations.[4] He can dwell on them in any order he pleases. The feeling of sacredness remains the same—deep and steady. He can even string them up into a garland of mental pearls and make a reverent offering of it as part of his daily devotions.

We know what happens when a person loves equally all the members of a group. He creates for himself a mind-made heart, a new, invisible life-centre whose energy controls, nourishes, and inspires all. There is no fear of loss for his little personality although he ceases to focus his attention particularly on it any further. On the contrary, it stands to gain most, as the highest values, in a way, fill it to overflowing before they enter into the lives of others. Is it possible for a power-house to suffer for want of light when the current supplied through it is actually being used for various purposes in distant homes? Among the effects of unwavering love two may be clearly distinguished. First, it falls silently on the noble traits dormant in its recipients, and makes them sprout and develop into healthy plants. Passing quickly through the inevitable stage of trial and error, the persons who receive constant encouragement seize every opportunity to express their inborn talents and ultimately perfect them. Secondly, love is the mightiest force for coordination and harmony. From the start, as these talents emerge, the loving heart, with equal, effortless grace, penetrates them like a silken thread, and holds them together as a precious ornament for the benefit of one another and of the world. Spiritual vision and love always carry with them the delicate touch that awakens and coordinates the dormant gifts of those coming within their range.

The instrument for instilling the spirit of coordination among the masses has for the most part been oral tradition containing stories and parables. The sages who composed them set the model in self-effacement by mentioning little about their own lives. They wanted that men's endeavours should be directed towards their inner refinement. So they made literature, art, social customs, and festivals help in the realization of the Cosmic or Divine element in the human personality. They resorted to poems, songs, ballads, and interesting anecdotes so that even children might learn them with delight. They would constitute a mental useful storehouse from which useful suggestions for day to day conduct might be freely drawn in later years. We often fail to see this educative value of mythology; for we still cling unconsciously to the ideas that made the history of advanced nations look very much like a chain of political intrigues, military conquests, and empire-makings! Thoughtful people are now seeing that seeds of aggression, sown under whatever pretext, must in due course produce an abundant harvest of inescapable bitternes and retaliation on a global scale, This is bound to lead to the realization of the truth that ancient sages saw and taught, viz. that humanity is at bottom a single indivisible unit, and that the intensification of the spirit of peace and goodwill within oneself is the shortest and surest way of promoting the cause of peace and culture all around.

That unregenerate men may use power for carrying on ruthless exploitation even beyond earth's limits is the theme of a well-known Indian story. Three brothers, Tarakaksha, Kamalaksha, and Vidyunmali undertook technically perfect disciplines and secured far-reaching concessions from Brahma, the Creator. These enabled them to dominate the heavenly, interstellar, and earthly regions from their three cities made respectively of gold, silver, and iron.[5] The contract stipulated that Death could overpower them only if anyone could manage to pierce them all with a single arrow just when they would meet together once in a thousand years![6] Having concluded this unique pact, they felt themselves secure and enslaved the three worlds for long. The pains of the oppressed gradually gained in volume and mounted up and made Siva, the Oversoul, break His meditation to end the Reign of Terror and protect the virtuous. Unable to bear His strength to reinforce their own, the celestials gave Him half of theirs instead. But He stood in 'need' of proper equipment, He said. It is here that the story imparts its lesson. It says that, recognizing the magnitude of the task, the entire earth gladly became His chariot, with the sun and the full moon fixed up as its shining wheels.[7] Scriptures, with their power to penetrate the subtlest levels, acted as horses, and Brahma, the Master of creative forces, with the ability to look in every direction with his four faces, willingly took up the steering work.[8] The foremost among rivers, mountains and the like cooperated in different other ways, and Vishnu, the Redeemer, became the shaft to complete the task at a single stroke.

That this example of total cooperation is meant to be copied by us in facing our difficult problems is shown by the author of the *Mahabharata* himself even through Duryodhana who persisted in wickedness counting on his military might. The context is worth noting. When Karna was installed as Commander-in-chief, he insisted that King Salya should act as his chariot-driver. Salya who felt that he was 'equal' to Karna took this as a personal affront and decided to 'walk out'. Duryodhana then narrated this story and said: 'Surely the success of the shooting depends in the steering. As Brahma did this great service to make Siva succeed, can you not cooperate with Karna in the coming decisive fight with Arjuna who has had Krishna himself as his able charioteer from the start?' Salya was pleased with the implications and he climbed into the charioteer's seat.[9]

IV

Poverty, hunger, disease, illiteracy, want of fair opportunity for all, insecurity, fears of various kinds — these are some of the evils afflicting humanity on the physical, mental, moral, and spiritual levels, as all thinking people can easily see. In the grim fight against these, everyone's cooperation is needed. According to his particular talent, each willing person can take up any of the million functions, like that of the chariot or its wheels, each of them being not merely 'honourable' but equally essential for the success of the whole. Our motto has to be: Unity, Synthesis, Equilibrium. For India, particularly, this 'Unity' has to be of: 'every Indian man and woman; of all the powers of the spirit, dream and action, reason, love and work, Unity of the hundred races of India with their hundred different tongues and hundred thousand gods springing from the same religious centre, the core of present and future reconstruction'.

And for everyone without distinction it has to be:

'Unity within the vast Ocean of all religious thought and all rivers past and present, Western and Eastern'. Unity of 'all the paths of the spirit: the four Yogas in their entirety, renunciation and service, art and science, religion and action from the most spiritual to the most practical'. 'Unity along all of them simultaneously'.[10]

19. Formula of Rousing and Refining

The mind is everything. If the mind loses its liberty you lose yours. If the mind is free, you are free too. The mind may be dipped in any colour, like a white cloth fresh from the wash. ... If the mind be kept in bad company, it will colour one's thought and conversation. Placed in the midst of devotees, it shall meditate upon God also. It changes its nature according to the things amongst which it lives and acts.

—Sri Ramakrishna

I

Ordinarily, air is 'light' and 'non-resisting'. Small insects, almost invisible to the naked eye, can hop from one place to another and pass through it with ease, with the help of the tiny muscles of their legs. But if the insect has wings, air stands 'rigid', as it were, receives their beatings and permits steady flight. This rigidity, however, can become most deadly to man and his properties when, instead of remaining still, air begins to move at eighty miles an hour, along a ten mile front! Those who had occasion to carry relief to cyclone-struck areas know the extent of damage this 'light' element that surrounds us can cause within a short time.

Thought exhibits some of these features. When we leave the mind to itself, without making any effort to direct it, thought forms emerge and combine in strange ways. They roll and curve like puffs of smoke from a dying fire. They look harmless and, sometimes, even interesting like butterflies flitting in the morning sunbeams. But the consequences can be terrible if their 'airy' waves develop into a passion which spreads from one individual to another, till opposing nations are caught in its violent eddies and whirlpools. Wars and bloodshed start as little breezes in ambitious minds. But when left unchecked, they slowly assume the proportions of a wide-spread storm which spends itself in wrecking homes, killing and disabling millions, and destroying works of art and culture. The next generation or two would find themselves thrown into a sorry plight. They would be compelled to struggle hard to rebuild what was wantonly razed to the ground during hostilities. If still the general pattern of thoughts remains unchanged, the aggrieved party would surely plan some sort of revenge to 'retrieve'—as they would put it—the honour supposed to have been lost earlier! The vicious circle would thus be continued indefinitely. Uncontrolled thoughts have a way of percolating, and ultimately sweeping away, society's protecting bunds in the shape of mutual love and helpfulness, or the religious values of the Fatherhood of

God and the brotherhood of man. Therefore, from the earliest times, sages who had at heart the welfare of all mankind have laid the greatest emphasis on the regulation and purification of the tremendous energies flowing through the mind. Every aspirant is expected to struggle hard in his own way to detach his mind from the external world and to turn it Godward. The reason for such a discipline is not that activities on the physical plane as such, or the presence of other people nearby are objectionable, but that there is need to make special efforts to create, and hold aloft, an all embracing and sublime Ideal to which all activities and contacts can be intelligently referred then and there, without fail. Like every other work of skill, the creation of such an Ideal is possible only if thought can be lifted above the craving for sense enjoyments, and trained to move freely, and feel quite at home in a world of moral and spiritual values. When guided by such a pervasive Ideal, mind becomes our best friend, while without it, the same mind becomes our deadly foe.

II

There is one aspect of the personality that is common to the man of uncontrolled habits and the perfect sage. It is the fact of being connected with bodily exertion and of actively participating in day to day affairs in their respective fields. But while the movements of the one are prompted by the motive of securing for himself whatever promises satisfaction to his senses or vanity at the time, those of the other carry the ennobling touch born of the clear recognition of the sacredness of all life and the unity of existence.

If two people can have the same set of ideas, arranged

precisely in the same order, their inferences, convictions, and behaviour are bound to be identical. The trouble is that they are seldom so arranged. Hence people think and act in diametrically opposite ways although their environment contains all that is required to make everyone virtuous and holy. In many cases, a person takes his first step in self-control when he has carefully observed the sequence of changes within him and put them together in a causal chain more or less as follows : The sense organs are so made as to be able to bring reports of any attractive object falling within their range. If there is no pressing work for the mind, it dwells on the special charms of any of those objects. When this is repeated, it gathers momentum and its influence automatically spreads to the next higher level of the personality. There it takes the form of a steadily rising desire to possess the object. From here on the turns of thought become extremely complicated. For, when many people desire to seize the same object, a clash becomes inevitable. That means enmity, anger, and a state of mind in which the memory of better principles of conduct can hardly arise. Thus, since all available and relevant facts and views fail to get into the picture, the decisions arrived at and the actions undertaken go wrong, and lead to varying degrees of pain, loss, or destruction. Man is man only so long as his internal organ, Antahkarana, is fit to discriminate between right and wrong, good and evil, useful and harmful. When it is unable to do so, the man is ruined or debarred from attaining human aspirations.[1]

According to this reasoning, it is unchecked 'brooding' on the beautiful side alone of sense objects that helps unwanted elements to come out of their 'shells' and enter the thought stream. If we are fully convinced of this, we shall always be vigilant. Instead of remaining passive, we shall travel all along the line and take note of the forms those elements assume at different levels. We shall then learn to tap the energy that gives them life, and convert it in ways that benefit ourselves and others. We do the same thing with wealth. All the products of a nation's creative efforts can be estimated in terms of money or purchasing powers. Wicked rulers may waste it in securing the services of agents whose business is to accentuate differences of language, race, or religion among masses of people in adjacent lands, till all of them drift into war and destroy themselves as well as the sources of production! Through wise policies, on the other hand, it is possible to utilize that very purchasing power to provide better facilities for the spread of knowledge, to promote arts and culture, and even to improve production as a whole. In actual practice, the question resolves itself into one of increased spending for right purposes; when supplies are fully diverted into good channels, bad ones must sooner or later dry up of themselves. The principle that, by continued stress on the desirable, disconnection from undesirables is brought about without striking a single blow at them, is at the back of most exercises in mental purification. This is hinted during the brief reference to the process whereby the senses can be pulled back from their objects and made to 'imitate, as it were' the nature of the mind. 'The senses', it is stated, 'are restrained, like the mind, when the mind is restrained'. As this is too terse to be easily understood, the common example of the bees is cited immediately below. 'Just as bees fly as the queen flies up, and sit as she sits down, so the senses become restrained when the mind is restrained'. In other words, to the extent we create a lofty Ideal and implant it within ourselves, the various aspects of our personality, mental or physical, will 'settle' round it, get charged by it, and faithfully reflect its glory in the course of our daily work. Since it acts on all of them simultaneously and in equal measure, this method of control is the surest and best. Other controls involving a single sense, limb, or aspect have necessarily to be supplemented, while this control acting directly on the intellect, emotions, and higher receptivity does not 'stand in need of employing any other means'.[2]

III

For quick check-ups we require short formulas. Even when our car fails to start, we are forced to use a few of them. We try to find out what has gone wrong by conducting 'tests' along two or three 'lines' kept distinct in our minds for the sake of convenience. First, we surely examine the fuel side—stock, supply pipe, and pump. We may next take up the ignition side—battery, wiring, plugs, and cleanliness of the various 'points'. If still we are unable to detect the mistake, we may pass on to the carburettor, and so on. Similarly the physician of the traditional Indian school also has his own 'code' for classifying his patient's symptoms. One technical term covers the assimilative system—excess or deficiency of digestive juices etc. The second means tissue formations, which include such opposites as swellings and tumours, and atrophies. The third embraces all 'movements', related to joints, muscles, nervous impulses, or difficulty of emotional adjustments. He has naturally to arrange his drugs too in accordance with their power to restore the equilibrium of the three vital 'sections', as seen by him. Such divisions are made primarily for convenience. They are not without a certain reasoning behind them.

In the matter of mental control also, a threefold division is possible. It has to be based on three easily identifiable kinds of ideas and emotions that every man is likely to experience at some time or other. Of these, the lowest kind makes a man sluggish and ordinarily averse to hard work, especially mental. But when he chooses to exert, his tendency may be to cling doggedly and without reason to any single idea, as if it were all. Or he may rush headlong into action without understanding the need to pause and consider his own ability, or the loss and injury that may be inflicted on others. He may be fickle and stiff-necked by turns, and as a general rule, too indolent to shake off the habit of looking at things from the wrong end. When these symptoms are found, we must conclude that the mental mechanism is still in the lowest 'gear' in which Nature had left it at birth! Such moods, outlook and behaviour are called 'Tamasic'.

The next higher kind is called 'Rajasic' It makes egocentric ideas dominate the mind. The man who is goaded by them will always aim at personal gain. He would gladly undergo severe hardships, even carry on prolonged religious austerities, in order to secure wealth and sensual pleasures. Greedy and cruel, he does not hesitate to encroach on the rights of others. He runs into extremes — of joy when his schemes succeed and of utter misery when they fail. It does not strike him that what he thinks to be enjoyment is in fact a veritable trap-door through which he loses his strength, intellectual vigour, and psychological stability. He must indeed be a most foolhardly driver who is unable to notice that his chance hits have put his machine in the 'reverse gear' in the evolutionary plane!

The third in the series is the 'Sattvic' mood. As any text book on spiritual topics will show, Sattva endows the aspirant with mental firmness and vigour. It leads to the steady rise within him of qualities like fearlessness, uprightness, serenity, modesty, compassion, and devotion to study and worship. They gradually purify and enrich his personality. As they penetrate into deeper levels, they establish 'irreversible' patterns of reaction out of the very energies that previously produced only Tamasic and Rajasic moods. When purity reaches its peak, the mind becomes fully receptive to the highest Truth, the One indestructible Reality in all beings. The intellect, thoughts, vitality, and sense organs henceforth lose their separate existence in a way; for they have now become equally faithful instruments to express that Oneness in their respective spheres of work. That this transformation has a reality, far surpassing that of the physical body and the material objects surrounding it, is verifiable directly by the sage himself whenever he is inclined to look within, and indirectly by others who live so close to him as to be able to observe the turn of events within his 'range'.

IV

The object of bringing all mental movements under three heads is clear from the degrees of cultural advance inferable[3] at the back of the qualities included in each. The simplest principle of control is that wherever Tamas is seen to be operating, steps should be taken immediately to replace it by Rajas. Vigorous activity is the best antidote to sluggishness and stupor. Selfish activity has no doubt its own dangers, but it has one relieving feature while indolence has none. For, selfishness always carries with it not only the desire to forge ahead, but also the determination to protect itself while engaged in running after pleasures. Sooner or later, Nature will lead the selfish man to a cross-road. He will then see that he can gain his further objectives by peaceful means which may be a little slow in fructifying. Or he can resort to violence or intrigue in the name of speed, and risk everything, including previous gains and even his own life. Confronted by these alternatives, he will be compelled by his self-interest itself to pause and reflect. The difficulty is only in picking up sufficient courage to make the first right choice. After that, he would see the advantage of adopting the path of love and gentleness to achieve his legitimate ends. Each subsequent adjustment within himself would mean a little more widening of the aperture to let in the light of Sattva. Before long, he would begin to treat day to day problems as excellent opportunities for reacting quickly with virtuous 'drives'. When this attitude takes firm root in him, he would play the game of life with power and grace, distilled out of the very energy that used to work havoc inside him before.

That mental refinement is a kind of distillation from crude sources was well known to ancient teachers. What more dramatic example of it can be found than the way in which Krishna dealt with Arjuna's sudden dejection before the starting of hostilities at Kuruksetra? This impending slaughter acted as a powerful stimulus, and made Arjuna, although a hero of many battles, acutely conscious of the uncoordinated streams of valour and virtue all along flowing within him. That was evident from his prostration at Krishna's feet and his earnest prayer for guidance, in spite of his feeling at the time that a mendicant's life would be better than a military victory stained with the blood of relatives and preceptors. Krishna too saw the same facts and entertained the same love and respect for the fighting men on either side, as Arjuna did. But he had the special ability to integrate every external event, however terrible, and plan of action, however painful, into a well-ordered Cosmic Scheme, in which earthly values of gradual evolution mixed harmoniously with the eternal Perfection of the Supreme Lord. Words spoken and discussion carried on in an atmosphere charged with such a penetrative vision could not fail to produce the final tranforming movement in the fairly 'processed' materials present in Arjuna's noble heart. If we turn to the lives of the great prophets and their immediate followers, we shall come across beautiful instances of conversions and transformations, some sudden, others slow, the variations in speed being due mainly to the different proportions in which Tamas, Rajas, and Sattva stood mixed up in their thought stream at the time.

Students of the popular drama, *Sakuntalam*, will remember how the celestial charioteer Matali employed the sound psychological principle of whipping up Rajas in order to neutralize Tamas. He found that something sensational had to be done to remove the stupor into which King Dushyanta had fallen and to make him fit to fight on behalf of the gods. With a touch of grim humour, Matali who knew how to keep himself invisible, seized the innocent jester Madhavya, pulled his neck backwards, almost 'snapping it into three parts like a sugar cane', and shouted in threatening tones: 'Here I am, thirsting for the blood gushing out of your throat. I shall kill you now, as a tiger kills its struggling prey. Let Dushyanta who wields his bow to remove the fear of the afflicted rush to your rescue!' This ruse had the expected result. How could any hero look on idly when ruffians attacked members of his household and he was himself called by name and challenged? He decided quickly to send a missile that could locate an unseen enemy and slay him wherever he might hide. Having achieved his purpose, Matali appeared before the king, bowed down to him and, after putting him in his normal mood, explained: 'I found Your Royal Highness extremely dispirited. It was to rouse you into anger that I acted in such a strange way. To make the fire blaze forth, we have to stir it; and to make the snake spread out his hood, we have to poke him a little, Similar is the case with human beings. They can get into their highest spirits only when sufficiently provoked'.[4]

The general rule, thus, is that when internal balance is upset, we have to 'counteract Tamas by Rajas, then conquer Rajas by Sattva, the calm beautiful state that will grow and grow until all else is gone'.[5] But as long as Sattva is weak, and the mental scene presents nothing more than a prolonged tussle between Tamas and Rajas, the statement of the wise that 'the mind alone is Ignorance'[6] is literally true. When Rajas predominates and sense enjoyments are eagerly sucked in from all sides, the 'mental sheath' may very well be compared to the sacrificial fire of ancient ritualists. The five senses will then correspond to the five officiating priests, the innumerable desires imbedded in the mind to the fuel that keeps the fire burning, and objects of pleasure to an unbroken stream of oblations.[7] What can be expected to result from such a procedure except a tightening of existing bonds? It is to rouse men from their complacent attitude and make them aware of their danger that poets have conveyed their warnings through the use of striking images. One briefly-worded caution says: 'In the forest-track of sense pleasures, there prowls a huge tiger called the mind. Let good persons who love Freedom never go in that direction!'[8]

V

Every warning, howsoever expressed, is bound to throw the listener on his guard in an instant. It cannot but wake up his sleeping faculties and make them spring into position— alert, poised, and ready to act, like a whole regiment with arms shouldered, waiting for the next word of command. When this is over, the problem changes into one of utilizing the energies whose downpour is heralded by the sudden flash of vigilance. Ancient teachers have wisely provided the necessary canals. They have followed up their warnings with positive directions, and assured success to those who adhere to them. Like skilful painters who balance each dark shade by a high light, these sage-poets have placed by the side of every prohibition its appropriate counterpart in the shape of some practical step for rearranging the pattern of thought. The very fact that they have spent their precious time to exhort us ought to be an eye-opener to us. In the first place, it implies that we have the freedom to change whatever is undesirable. Secondly, it shows that the most basic of all changes—that from which others are derived later—is the conscious introduction of any convenient virtuous thought to neutralize an acknowlegedly bad one.

We know the important part played by the initial 'suction' of fuel-mixture in an internal combustion engine. What we call 'thought' performs a similar function in our personality. Take for example, the familiar 'desire' to walk to the nearest door. What happens on the conscious 'dial' or 'screen' is the presentation, in advance, of mental pictures of our body executing the relevant movements.

We also 'hear' a mental talk urging us to carry them out. If we do not 'act' immediately, it is because, for some reason or other, fresh pictures and talks have entered the field and cancelled previous ones. If our power of observation is sharp, we can watch the subsequent 'audio-visual' events. Or, cutting off the expected 'forward' movement, we can recall earlier 'bits' and combine them in any order we like. But whatever takes place in the 'surface' mind, under control or without it, 'seeing' and 'talking' do not leave us. What the teachers realized, and want us too to realize, is that something else, more vital and 'basic', happens at the same time, in the deeper recesses of the personality. That is the 'suction' of life-energy in its purest and most creative form. We may call it Cosmic Prana. Under suitable conditions, it is capable of moving the ethical, artistic, and spiritual wheels with which every mind is equipped from the start. If a person is 'willing' to undertake the prescribed disciplines, he can employ the resulting currents to overhaul the related environment—his own mind and body—to the maximum limit, and to a lesser extent, the external world abounding in people whose ability to respond to higher values may not be adequately developed. 'Thought' in its entirety is such a complicated process that while it undoubtedly uses and 'exhausts' this Prana from one side, it also manages to draw it in freely from the other side[9] which is immersed in the Universal Fund of all Energy. The speciality of thought, as distinct from ordinary energy, is that what we mean by such terms as desire, meaning, or purpose and has the unique gift of filtering out all other possibilities and 'picking up' just those elements of power which correspond to the 'intentions', either allowed to continue unchecked, or deliberately kept up by us for attaining the Highest. Looked at from this standpoint, 'mind' cannot be permanently labelled 'the abode of ignorance'. For with the change in intention, the character of the thoughts, and therefore of the mind, undergoes a total modification. If the mind caused bondage previously, it can in an altered set-up, prepare the way for Freedom and Peace. There is nothing unusual in this, says the poet: 'Threatening clouds are brought in by the wind, but again they are scattered and driven out of sight by the very same agency. So it is with the mind; when pure, and divested of Tamas and Rajas, it conduces to Liberation and Insight'.[10]

The path of any newly-risen intention, however, can never be quite smooth. For, its predecessors would have adapted the internal mechanisms to suit the acquisition of objects and satisfactions matching their own inferior moral and spiritual content. It is in the nature of old plans, fittings, and ways of handling available resources to continue to operate till they are approached from the right angle and readjusted into a new framework without serious inconvenience or damage. And this means hard work—the patient transformation of the emotions and outlook connected with the earlier order, which has now to stand in the category of Rajas or Tamas. The Sattvic elements employed to carry out this important task should have a preponderance of discrimination and dispassion. The former is needed to help in deciding what nobler levels lie higher up, and the latter to re-educate the mind and facilitate the easy shifting of emotions into them step by step. With these two qualities functioning as its powerful wings, the new intention can make its controlling and co-ordinating flights wherever it likes. Far from impeding its onward sweep, the 'rigidity' of old habits from within and of adverse situations outside will only serve to aid it by receiving the 'beatings' of its wings and giving them their forward thrust. For the hero who aims at the conquest of 'Self'—which means also a wise and creative attitude towards what was earlier classed as 'not-Self'—resistance from any side, internal or external, can only act as a welcome incentive for further efforts and greater harmonization.

It is not difficult to see that ancient sages looked at Liberation not as a 'retreat' in the crude sense we sometimes give the term, but as an advance, not as a mean shrinking, but as an intelligent expansion. In some places, it has been presented, most poetically, as a 'damsel' whom one might wish to meet and cherish as one's own, or as a delighful 'creeper that grows on the top of a tall edifice', like a temple. Since nobody would like to remain in dependence, it has been quite significantly described as 'the suzerainty of absolute Independence'. And to every thinking man who is troubled at heart by the mounting problems of the modern world—generally left unsolved, and in many cases, dangerously aggravated by current racial, economic, political, military, as well as religious programmes— a refreshingly safe and fruitful line of action will be opened up if he can be convinced that spiritual Freedom involves the positive and unshakable realization of 'everyone in oneself, oneself in others,' and all together in a supreme Protecting Principle which religions call God.

Nothing can 'obstruct' the mind functions of a sage who gets such a realization. He would depend no more on 'conditions of place, time, posture', moral discipline or specific objects of meditation.[11] But, being guided by his ever-blazing Illumination, he would never violate the principles or the values mastered through a faithful observance of such restrictions earlier. His thoughts, words, and deeds can henceforth move only in one single direction : To achieve the welfare of one and all without distinction. If the old world gained from such insight, the modern world stands to gain much more from it now.

20. Graded Forms and Levels of Aid

I

There are different ways in which we try to control others. The simplest and the most crude is to use physical force. We adopt it, almost instinctively, in the case of animals. If a bull refuses to drag the plough, our first reaction is to whip him or twist his tail. Being helpless, he chooses the lesser of the two pains and does the allotted work. Brute force, as is well known, is the main source of strength of all anti-social characters. Newspapers carry reports of armed robbers breaking into rich men's houses at night, even in big towns, killing those who resist, and carrying off all valuables. Society's defence against them consists in the appointment of armed policemen. When they overpower dacoits, handcuff them and drag them to prison, we see a legitimate employment of supeiror physical force to maintain law and order.

Turning to human groups called nations, we come across relationships that are complicated, blurred, and often wantonly ignored. Look at any war of aggression. At bottom it is house-breaking on a colossal scale. The danger does not end with the destruction of lives and property, inevitable during the military action. For it is followed by the 'elimination of the war potential'. It means the enslavement of the conquered population and a highly ingenious system of impoverishing them for generations together. The idea is to restrict their manufactures, industries, and trade in such ways as to prevent them from accumulating a surplus that can be converted into the instruments for a war of independence afterwards. But as long as there is no stigma attached to conquests—rather, as long as historical and other traditions hold them up as brilliant examples of manliness and intelligence—there is bound to be a perpetuation of the feeling of bitterness among the victims, resulting in violent attempts to shake off their yoke. If there is glory in a conquest, there must be greater glory in achieving liberation; and so the chain of fighting is kept up. As a means of control, undiluted force is thus positively injurious outside a very narrow field. For the spirit behind it has a way of reincarnating itself in progressively wider areas and in increasingly destructive forms.

Education is a more reliable method of influencing others. It combines many advantages and leaves no bad effect behind. Its recipients, individuals or communities, get a widening of their intellect according to the subjects taught and remain grateful ever afterwards to those who instruct them. With the enormous advances made in science and technology, there is an immense scope for the spread of knowledge to remote corners of the world.

To millions in under-developed areas, such knowledge would come as an unprecedented blessing. It would result in a better utilization of their natural resources and in an all-round improvement of their standard of living. It would teach them, in the first instance, to get a better yield of corn, vegetables, and fruits from their lands and to raise a better breed of farm animals. These would enable them not only to obtain abundant and nourishing food for themselves but also to save some fair portion for sale or to give in exchange for other articles they require. Once a start is made in this line, local talent, lying dormant for want of proper opportunities, would come forward and play its part in erecting good houses and establishing well-equipped schools, hospitals, and even centres for research.

There is a general movement among powerful nations to speed up this kind of service in areas which suit them most at the present time. No doubt, there are serious stumbling blocks in the way. Processes of manufacturing important goods are closely guarded secrets. The profit motive prevents a free dissemination of such useful information. Then there are various political and other considerations which act as 'traffic jams', as it were, and hold up the vehicles carrying the 'know-how' personnel. Under certain combinations, these very considerations, curiously enough, clear the obstructions along some roads, and then different nations speed along them to gain spheres of influence in exchange for technical aid! Knowledge somehow finds its own level. The unseen hand that paves the way for its rise in one place manages to create such situations that self-interest itself compels the knower to carry his precious gift to other places in due course. There are at the same time fields like art and culture where a policy of exclusion serves no purpose and where competition leads to the progress of everyone concerned. It is a happy sign that in those fields cooperation is steadily on the increase. Many countries are now linked together by programmes involving exchange of professors and educational tours of large numbers of students specializing in different subjects of study. Amounts spent by one country in giving scholarships to students of other countries is always a sound investment. It builds up an inexhaustible reserve of gratefulness and goodwill in foreign lands: and who does not want it? As against it stands that kind of expenditure which flows into ways that increase fear and suspicion, lead to actual hostilities, bloodshed, and destruction of cultural values, and above all, leave a legacy of hatred lasting for decades, if not for centuries afterwards.

II

Let us now imagine ourselves to be the recipients of help and see what we would like to get and to experience within after such getting. Food, shelter, and medicines being primary requisites for all, we would certainly be thankful to receive them during floods, famines, epidemics and similar calamities. Even at other times, outright gifts can come in through broad-minded people who have an eye to detect the pressing needs of those living around them. Gifts, however, have a subtle way of pulling down the self-respect of their receivers to some extent. That is why the vow of non-acceptance of gifts is taken by sincere aspirants from the very commencement of their spiritual disciplines. If there is to be no feeling of embarrassment but only the legitimate glow of rising self-reliance while viewing old events in retrospect, we should cease to treat helps as 'free' gifts at any stage of our onward march. It is a rare privilege, whether we are beneficiaries, or not, to contribute our mite towards that sum total of services without which society loses its cohesion and the chance to develop to the maximum the varied talents of all its members. Any help given by others — separately as individuals, or united into an organization — has its value not only because of the tangible forms it can take but also because of the love and sacrifice that prompt it. He must indeed be a blind man who sees only the limited forms but not the unbounded spirit behind them. So, if circumstances force us to accept the forms, we should look upon it as a God-given opportunity to imbibe the spirit as well, and decide to express it in our own dealings with others later. This is much more than a simple question of economics or of paying back a badly-needed timely loan. The attitude involved here is one of capturing the higher values of pure and unselfish action and of driving it into the habit level, so that the whole personality may become an open channel for it thenceforth.

Help can be graded according to the nature of its forms and the ways in which it is offered. Every service that enriches our mind surely stands on a higher footing than the supply of material goods, however valuable in themselves they might be. The latter, as is well known, cease to be available to the giver after their transfer. But ideas and skills that constitute the former have the unique power of spreading and flourishing the more they are passed on to others. In this respect, they are like the flame of a candle that enables thousands to be lighted from it, without itself suffering diminution in the least.

The method of presentation is equally important. There was a time when people behaved as if new ideas were to enter like an army of occupation. As long as that picture coloured the imagination, the teacher acted like a military leader. His first step was to soften up the area of resistance, viz. the minds of the students, by demolishing the cultural structures found therein. That pattern is slowly changing. It is being generally recognized nowadays, at least in theory, that there should be nothing negative, irritating, or threatening in the manner in which even the most excellent ideas are presented. We all have a certain amount of pride about our families and what we consider to be the traditions of our community, country, creed, or race. That pride is quite consistent with the conviction that what our ancestors thought and did in their days must be considerably altered and supplemented by us to tackle the problems that confront us today. That very pride can act as a dynamo of power and enthusiasm if properly tapped. It can make us cheerfully and resolutely undertake difficult tasks whose completion we can never see in our own life-time. We shall bring into its humble beginnings the faith and satisfaction that, when the programme would be fully carried out, its successful termination will add to the glory of our forefathers and the tradition they handed down to us. We shall view our present limited share in the work in that wider perspective and value it as an essential link between the past and the future. It would be unwise to shake that legitimate and healthy pride in any attempt to teach modern subjects. Destructive criticism of ancient ways does not add to our mental clarity while trying to imbibe new ones. The most effective teaching is that which stimulates all that is noblest in the student and uses that as the motive power to make him think along original lines. 'In language and literature', says Swami Vivekananda, while talking about the right method of education, 'in poetry and arts, in everything we must point out not the mistakes that people are making in their thoughts and actions, but the way in which they will be able to do these things better'. 'If you can give them positive ideas, people will grow up to be men and stand on their own legs'.[1]

Even about enriching the mind, the Swami's ideas are worthy of note. Education, he points out, is not the amount of information that may be poured into our brain and may run riot there, undigested all our life. What is needed is assimilation, the building up of our character, making those ideas the basis for our plans and actions. 'If you have assimilated five ideas,' says he, 'and made them your life and character, you have more education than any man who has got by heart a whole liberary.[2] What we want is that kind of education 'by which character is formed, strength of mind is increased, the intellect is expanded, and by which one can stand on one's own feet'.[3] The secret of assimilation and even of the ability to discover new and important facts is the power of concentration. The Swami expresses it very forcibly when he says, 'If I had to do my education over again, I would not study facts at all. I would develop the power of concentration and detachment, and then with a perfect instrument collect facts at will'.[4] 'The world is ready to give up its secrets, if only we know how to knock, how to give the necessary blow. The strength and force of the blow comes from concentration'.[5]

III

Does character ever become steady and perfect

without spiritual insight? It may appear, at first sight, that the only requisite for being service-minded is to keep the formula that we should look upon others as we look upon ourselves. Even without studying scripture, it is possible to arrive at the idea that, like us, all creatures wish to get what is agreeable and to ward off what is painful. There is, however, a vast difference between an intellectual acceptance of such an idea and the process of making the entire personality a channel for the effortless and unconditional flow of love and goodwill for all. If we analyse our behaviour patterns and unflinchingly trace them to their deep-seated sources, we shall come across a number of emotional tangles and egoistic pulls, ordinarily lying dormant. No doubt, as a source of power and enthusiasm for acquiring knowledge and facing difficulties, we may count upon our pride about ancestors and country's traditions. But, unfortunately, that emotional nucleus contains endless possibilities for mischief as well. In most of us, the intellect can hold up the motto of equal treatment of others only during our calm moments. It is usually powerless to control the habitual upsurge of emotions when appropriate stimuli happen to rouse them into sudden action. We then behave like the proverbial parrot that can sing God's names when everything is peaceful, but cannot help shrieking in the true parrot fashion when a cat seizes its tail.[6] The entire course of spiritual discipline is meant to help us in two ways: to arrive at a stable, all-comprehensive Ideal, and to subordinate the various emotions to the intellect that upholds it to start with. Emotional springs are not blocked or destroyed, but only smoothly taken over and incorporated into the Ideal that henceforth ceases to be a special possession of the intellect alone.

It is significant that the *Gita* passage that teaches the equating of others with oneself comes practically at the end of the section describing the process and content of meditation.[7] Two facts stand out prominently here. First, regarding the content: What is to be seen, recognized, felt, and assimilated is shown to be the Unity behind what we fancy to be separate entities called our personal selves, others, and the Supreme Being. By continuous aspiration and inward churning, we have to evolve a sensitive limb and learn to lift it far above the coarse atmosphere charged by our rivalries and exclusive attitudes. Floating like a balloon carrying specially tuned instruments, it would catch from any direction the peace and sacredness of a wholly unified perspective and regularly transmit to us impulses that transform our daily life. Secondly, regarding the process itself: Words like 'withdrawal' are no doubt used, but it is clear that no spatial or compartmental 'cut' is meant. The exhaustiveness of the values involved will bear this out fully. For that alone is declared to be the true and final 'vision' where we see ourselves existing in other beings, and all of them related to us in a similar way. This is one formula. It is followed by another: the Supreme Being Himself, who is without parts, existing in all creatures or everywhere; and everything, viz. the animate and the inanimate, equally existing in Him. Last comes the stipulation that whatever we do we should stand upon this Unity and do it as His worship. Mutual love and service on the social level thus become blended with adoration and worship on the religious level. It is only when such illumination comes that equality becomes firmly established and spontaneously operative.

Because this type of discipline is unique, the books dealing with it use technical terms applicable to a world of relationships transcending, but at the same time comprehending and elevating, social, economic, political, or philanthropic relationships. Their direct object is not to explain these latter relationships, and we should not take it amiss if some books make no reference to them at all. And yet critics are not wanting who give narrow meanings to the technical terms used in describing spiritual discipline, and on the basis of such meanings argue that the society that produced those books looked down upon domestic, social, industrial, and patriotic activities, thereby betraying a woefully pessimistic and other-worldly outlook!

IV

The greatest service anyone can render us is to make us fully awake on the spiritual plane. The teacher's work in opening our inner eyes to the glory of the One Perfect Existence has been nicely compared by poets to the expert physician's art of applying medicinal collyrium to the physical eyes of a patient suffering from 'double vision.' Through interesting examples and parables, every great teacher down the centuries has tried to enable aspirants to become conscious of higher values by degrees, and build them steadily into the very texture of their personal lives.

Is it possible for a person whose defect is cured to experience 'double vision' again, in the sense of taking all teachers and all paths to be totally distinct from one another and leading to different goals, of which one alone is true and the others false? We shall quote from Sri Ramakrishna's teachings to answer this and a few other important questions. The gas-light, says he, shines unequally in different places. But the life of the light, viz. gas, comes from one common reservoir. So the true religious teachers of all climes and ages are like so many lamps through which is emitted the life of the Spirit, flowing constantly from one source—the Lord Almighty.[8] He points out the same truth through the picturesque example of the rain water falling upon the roof of a house and flowing down to the ground through pipes having their mouth-pieces shaped like the head of a tiger, or a bull. Though appearing to come out of a tiger's or a bull's mouth, it is only from the sky that the water really descends. 'Even so, the eternal truths that come out of the mouths of godly men are not uttered by those men themselves, but in reality descend from the kingdom of heaven'.[9]

Anyone who grasps this principle can never treat others as opponents and try to defeat or convert them by the force of superior argument. His sole effort will be to treat sincere aspirants with consideration and help them to get finer perceptions. To a Pandit who had been arguing vehemently with a Mr. Mani Mullick, Sri Ramakrishna said with a smile: 'Mani Mullick has been following the tenets of the Brahmo Samaj for a long time. You can't convert him to your views, Is it an easy thing to destroy old tendencies?' He then half-humorously narrated how a devotee of the Divine Mother, forcibly converted to Islam, found it impossible to pray in the new fashion demanded of him, as Jagadamba still filled him 'up to the throat'. Then the Master added: 'God has made different religions and creeds to suit different aspirants.' For there are, as all can very well see, different temperaments; there are also differences in the capacity to comprehend. When the same Pandit, later, hesitated to take refreshments before finishing his evening prayers, the Master sang in an exalted mood:

What need of rituals has a man,
What need of devotions, any more,

If he repeats the Mother's name
At the three holy hours?

The Pandit caught the spirit of the song and immediately consented to take the refreshments. The Master, however, remained true to his own principle and gently dissuaded him with the memorable remarks: 'No, I don't want to obstruct the current of your life. It is not good to renounce anything before the proper time arrives. When the fruit ripens, the flower drops off of itself. One shouldn't forcibly tear off the green branch of a coconut tree. That injures the tree'.[10]

The dominant note in all that Sri Ramakrishna narrated, explained, or chanted was the feeling of sacredness born out of his unbroken consciousness of the Divine, within and without. 'Why should the universe be unreal?' he asked and gave the answer himself by saying: 'That is a speculation of the philosophers. After realizing God, one sees that it is God Himself who has become the universe and all beings'. He also pointed out 'in a nutshell' the most direct means to attain such a realization. 'One must become', he said, 'like Sita to understand Rama, like Bhagavati, the Divine Mother, to understand Bhagavan Siva'. 'One must cultivate the attitude of Prakrti in order to realize Purusha—the attitude of a friend, or handmaid, or a mother'.[11]

Since the Master stayed in a temple, and even when he was not officiating as a priest, engaged himself in making garlands to decorate the image with his own hands,[12] it was but natural that most of the figures of speech occurring in his talks should contain picturesque references to flowers, garlands, lamps, and the moods of formal worship. Take, for example, his beautiful reply to the question about the source of his vast knowledge. 'It is true', he said, 'I did not study myself, but I have heard much. I remember all that. I heard the Vedas, the Vedanta, Darsanas (philosophy), and the Puranas from good and reliable scholars. Then I made a garland of them all (meaning, the books) by means of a string, put it on my neck and offered it to the lotus feet of the Mother saying: Here is all Thy scriptures, Puranas and the like. Please grant me pure devotion'.[13] This was in a line with what he had done earlier at the close of the Shodasi Puja. Then he had, as the culmination of his disciplines, given away for ever to the lotus feet of the Mother (specially invoked into Sri Sarada Devi) his all, viz. the results of his Sadhanas, his rosary etc., as also his own self.[14] Similarly, doubtless, he made a garland of the devotees, lay and monastic, whom the Mother brought to him for instruction—of whom a few had the priviledge of gathering round him during his illness to serve him and to form a more or less well-knit 'organization' with its twin motto of working resolutely 'For one's own liberation and the welfare of the world'. About the unique power the Master wielded in the entire realm of the Spirit, Swami Vivekananda made the following significant observation; 'It is not a very difficult matter to bring under control the material powers and vaunt a miracle; but I do not find a more marvellous miracle than the manner this mad Brahmana (Sri Ramakrishna) used to handle human minds, like lumps of clay, breaking, moulding and remoulding them at ease and filling them with new ideas by a mere touch.'[15]

21. Opening up of Inner Springs

Orthodox people adopt a special way of greeting one another. It is nowadays observed mainly on ceremonial occasions, and particularly when a junior makes obeisance to a reverend senior. It takes roughly the following form: 'Respects to you, sir. I am..., by name, — a descendant of Sage.'... The blanks, when duly filled up, will contain terms like' 'Sarma', 'Varma' and the like, indicating the social position and other details connected with the accosting individual. The senior is expected to reply, 'May you be long-lived, O amiable one,...!'[1] He is then to raise his hands in the attitude of benediction. If the motive for the interview is a sincere desire to learn anything, the relationship is certainly altered. But the conversation would be interspersed with polite and pleasing expressions conveying the love and gratitude of the student to his teacher and, likewise, the teacher's solicitude and appreciation to the student. Well chosen words serve a twofold purpose: They express the feelings that are already sweeping the mind; they also help to evoke the desired feeling and to strengthen it by the force of repetition.

Ancient teachers knew the value of time. They realized that it ought to be looked upon as a God-given opportunity to be employed, without the least waste, for the attainment of the highest wisdom. So they built up a tradition which made it an act of great 'impropriety' for anyone to express his doubts or to frame his questions in roundabout ways, using words or phrases which could be easily dispensed with. Problems which appeared difficult to the student could be presented with all the directness at his command. It would by no means inconvenience the teacher. For no problem would be absolutely new to him. He would have come face to face with it himself during his early struggles. He would also have, later, seen many a person who had to go through the same phase of mental development. The books might describe it as the 'duty' of perfect men to impart without reservation whatever knowledge they had gained through their prolonged disciplines. But even apart from rules and regulations, it was, and is, but natural for men of insight to move of their own accord to alleviate the distress of those coming within their range.[2] And what greater service can there be than the removal of doubt and fear in all their different forms? Wealth, relatives, doctors, and the government are surely competent to eliminate certain kinds of fears. But those springing from painful discords within the mind and unexpected strokes of adversity form without will ever be outside the scope of such agencies. They can be effectively tackled only by persons whose thoughts, words, and even looks carry with them the awakening and assuring touch born of unbroken illumination.

The nature of an ideal meeting and conversation aimed at the destruction of such fear is beautifully brought out by Acharya Sankara in his *Vivekachudamani.* In the description of the student's mental condition, there is an abundance of words indicating the strength of his afflictions. He is intensely aware of the violent movements in the physical, mental, and emotional worlds. He is not able to find a point of equilibrium among them. It seems to him as if he is in the midst of a rapidly encircling forest fire or the surging waves of an angry sea. He is overcome by terror and has repaired to the teacher in order to learn from him how to free himself from it. That very approach has, probably, been the result of an initial trust engendered by the kind look in the master's eyes and the habitually imperturbable calmness in his face—characteristic of the type so arrestingly carved on stone to represent the countenances of the Buddha, Jain saints, and many of the deities and Rishis of the Hindus. Every sage knows the creative efficacy of a well directed talk; and this teacher selects his opening words themselves in such a way as to reinforce the disciple's existing confidence, and to help him to gain some solid footing within himself. 'Don't fear!', he says and quickly follows this up with a succession of short sentences, each word of which acts as a pleasing, stabilizing tap on the aching and shaky points of the student's personality.[3]

II

We often judge others by observing their behaviour in a few contexts and framing a convenient theory to include what we hastily sum up as 'all the facts'. We arrive at these latter mainly by scanning people's spoken words, watching their restlessness, and enquiring into their discomfitures in the domestic, economic, or social spheres. Since no individual would have grown up without experiencing some serious defeats and disappointments, we shall never find it hard to collect a considerable number of the facts we want. There is a commendable simplicity in our procedure. Our first step is to make an exhaustive list of all the unhappy incidents in the life of the person to be judged, beginning from his earliest memories as a baby. The next step is to connect them causally with his religious or philosophical pursuits! Thus, if he seeks peace, we jump to the conclusion that it is because he is afraid of struggle; in short, he is a coward. If he prays, it must be because he has not yet outgrown his childish tendency to lean on an obliging 'parent', earthly or celestial. The defect in his upbringing was that he was not taught from his earlier years to assert his manhood and to stand upon his own feet. As for his yearning to be — or his fancy that he has been — blessed with a 'vision' of the Kingdom of Heaven, it can only be the direct outcome of an unconscious drive to fly into a world of mental glory to balance his sense of inferiority and humiliation in the physical world of men and actual events. Running along this single track, we have no other alternative but to try to explain away spiritual endeavour itself as a pitiful survival of unhealthy infantile reactions, as a shameful retreat unworthy of adults, or as a colourful play of the compensating mechanism!

Sages who have fathomed the depths of human consciousness, however, have their own way of estimating people who resort to them for help. According to them, it is a sign of dullness to run after externally attractive objects without considering their essential worth and the transformations that attachment to them can undergo when opposed by others engaged in the same game. On the other hand, sages treat it as a sign of higher sensitivity in anyone to be able to see ahead the lowest levels to which selfishness and the craving for sense pleasures can lead, and the flowering of the personality attainable by a systematic sublimation of mental energies. A little reflection is enough to show that our internal apparatus is an exceedingly complex structure. We may say that it functions more or less like a dramatic company with its own stage, movable scenic fittings, adjustable lights, planners, composers, actors, an invisible audience whose voices periodically applaud or condemn and, above all, a supreme witness who always presides and permits![4] What we call sensitivity is one of the most precious qualities emerging and becoming strengthened in the course of the drama as a whole. It alone can reach, touch, record, and transmit the perfection man can ever realize. With its dawning, the aspirant begins to perceive first dimly, later on clearly, what happens to the creative forces that are sucked in by the mere 'pull' of thought. These forces are the same for all. But each person's character—his 'fixed' notions or values, operative at any time—acts in unsuspected ways as a subtle device to deflect some of them and distort and convert others. What is found *in* or *as* the environment, particularly that part of it which brings joy and sorrow, or friends and foes, and aids a person's progress or downfall, is precisely the final condensed 'form' of those forces, presented back to him in as intimate a manner as when he received them and processed them earlier—may be five, ten, or even twenty years back. Any teacher, with his heart fully blossomed, would be delighted at the budding sensitivity of the student, in whatever form he might express the nature of the pressures that make him seek redress.

The teacher too makes his judgement by observing behaviour. But his analysis goes deeper than the ordinary psychologist's. The facts he gathers are, therefore, greater in number, subtler in character, and more effective as harmonizers of the personality. What he grasps directly without depending upon graded steps in reasoning, he later corroborates by arguing thus: 'This student has come to the conclusion that all objects of the physical and mental worlds are transitory. To be thus able to see that everything is in a flux, the 'observer' must needs be standing on some platform which does not move, or change its values, like the rest. Whenever he complains that he does not find an equilibrium, he is actually looking around from that stable position. To that extent he is on the right line, and deserves to be congratulated. The trouble with him is that he does not know what place to assign to the fluctuating things—objects, events, and memories of the past, painful problems of the present, and their possible recurrence in the future'.

III

To put it in a general way, re-education must proceed along two lines. In the first place, the student has to be made to turn his attention to the one indisputable 'fact' he has been ignoring all the time, namely, the presence within himself of the non-fluctuating 'observer' who can never become an 'object' of observation to anyone. It was with that observer as the basis that he could discover the evanescence of all that came within the range of his observation. Even when a person says to himself, 'This tempts me; that frightens me; that is included in this; this is not different from that', the consicous principle that makes him aware of the different relationships remains perfectly unchanged. There is neither increase nor decrease in Its content, although significant changes take place in the personality, coinciding with each of the perceptions. The teaching must contain arguments and examples to drive home the truth that he is this principle, that he, or It, is essentially non-attached, and that discipline is not meant to create non-attachment and freedom in the literal sense of the terms. At some stage or other, the student must be helped to realize that 'the Self is not a thing to be reached, got rid of, or acquired'. For, 'if the self be quite unknown, all undertakings intended for the benefit of oneself would be meaningless. It is indeed not possible to imagine that they are for the benefit of the body or the like, which has no independent consciousness of its own. Nor is it possible to hold that pleasure is for pleasure's sake and pain for pain's sake. All efforts secular or religious, carried out of one's own accord, or in obedience to the suggestions of others, are at bottom aimed at the benefit, fancied or real, of some 'entity' covered by the notion of 'oneself'. 'Therefore, just as there is no need for an external evidence by which to know one's own body, so there is no need for an external evidence by which to know the self who is nearer and more intimate than the physical body'. 'It is,' then, 'not for the knowledge of the self that any effort is required; it is required only to prevent us from regarding the not-self as the self'.[5] With the aid of a competent teacher staying by the side, it can never be difficult for a diligent student to locate within himself the different shades of meanings and values corresponding to the technical terms employed in the discussions.

When the student is intellectually convinced about the

truth related to the ground covered thus far, a host of other questions will surely spring up and demand satisfactory answers. The gaps in his knowledge will, among other things, take some of the following forms: 'Why do external events go against my interests even when I am scrupulously correct in my attitudes?' There is bound to be a closely allied doubt concerning his own mental world: 'Why do thoughts, fancies, and emotions which I know to be base sweep through my mind when I do not expect them, and even when I consciously try hard to get rid of them? Why also am I unable to organize all my inner faculties round an Ideal which appeals to me as the nobelst and which, in my calm moments, I resolve to uphold in the face of every obstacle and danger that may confront me?'

This brings us to the second direction that the teaching has to take. For, these are questions centering round the methods of purifying the personality. Here every religion will be found useful: for each has well arranged frameworks of disciplines to suit people of different temperaments. But even here, an intellectual understanding, and a constant loving remembrance of the glories of the Self do help the aspirant considerably in sublimating his mental energies. Its immediate effect is their conversion into spiritual qualities and higher receptivity. Its long range result is the building up of new and desirable habits which, in due course, neutralize old ones and alter the entire outlook, without undue stress on the negative method of 'detaining' undesirable aspects of character and making frontal attacks on them.

IV

The first requisite for success in this work is an initial high level of sensitivity on the part of the student. That he has it, is clear when he complains that he fails to find a stable point anywhere in the 'field' of perception, external or internal. For it implies that he has repeatedly 'moved' into the position of the 'pure' witness — the Drk, as distinguished from the totality of Drsya.

It is no wonder that in the beginning, the student is unable to see the phenomena within him in their true light. for his attention is not yet disengaged from the notion of his being caught up in the Drsya, and of the necessity to plan an escape from it. We too are likely to miss its significance. For, ordinarily, our ideas run along two lines. We may imagine the ideal condition to be one of absolute sameness, homogeneity, and featureless immobility of the Drsya, induced by a relentless conscious effort in which human emotions, however exalted, ought to find no useful place. Or we may equate perfection, rather vaguely perhaps, with the ability, by sheer will, to crash through all delays and resistances in the Drsya, including in this category the 'moving' aspects of ourselves and others. Some of us may even imagine that if there be a number of spiritually advanced men in any country, its social, economic, and political problems — should they arise at all — would be solved smoothly, and all constructive programmes would proceed strictly in accordance with the schedules made, and even ahead of them! At the back of the mind, there may be the idea that oppositions must 'melt' and disintegrate when exposed to the deep-acting 'power' emanating from stepped-up mental forces. During pre-Independence days in India, there were many who used to argue, in all sincerity, and maintain that poverty, foreign conquest, and other evils were the clearest evidence that the springs of spirituality had dried up, or that spirituality itself, as a 'power', existed only in the high-strung imagination of persons who lacked the courage to wrestle with Nature and ultimately make her a willing servant.

Wherever these ideas hold the field, there will be a tendency to mark only the surface movements in the mind of the student and the peculiar idioms and phrases in which he happens to give expression to them. The experienced teacher, on the contrary, would see deep down into the personality. He would have his eye on the grand tower from which the student is actually making his observations and judgements. How can he fail to appreciate the fact that in the moment of trouble the student retains enough discrimination to resort to some sage for instruction? There are a few distinct ways of reacting to a keen awareness of the want of equilibrium all around. One is to speak of fear and match the talk by an actual flight, condemning oneself and life itself. Another is to fight recklessly without examining the nature of the forces involved. A third is to consult someone who is living in the midst of the same forces, yet has triumphed over them, and is willing not only to teach how he did it, but also to permit others to stay with him and watch from close quarters how he maintains his Ideal in every context. When a student has chosen the path of consultation, it convinces the expert that the nucleus of coordination has sprung to life and begun to send forth its delicate shoots in search of proper nourishment and support. His first concern, therefore, is to supply them in the particular forms suitable to the occasion. He too is a cultivator. Like all farmers, he too knows that the manure and other materials he may add from the outside will be duly transformed into appropriate leaves, flowers, and fruits by the unique 'genius' of the plant itself. No cultivator ever dissects the first shoot or tendril and condemns it on the ground that it has no resemblance to the ripe fruit he wants to get. Nor does he suppose that a few fruits he may throw at the foot of the plant once or twice will, immediately and without assimilation, reappear as the harvest—and a plentiful one at that! Thus, no spiritual teacher wastes his time by cutting and scrutinizing the actual sentences or figures of speech used by the student who approaches him. He would only direct his welcoming look to the individual 'spirit', standing before him in all his perfection, and greet him with the love and respect due to him.

This is the significance of the manner in which the teacher in the *Vivekachudamani* is described as addressing his student. The sage unreservedly calls him, 'O learned one!', and then proceeds to give the much-needed psychological support with the quiet assurance, 'there is no danger for you!'

V

The old Indian tradition believed in awakening the student to a progressively higher level of values, never in coercing him or in thrusting ready-made values upon him from outside. It is easy to see the principle behind it. If a person is found to pin his faith on some form which is crude, only harm can come from laughing at him or trying to shake his faith as such. He can be helped only if wise men mix with him and demonstrate a better way so that his enthusiasm may grow and his perceptions become finer. What appears at the surface as the sprouting of faith, centered on whatever object, is the first indication, though somewhat blurred, in the psychological field of what is, at its base, the sure descent of God's grace on the spiritual plane. What the teacher can, and ought to, do is to draw the aspirant's attention to a well graded set of ideas, arguments, and examples. When mixed with the student's previous notions, they will assist him in creating a better order in his mind than before. Some of his outstanding doubts will then be solved without further external aid, and he may henceforth plunge into the pursuit of truth with an added faith and determination. Since the teacher's vision of his Ideal pervades and unifies not only all that he contacts but also all that he thinks and does, the work of instruction on his part and the growth of faith on the student's side will be viewed by him only as two equally adorable modes in which Its many-sided glory is manifested in the world of men.

Worship is not exhausted by what is usually conducted with lights or incense in front of an altar. Its essence is the unbroken feeling of the presence of the Lord. Each person will feel it in more extended fields in accordance with his inner capacity to perceive subtler truths. The barest minimum is to be able to feel it in one's own heart and in any consecrated place. If this stage is gone through properly, the yearning to have a realization transcending and harmonizing the 'categories' of philosophical analysis is sure to open up his inside and point out to him 'newer' flights of steps to reach much higher levels. It may be taken as a general rule that when one plane is 'conquered', the resulting 'visibility' will naturally extend to the immediately higher one that has to be mastered, as well as to the methods that the aspirant can profitably adopt.[6] Progress in wisdom can never mean exclusion and irrational rejection of the love and reverence previously employed in selected areas; it must, on the other hand, mean their effortless and graceful application to every person, material, and act of service as and when situations arise. The home and the office, then, become as 'sacred' as the formal place of worship, while teaching and administration become channels of whole-hearted adoration as much as verbal prayer or silent meditation. Illumination, once attained, remains steady at all times, irrespective of the kinds of physical and mental movements that genuine service demands.

VI. SERVICE

22. Coordinated insight and service

Most of us ordinarily start serious experiments in self-control as a remedial measure against the pain and frustration caused by events of the external world. There is nothing contemptible in this. Besides, later on, when disciplines proceed, the motives are altered, purified, and put on nobler levels.

Nature herself gives us valuable hints about making a controlled swing from troubles to peace. We shake off our daily fatigue by passing into dreamless sleep. From the waking standpoint, we conclude that our 'overworked' senses and mind were then withdrawn from their usual activities. 'Exhaustion cannot be removed by any other means than this resting within one's self. So it is quite reasonable to say that in that condition the man has gone to his own essence'.[2] 'A bird, fastened by means of a string to the hand of a bird-catcher, flies in various directions in order to escape from its bondage. But not finding any resting place anywhere else except the hand to which it is tied, it at last returns to it and settles down on it. Our mind and senses behave in the same way,' The human soul, limited by the mind, flies about experiencing joys and sorrows in the waking and dream states. It is impelled by desires and driven into struggles. Exhausted, and not finding any resting place in those states, it finally enters the 'self of pure being,' the substratum of all causes and effects.[3]

Comparing the characteristics of the three states, we infer: In waking and dream there is differentiation of names and forms. This short formula includes also the distinctions of number, quality, actions and the like. Differentiation is experienced through the intelligence of an individual self. But individuality itself disappears in what is known as deep sleep. Had it been permanent and independent, it should have remained recognizably present all through. It could not have disappeared. Therefore, even when it rises up and functions, it can only be a reflection of a subtler, all-embracing Entity which projects it, sustains it, withdraws it with all its valuable attributes intact, and can again manifest it in accordance with a law superior to those operating within the three states. In fact, what appears from the waking ego's level as the individual's deep sleep indicates that the supreme Deity which 'entered' into reflected intelligence as an individual 'withdraws' into Its own self, divested of such a reflection.

The perception of this natural 'withdrawal' from manifested duality can thus become the first step in a planned withdrawal from ego-centricity— that useful field which induces discrimination by duly giving back every wrong thought transformed into a sheaf of inescapable troubles!

The next rational step in this approach is to put all pain-causing attitudes into one group and systematically cultivate their direct opposites. All religions instruct us to practise devotion, self-surrender and other positive virtues. Their steady welling up within our hearts, and their capacity to resist evil are facts which can be verified — unmistakably from within by ourselves, Pratyakshavagamam, and quite often from outside by others who watch our reactions. These qualities proceed from God and become the easiest means of realizing Him. They can be rightly called 'divine attainments'. Whatever 'withdrawal' takes place during their cultivation is only from the source of evil. The essential movement of the personality which it entails is ennobling and dynamic. When its effect penetrates into the habit level, it eliminates the opposites and remains abiding.

II

The starting point, however, can be different. We do not wish to be in ignorance. In whatever field we find it, we want to destroy it. The result is an intense struggle which sooner or later culminates in knowledge. We may, for convenience, 'plot' the following points to indicate the course it takes: the sprouting of the desire to dispel inner gloom, extension of the struggle into various fields, the retention of knowledge after it arises, and the application of it, later, in appropriate ways as circumstances require. There is no single term in current use, — other than 'Self', or 'Truth', or 'Reality' — to indicate the invisible Source which seems at one stage to lie 'under' a veil of ignorance, but which is capable of expressing itself as desire, as struggle, as the achievement of wisdom, and as its effortless manifestation wherever necessary. The difficulty becomes greater when we wish to bring within our generalization not merely the attainment of wisdom by conscious human effort, but also the apparently 'unconscious' movements by which even animals and plants exhibit the perfection possible for them. We may call it, if we like, 'the subtle pure being'. Even then, the doubt crops up: how does this gross universe, consisting of the earth, etc., with duly differentiated, names and forms proceed from the extremely subtle pure being devoid of them all?

One way of searching for an answer is to observe nature herself at her work, to take some example of what she does on a large scale almost everywhere, and try to grasp the principle. It is no wonder that one of the Upanishadic teachers used the common seed of a tree to drive his lesson home. 'What do you see inside it?' he asked after the student, his own son, had broken it as ordered. 'I see nothing, sir', came the reply. Then the father said: 'On breaking this seed, you did not see the subtle essence. But it is there all the time. It is from that subtle essence that this large tree supplied with all these—large trunk, branches, twigs, leaves, and fruits—was produced and continues to grow up'. 'In the same manner does this gross universe with all names and forms differentiated proceed from the subtle essence'. And he related it to the life of the student by adding, 'That is the True, That is the Self, That thou art, O Svetaketu.'![4]

This part of the teaching does not stop with the idea of the final goal as a state of peace. Here there is the addition of the vital concept of knowledge as well. It is intended that the swing of the personality must be from ignorance to knowledge. We know from experience that when mastery is acquired in any field, its manifestation is assured and effortless wherever needed. What is withdrawn in the process is the resistance, or the sense of struggle which we felt prior to its rise. The possession of a fine lens and a screen is not enough to get the clear, real image we want. Proper direction and accurate focussing are necessary. The appearance of blurred figures is not an occasion for lamenting. It merely indicates that further adjustments are to be made. The same is the case with the clouds of ideas including doubts, that ordinarily appear in our mind. By shifting a few positions from within, clarity can be achieved. Correct values and relationships would then come into view. Discipline consists in removing faulty outlook, technically called 'dirt'. This term is highly suggestive. We do not complain on finding dirt on our lens or mirror. Dirt is not inherent in its structure. It is only on the surface and a little cleaning will remove it. So too with the mind; resistance is simple impurity. Discipline is the cleaning process. 'The more this impurity is reduced, the greater becomes the light of wisdom, which reaches its culmination in unwavering discrimination'.[5] The 'release' involved does not mean cessation of activity as such, but of the necessity, or the compulsion, or even the possibility of 'adding' anything further to what is gained. Mastery implies that qualitative perfection. The sun of mastery sheds his transforming rays always and in all directions. They may be received or shut out as people like.

III

Since cleaning is going to be thorough, all aspects of the personality—intellectual, moral, and emotional—are bound sooner or later to be affected by it. The simplest rule is to begin purification of every area that by turns becomes actively engaged in daily work. When we are seated in a quiet prayer hall, the distractions we experience come only from mental impressions and wild fancies. As distinct from it, we may say, the control during actual contacts with different people and events is a regular 'field work'. For it requires that we should note the effect of each stimulus from the external world and then and there set right wrong reactions that may rise up within us. These repeated internal encounters are troublesome and tiring in the beginning. But they turn out to be easy and useful as days pass. We shall take kindly to this discipline, if we can convince ourselves that it is the higher quality and penetrating power of our reactions that knocks out the supply base of all hindrances and enables us to disarm stragglers.

For the sake of economy of control, harmful reactions can be considered as the outcome of a wrong attitude towards life. We may call it an aggressively separatist attitude. It tries not merely to secure all good things for oneself, but also grudges anything good going to the share of others. From it develop intolerance, jealousy, malice, deception, fight and, finally, slaughter. Then also, actions intensify passions, and stepped up passions lead to greater violence. As long as this drama is enacted, we cannot expect Truth to enter the stage.

Truth, as we have seen, is the creative and cohesive principle behind man and nature. When our adjustment will be complete, our individuality will function like the focal point with cosmic creativity and protecting love on one side and their potent real images on the other, falling on whatever corresponds to the screen to catch them. Individuality by itself is not an evil. What matters is how it is poised—the elements permitted to pass through it, and the sensitivity or harmfulness of the aims and objects associated with it. Disciplines, therefore, are not directed against that aspect of 'separatism' which keeps up a psychological centre of illumined action.

To neutralize unwanted reactions a fourfold vow is obligatory on all.[6] The application of its different limbs is closely connected with the nature of the stimulus from the external world. For example, we may come across someone who is happy. Probably a son is born to him or he has just entered his newly constructed house. There may be faint tremors of jealousy in our mind on seeing his happiness. This vow requires us to replace them by deliberately rousing the feeling of friendliness, Maitri. Since the harmonization of the entire personality is needed to induce full receptivity to Truth, we must make our newly found joy express itself through the physical body forthwith. We must walk up to him and cooperate with him in whatever way he likes. Or it may be that our neighbour is in pain. We may be tempted to smile in satisfaction on the ground that he richly deserved it. But this satisfaction is our enemy. By condemning him, we encourage in us the tendency to sit in judgement on others or to injure them as our fancy dictates. We make our inside coarse. To stop it we must immediately learn to visualize Truth as the protecting power behind his ailing figure. Here too we must follow up our helpful idea with some practical step, like sitting by his side and speaking words of cheer and hope. Active sympathy, Karuna, when continued, roots out the desire to injure others. Our neighbour may be virtuous. Probably, he is engaged in an auspicious ceremony, adopting methods different from ours. This may cause us to feel jealous, or to criticize him because of the minor differences in the procedure. This uncharitable attitude clouds our own mind. It should be broken without delay. This vow asks us to capture the holy mood from our neighbour, by resorting to the formulas with which we are familiar. This is the practice of Mudita, joyful association in auspiciousness. Lastly, there may be something unholy happening in our area. Whatever reasonable step we take to stop it, our inner movement should not be one of partiality or of taking sides. This is technically called Upeksha. It does not mean utter indifference, as it may appear to be when carelessly translated. It means the taking of the 'middle path' in which we put down our impatience and self-righteousness. It is a call to us to restrict our attention to the welfare of the parties in front, exactly as we ordinarily do for ourselves. The pattern for our thought would then be on the model: Let all be happy and peaceful! Let none fall into grief!

It is fitting that when our goal is Truth, the means too should be characterized by the observance of truth in our daily dealings with others. Often we knowingly keep thought, speech, and action in separate compartments. We do not allow the movements in one to coincide with those in the rest. The vow of truth harmonizes the three sections by making 'word and thought accord with facts'. 'Facts are what have been heard, seen, and inferred as such'. 'We speak for transferring our thoughts to another, to create in other minds the knowledge that is in us'.[7] One more stipulation has to be made. The knowledge transferred must be for the good of others. If not so uttered, the speech contains only a semblance of truth. 'Take, for example, the case of a man who has taken a vow of truth being asked by a gang of robbers if the caravan they are pursuing has passed that way. Suppose the man has actually seen it and therefore gives an affirmative reply. This utterance of his may be technically true. But it is not so in reality, as it tends to the injury of others'. In each context we have to see whether our speech and act help in the realization of the supreme protective power behind the universe—which is the goal of all endeavours—or only hide it further from view.[8]

IV

Actual practice of mental discipline becomes quicker and easier if there is a healthy cooperation between advanced seekers and beginners. In some parts of India there is a pleasant ceremony coinciding with the movement of the sun into the sign of Aries (Mesha). During the night itself a small altar is erected, with a metal mirror in the centre, and flowers, grains, fruits and other auspicious articles arranged around it. A lamp is also kept in the correct position, but not lighted. In the early morning the eldest member, after washing his hands and face, gropes his way to the lamp, with closed eyes, and lights it, Adjusting his position on the prepared seat he then opens his eyes, sees his 'self' in the mirror, and next the flowers and fruits gathered by human effort. Afterwards, he leads the other members who also come with eyes closed, and, next, see them all in the prescribed order: See the Self first, other things next! This ceremony is thus highly symbolic.

Each person's progress is largely dependent on his own efforts. Acharya Sankara brings this out nicely in his *Vivekachudamani.* It is no doubt possible, says he, to get rid of the load on my head if an obliging friend agrees to transfer it to his. But my own hunger and thirst are not so transferable. I myself must eat and drink to remove them. So too, if I am ill, I myself must take medicines and observe diet restrictions. Another cannot do these for me by proxy;[9] hence the necessity for systematic personal exertion in spiritual matters. And yet, by a careful grouping of energies and talents, we can create an environment favourable to the progress of all participants. The family is the simplest of such units. Its head has to combine in himself (or herself) parental love and the functions of a teacher and administrator. By patient explanations and by his personal example he gives the intellectual background for the younger members to discipline themselves. Herein he is the teacher. Youthful emotions, however, have a way of sweeping aside both reasoning and prudence. To regulate the volume and force of their flow, there is the necessity to create an effective system of canals, bunds, and barriers which cannot be crossed or broken with impunity. In planning and maintaining these checks and controls, the head of the family does the work of an administrator in howsoever small a scale.

A much more complicated unit is the State. Its efficiency depends on its head and his assistants working together as a team. Let us take the king or the ruler as an example. He must combine in himself a variety of qualities. In his private and public life he must so conduct himself that people would long to approach him because of his welcoming heart and his ability to bring out the best from one and all. But he must also carry about him such a deep, impenetrable, and solemn atmosphere as would prevent the people from thinking and acting in ways that might ruin themselves and the State. He must be like the ocean, *Adhrsyas-cabhigamyas-ca yatha-ratnairivarnavah*— inviting because of the pearls it contains, but forbidding at the same time because of the dangerous creatures holding sway within its depths.

As an example of what should be the train of thoughts that any good administrator's genuine virtues should normally create in his subordinates and attendants, we refer briefly to a few passages from the well-known drama, *Sakuntalam.*[10]

The king has just got up from the judgement seat and has retired for a little rest. But he has to be disturbed since Kanva's disciples and Gautami have come along with Sakuntala to have an interview with him. Aged Kanchuki says within himself:

Even though a matter of sacred duty must not be deferred by His Majesty, how can I announce to him the arrival of Kanva's disciples ?. It will only put him into trouble. What he wants is rest. Or, perhaps, the office of governing subjects is one which does not give any scope for rest. The sun has his coursers yoked but once; the wind who carries scent blows day and night; and the burden of the earth is ever borne on his head by the celestial serpent. Even so, surely, is this ever-recurring duty of him who collects the allotted taxes from his expectant subjects'.

The king too, on hearing that they were people from the hermitage, immediately takes the necessary steps to receive them with proper honour. He then says within himself:

'Everyone is happy on getting what he wants. The case of the ruler is different. Whatever anxiety he may have had earlier is no doubt removed when he actually gets the throne. But the problem of discharging his responsibilities harasses him after that. Indeed, the administration of a kingdom, which is in one's own hand, is not so much for the removal of fatigue as for creating it! It is like an umbrella which is meant to give good and comforting shade, but whose heavy handle one has to carry in one's own hand all the time!'

23. Mental preparation for Efficient Service

I

Actual work gives the best training. Every work implies the overcoming of some resistance, obstacle, or unfavourable factor present in the environment. Whatever theoretical knowledge we may have of these resistances, we do not realize their exact nature or strength unless we put our own force into the environment and mark the reactions. It takes some time even for a diligent experimenter to coordinate his theoretical knowledge with his direct awareness of the play of forces about him. In many cases, what is practised in a controlled area constitutes only a bare preliminary step. It must be followed by quite different steps, taken in more and more open areas where one may encounter unexpected forces at every turn. Everyone knows that it is one thing to learn to drive a car round in a vacant meadow, but that it is a far more complicated matter to be able to drive it safely and with ease along crowded streets during 'office hours', when traffic, as they say, usually reaches its 'peak'. Herein comes the need to take the help of a competent guide—the need to watch his actions and listen to his verbal instructions till they enter the mind of the student, penetrate into his habit level, and without fail suggest to him the right course to adopt in all contexts. All skills come under this category—particularly those related to activities affecting the time and energy, the progress and fortunes, of large sections of the public.

We may take the example of a trained school teacher, to begin with. He has to finish a certain set of subjects or topics in the course of the year. He may lecture, give home exercises, or take other measures, as he chooses, but the net result must be to bring his student to the required standard of proficiency before the twelve months are over. His one advantage is that every student is ordinarily anxious to come up to the expectation of his parents at home, of his companions in the classroom, and of the teacher himself. What happens, however, is that this initial anxiety or eagerness becomes dissipated by a number of factors which the young man may be unable to control unaided. Depressing influences, antagonistic to studies, can come from the knowledge of the family's economic difficulties or from irritations caused by unsympathetic neighbours. They can also come from conflicts originating in the playground. When left unresolved, they have a tendency to rankle in the minds of the opposing parties and to distract their attention even while listening to the lectures in the classroom. Lastly, there is the onrush of tremendous energy at puberty, creating serious problems unless properly canalized.

The successful teacher is he, who takes note of every factor and gently puts in a word here and an explanation there in the midst of casual talks. If he can help his students to get a better perspective, they will alter their conduct of their own accord in due course. Many who rose to great heights started their careers from very humble beginnings. They were either poor, or had to fight against severe odds to complete their education. They had to struggle hard to create the facilities for doing research or producing works of art. Physical disabilities like blindness could not daunt them, nor could financial handicaps like huge debts, or persecution, religious or political, dry up the springs of their enthusiasm. Greatness came to them, because they called it forth from within themselves. Adversities only made the calls more insistent, and the inner responses abundant and creative. The wise teacher knows how to present the lives of eminent men and women to his students in such ways as to stimulate their imagination and make them frame 'heroic' ideals suited to their inborn tastes. He knows also the value of taking active interest in their games and outdoor activities. Desire to develop a powerful physique, to excel in singing or painting, or to become impressive on the platform or the stage is as strong in growing minds as the impulse to master the prescribed text-books. That teacher alone serves most who discerns the total range of the student's personality and emotionally plants himself at its very centre. To the extent he can do this, his words and suggestions will become capable of awakening dormant virtues. There can be no greater source of encouragement to his students, no better incentive to the re-grouping of mental powers, than the consciousness that their revered teacher taps them only on their bright sides even though he knows all their failings as they themselves do. The energy needed to hold steadfastly to the idea of their all-round progress, as if it were an accomplished fact, is not much more than what is needed to detect and accurately hit the sore spots of their character. Surely, they would not be cunning enough to hide them from the experienced eyes of elderly men.

There is, however, a world of difference between the results of the two efforts. To the teacher, it must be the most enjoyable of disciplines to dwell in confident expectation, and to be the actual witness, of the steady unfolding of his student's inborn gifts. In due course, his whole inside would become so charged with positive thoughts and active goodwill that Nature would respond by bringing to him individuals of different types to be benefited by his benign influence. As for the students themselves, his trust-inspiring presence would constitute an unfailing source of strength at all times. It would reinforce their self-reliance and suggest to them most original ways of tackling their problems. They may get into trobles owing to faulty observation or hasty judgement. Or some emotions may prove to be turbulent, and in a misguided frontal attack on them, they might miss precious opportunities to develop skills which could balance them from the start and ultimately neutralize them altogether. But whatever might be the nature of the discord, the teacher's talks and example would instil into them the habit of returning with redoubled vigour and determination to the task of mastering the forces involved. To those who are thus trained, defeat can never be the cause of fear or shame. It must ever be the signal for greater vigilance and more intensive effort.

II

The home is as good a training ground as the school. In some respects it is even better. Corresponding to the teacher in the school, we have in the home the father, the mother or some other member who stands at the helm of affairs. In the school there is some homogeneity, since the students in a class fall more or less into the same age group and have common subjects to learn within the prescribed time. In the house, on the other hand, we have people of different ages, temperaments, and capacities or willingness to work. The complications caused by this very diversity tend to call forth a greater variety of abilities from the head of the family than the problems of the school do from the teacher. While the school is meant only to teach and not to maintain the students, the family as a whole has to function as an earning unit all the time. Each adult has to carry out regularly a certain number of services connected with the supply of food and other amenities for the entire group. The head has to infuse his own zeal into the others and make them work, earn, and save as much as possible. One member may work in a government office or in a private firm, His salary means a steady income, though probably small. Another may grow food crops if the family has lands of its own. Adverse weather or pests may affect this type of work, as all cultivators know. Or, if there is the necessary talent, the family's surplus may be invested in a business concern of their own. But whatever course is adopted, it is clear that the education of the children and the improvement of the prospects of the family depend on the creative output of all the members put together. If one works less, or falls ill, the burden on the others proportionately increases, Love is a factor that can smoothen rough edges and render hard work pleasing. But it is easy to see that if the head of the family is unable to combine his love with a resonable measure of sternness and discipline, the team spirit will be broken by the undue laziness of some of the youngsters and a general discord among the rest.

To achieve the best results the parent has to play the part of an educator within his small circle. His talks and actions must be such as to rouse the enthusiasm of the rest and centre it round some powerful symbol like the prestige of the family, love for the community, one's own perfection, or devotion to God.

As each class is related to others in the same school, and as schools themselves are related to one another, so houses too are connected by various ties to other houses to form villages, towns, and bigger groups. Through friendships with people living in different localities, through social gatherings and festivals as well as through business dealings, these ties become so strengthened that the consciousness of belonging to bigger and bigger groups gradually dawns on every member of any household. It is the duty of parents to speed up this process and to devise measures to see that their unit stands abreast of others in respect of general culture, if it cannot actually form a model for them to follow.

If we go round the country, we shall come across a few families which for generations together produced a series of eminent personages—artists, industrialists, social workers, political leaders, or saintly characters. It must have formed part of their family 'tradition to introduce in the ways of thinking and feeling—naturally of talking and acting—of its members certain elements of refinement and of higher values which formed an effective mould to shape the lives of its children from their earliest years. Continuous efforts in this direction produced, as it were, an invisible 'suction' area that regulated not only the training of the family's members and attendants, but even their entry into it through the apparently simple processes of marriages, births and the appointments of tutors or guides. The Hindu mind will easily see in such phenomena clear vindications of the law that steady aspiration exerts an irresistible pull, and brings into the area of the aspiring person those entities and situations that fairly correspond to the essence of the aspiration.

If the heart is moved by a passion for loving service, there is no reason why students, patients, customers, and assistants should not flock to a teacher, doctor, merchant, or social worker. What happens is that in most cases the mind of the serving person is not thoroughly purified. While extending a cordial welcome to those who join his party or come for his help, he entertains feelings of suspicion, jealousy, and enmity towards other 'leaders' in the field, whom he regards as his rivals. The formation of a well-knit organization for service of any kind is delayed or prevented to the extent that the attractive power of love is nullified by the opposing pulls of base emotions. How can the flow of favourable forces be continuous if the virtuous inclinations implied in the attitude of service are constantly marred by the oscillations of personal likes and dislikes?

III

Let us now turn to a much vaster type of training ground, viz. groups of villages situated in out of the way places. Thoughtful people have all along recognized that greater care should be bestowed upon them and that active measures should be taken to carry the benefits of education to them as a first step. But formidable obstacles stood in the way.

Those who got higher education had a natural disinclination to remain in villages. They wanted to be in places where they could enjoy the conveniences to which they had got accustomed when they stayed as students in fashionable cities. This meant that they should earn enough money. They could do it only by working in towns where government offices were located or big commercial firms transacted their business. The movement was not, therefore, into the villages, as desired. It was rather away from them. For, village youths who could afford to defray the necessary expenses started moving into important towns, first for gaining education, and later, to settle down permanently to earn wealth like others, as well as to enjoy the facilities which they could not easily have in their distant homes. Those, however, who had extensive lands for cultivation did go back to the villages. They became instrumental in establishing schools and creating various other amenities for the benefit of themselves and the people living all around.

In pre-independence days in India, it was not easy to carry on constructive work in villages. Those who represented the alien rulers were a few local men. While one kept a list of the lands and collected taxes, another settled disputes by holding a miniature court. Some villages had no policemen; they did not need any. The cultivators, weavers, smiths, washermen, and petty shop-keepers who formed the bulk of the inhabitants knew the advantages of living in amity with one another.

There were many things to be done to make their lives more fruitful. In fact, one could draw up a pretty long list of them arranged under such convenient heads as medical aid, irrigation facilities, cheap agricultural loans, better opportunities for marketing their produce, and so on. As against these, there were a few improvements made here and there by the people themselves. For example, the main street was kept in repair by the village association (Panchayat) with the free labour available locally. Some pumping engines and transport lorries had come into the area. They were puchased for personal use by the richer men who were also willing to rent them out for the use of others who were able to pay, and so on. These heralded something better to come next. But there could be no substantial advance on all fronts, unless there was a radical change at the very top and a passion for service descended from there right down to the lowest layers where the masses lived and toiled hard. The result was the struggle for national freedom.

During the days of the struggle, the leaders of the village had a difficult part to play. The house of the rich or influential person who had spent his time, energy, or money to set up school or a dispensary or owned an engine, a lorry, or a car kept its doors open for a variety of guests. National workers went there for food, shelter, and even for funds and moral support. Officers who had the total welfare of the nation at heart, but whose loyalty to the government prevented them from openly showing it out in all respects, invariably halted there on their rounds to push through whatever plans of improvement were sanctioned from above. On the other hand, there were also detectives and officers of an unsympathetic type who camped in the very same house, received hospitality like others, and tried their best to crush the national movement even if it meant imprisonment of the host and forfeiture of his property a few days later. Patriotism is a force that inspires men and women irrespective of their social status. Officials and non-officials, the rich and the poor, may respond alike to its influence. The difference lies only in the ways in which their respective sacrifices and services express themselves in tangible shape.

IV

With the attainment of independence, one main obstacle to the improvement of villages is permanently removed. The question now is one of patient constructive work. There is no need to discuss here details of the various schemes meant to increase agricultural production, start cottage industries, improve marketing facilities and so on. The government machinery can be trusted to do all that is necessary in these directions, subject to its two serious limitations,—lack of funds, and of an adequate number of trained persons to expedite, economize, smoothen, and co-ordinate the different stages in the translation of schemes into actual service.

One wise step that has been taken is to utilize the services of school teachers who evince exceptional powers of leadership. If they are able to rouse the enthusiasm of their students through formal teaching combined with a careful planning of extra-curricular activities, why should they not be able, with a little training, to put an altered stress in their general approach, and succeed in stimulating the creative efforts of the adult population of villages as well? What will be demanded of them will be a harmonization of the attitudes of a teacher, a parent, and an officer with the emotional identification of themselves as men born and bred up in the villages they visit. That should not be a difficult task to an educated man (or woman) who loves his less advanced countrymen. The National Extension Service is so arranged that he can get the necessary facilities for taking up a number of villages and organizing there Youth Clubs, Adult Schools and Women's Associations, or for conducting Rural Libraries and giving periodic film shows. The variety and extent of his programmes and work depend upon his resourcefulness and his ability to handle the masses in every context.

The trainess are usually graduates with teacher's diploma. Some are Masters of Art or Science. They are drawn from a number of States and grouped in convenient centres. It goes without telling that their mother tongues differ from one another. They also belong to different religions and creeds. A batch of sixty, for example, may contain Arya Samajists, Brahmo Samajists, Buddhists, Catholics, Protestants, and Sanatanists as well as Shias and Sunnis, coming from Andhra, Assam, Bengal, Bihar, Kerala, Mysore, Orissa and Tamilnadu—to put them alphabetically if one is interested in such analysis.

This free mixing of 'leaders' of constructive work on an all-India basis, cutting across the barriers erected by language and religion, is pregnant with brilliant possibilities. It is bound to be one of the most potent forces to achieve national solidarity. It stands in striking contrast to the harm done by misguided elements in the political field, who exhibit, here as well as elsewhere, an uncanny originality in singling out points of difference and emphasize them with a perverse tenacity till splits appear where oneness prevailed before. It is a crude way of looking at things to imagine that unity can be 'forged' by heaping discordant elements and hammering them with bitter arguments, violent denunciations or hostile mass demonstrations. Unity must be of hearts. The real leader must have a special eye to see in what respects it already exists. Without damaging these, he must get the clue from them as to the new areas into which it could be extended with the full glow of enthusiasm of all concerned. Before the will of the majority enforces painful cuts and divisions, he should be able to notice if any agency would be left in the minority or outside it to secure its whole-hearted love and co-operation afterwards. If there is none in sight and he cannot improvise one, the damage would indeed be irreparable for the country as a whole.

Many more problems will raise their heads and demand solutions from the social worker when he is actually in the field. Religion too will be one of them. The government, for its own reasons, may have declared itself to be secular in its outlook. But the worker has his own particular religious background which must influence his judgements in various subtle ways. The government school where no religion is taught and the home where a certain uniformity of religious belief is natural differ very much from villages where families belonging to many religious sections live in friendship side by side. When villages grow in importance, they will attract the attentions of disruptionists as well as aggressive proselytizers. When faced with such conditions, what is the duty of the educated organizer posted there after special training? It is clear he must have a firm philosophic background if he is to weather all storms and at the same time stimulate creative activity along all the healthy channels that true religious faith opens up in the minds of the masses. How can such a background be formed?

We hope wise people will have their own valuable suggestions to make.

VII. ATTAINMENT

24. Attainment, Delight, and Non-swerving

> Adopt means for the end you seek to attain. You cannot get butter by crying yourself hoarse, 'There is butter in the milk!' If you wish to make butter, you must turn the milk into curds, and churn it well. Then alone you can get butter. So if you long to see God, practise spiritual exercises. What is the use of merely crying 'Lord! Lord!'?
>
> —Sri Ramakrishna

> 'O Virtuous One! Realize your soul which is none other than that Supreme Light, seated in the triple forms of (individual) seer, his cognition, and the object of cognition. Realize it through proper discipline'.[1]

I

We speak of the external and the internal worlds. We do so for the sake of intensive study and research. All of us are not equipped with the same type of talent. Some with the requisite inborn gift can profitably specialize in exploring the world of matter. Others can, as naturally, plunge themselves into the world of mind. Systematic enquiry can help each set to discover how creative forces operate in the field of its choice. In both, the process adopted is practically the same. It is the triple process of observation, generalization, and verification. Success in any stage leads to the unravelling of truth—truth related to the layer reached. After certainty has come, the relevant force has to be mastered. It has then to be wisely used to serve human purposes, not harmful but beneficial, not unworthy but noble.

We may ask if the initial bifurcation of external and internal will not persist throughout. Will we not, as we advance, travel in progressively diverging areas, with no chance to arrive at any common meeting ground? Ancient teachers have given us the answer. They have pointed out not only in what direction the meeting ground lies but also that it is our duty and glorious privilege to press onward till we reach it. They have called it the Supreme Truth, or Reality. It is described as existing equally in both the worlds and at the same time transcending them. They have also claimed that, while both worlds show the possibility of evolving, Its perfection stands as the inescapable impulse for evolution, as its sustaining power and as its ultimate goal. The door for verification is ever open in a unique sense; for that starting ground itself—the very personality of man, the enquirer. Says Gaudapada: 'Having known the truth regarding what exists internally (i.e. within the body etc) as well as the truth regarding what exists externally (i.e. earth etc), the aspirant becomes one with the Reality, derives pleasure from it, and never deviates from it'.[2]

II

Let us examine more closely some of the valuable ideas contained in this terse statement with which Gaudapada's second chapter ends. To begin with, we shall take up the expression, 'become one with the Reality'. We can never become one with something that is entirely unrelated to, or beyond the reach of, our being. We learn mathematics or music. What does it imply? It implies that the relationships of figures or quantities, or the effects of sound combinations are not truths that demand only a casual intellectual assent from us. They are truths that can enter into us, penetrate into the deeper layers of our personality, and become second nature with us. We can afterwards turn them to good account, for the benefit of ourselves and others. Mastery, in fact, means the ability to use them so at will. The personality and its reactions to the varying pressures of the environment provide the field and opportunity for adequate verification. The verification of the Supreme Truth too is to take place, more or less in the same way. The one preliminary condition to be fulfilled is the purification of our psycho-physical mechanism through proper exercises. When its present selfish pulls and pain-causing twists are eliminated, it can act as an easy and effective channel for conveying Cosmic Creative Energy and converting it into 'forms' suitable for each context. 'Becoming one' is, thus, neither a flight into wishful thinking nor a misguided attempt to prevent the thinking apparatus from responding to the noblest impulses common for all humanity. It means just the opposite. It means the patient acquisition of a twofold skill : first, to purify and coordinate all faculties, thoughts, and emotions; and secondly, to so poise the harmonized personality that it spontaneously registers, and unobtrusively answers, mankind's yearnings as much as the situations warrant at the time. We have a tendency nowadays to measure the worth of any individual or movement in terms of sheer quantity or number. Has not the term 'million' a charm of its own? Thus do we often ask: How many among the 'masses' have been contacted by a candidate, lectured to from a platform, and made to 'vote' for the cause that we uphold? The larger that number, the greater must be the man; so we conclude. So also do we try to ascertain the vastness of the area covered by any programme that may be chalked out for constructive work, or the extent of the money expected to be spent when it would be taken up for execution! With size and bigness haunting our imagination, we are bound to look at the creative value of spiritual attainments from a wrong angle and, hence, come to totally false conclusions about it.

To put it briefly, the spiritually perfect person is one who habitually, 'sees' the Spirit in all Its glory in everyone with whom he has to deal—even in thought. When the physical eye and connected reasoning bring in the picture of a suffering or blundering neighbour, the eye of illumination, opened up by steady discipline, confronts it with the infinitely more powerful assurance of the Divine Presence. Every saint is, in this way, a 'centre' radiating positive influences, whether he is engaged in attending to his bodily needs or living in 'retirement', writing some books. That 'right thought' is a subtle creative force, who can deny? Do we not accept that the loving, forgiving, and expectant attitude of parents and teachers imperceptibly moulds the character of children and students who live with them? The thought-patterns of mature minds change the environment for the better. Even today physicians of the 'old' Ayurvedic system carry on their day to day work on this basis. The 'orthodox' among them may be few in number; but they are men of meditation. Their daily exercises enable them to see the Wisdom of the Heavenly Physician blended harmoniously with their own skill on the one hand, and the need of the afflicted on the other. They enter the consulting room, firmly established in the consciousness of the Divine Presence everywhere. The idea is simple. The mind that is kept in contact with the Creative Source of all Life not only moves into the truth, of its own accord, but also progressively awakens true, just, and beneficial responses from the areas to which it is directed. If that area consists of people who sincerely struggle for self-improvement, their responses will be quicker and more lasting. Others who are too indolent to change their ways or correct their faults will be unable to receive or assimilate much. All, however, will register some result; for no contact with a realized soul will be wholly unproductive.

But how is anyone to measure the extent of such 'results'? Where is he to look for them? There are insuperable difficulties in the matter of making a statistical study of the effects of a sage's eminence upon the general public. For the 'receiving' capacity of no two persons can be the same in all respects. Even when instructed by the same teacher about items of sense perception, we find a few students grasp him fairly aright, but a larger number misinterpret his meaning. Some interpret his words into the exact contrary of his view, and others do not understand him at all.[3] What then must be the divergence in the 'results' where the perception of subtle values and the transformation of the entire personality are concerned? It may so happen also that out of those who 'visit' a sage, a few who are receptive may progress in certain directions for a time and then apparently remain 'stagnant', whereas others who appear indifferent at the start may suddenly show signs of quick 'assimilation' later. Peters may 'deny' in unexpected contexts, and Sauls may take the lead in persecution; yet both may become changed beyond recognition as days pass. Then again, it is quite possible that only a bare handful of simple-hearted devotees gather round a saintly person in his own lifetime. But after hearing from them and being struck by their extraordinary calmness and sweetness, large numbers belonging to the next generation may proceed to record the Master's teachings and attain spiritual insight themselves. When they try to share their experiences with others, the message is bound to spread into wider and still wider circles. In this expanding movement, it may not be only pure mystics who take a share, but also men and women with diverse talents—scholars, poets, musicians, painters, sculptors, merchants, and even administrators. History shows that whenever there appeared an illumined soul of a high order—even though his career was brief like that of Jesus or Acharya Sankara—great cultural movements originated and continued to flow for centuries together, embracing in their majestic sweep countless millions spread over the earth.

Sages have sometimes been compared to the spring season.[4] The comparison is highly suggestive. When spring comes, it brings freshness and vigour with it. Not only big trees, considered mighty and useful by men, but even little plants growing unnoticed by them in some crevices on solitary hill-tops do get tender leaves and flowers suited to their own nature. The rejuvenating force of the season is the same; yet the visible and 'statistically recordable' changes in the 'receiving' entities depend upon the order of developments inherent in their structural patterns. Besides, spring, like other seasons, has its own rhythm and principle for its appearance. It does not stand in need of respectful invitations from anyone; nor does it expect even thanks from us for having given us its best. The idea is that great souls, similarly, radiate invigorating influences on all alike—that too, unasked, unobtrusively, and without the least expectation. We have to make one qualification, however. On spring's approach, all vegetation in the relevant locality bursts forth into a new song of joy and activity at the same time. But humanity's music of spiritual communion and service has a slower movement. For only those with adequate preparation are capable of being caught up by it. But by way of compensation, as it were, it has a way of gathering momentum with every new generation. As its wakening notes become repeated and their thrills penetrate farther, larger areas become affected; and greater numbers join the group with their special skills—thereby adding a richness, depth, and intensity of appeal that the original participants could never have dreamt of in their days.

III

So far we have seen that the Truth realized by saints covers what we, in the early stages of analysis, distinguish as the 'external' and the 'internal' worlds. Let us now turn to the second expression used by Gaudapada. He says that, having 'become one with the Reality', the sage 'derives pleasure from It'. We have to remember here that every scriptural text somewhere or other stresses this one point: that when the Self shines upon (or through, or as) the properly purified and poised mind, there is a welling up of unique joy. Words are ordinarily coined, or meant, to facilitate transactions of the sense world. Scripture is 'revelation' transmitted to us through teachers of the past. The maximum that any illumined teacher can do is to select the best from available words and combine them in ways that may help us to catch supersensuous truths. He may employ allied words in a series. Or he may add a succession of qualifying terms. These may enable the discerning student to experience higher values rising into a *crescendo* whose effect is unforgettable. The teacher can, thus, start with a simple statement that the sage 'enjoys, seeing the Self in the self by the self'. A commentator may add: The meditator has to adopt suitable disciplines (of Yoga) to prevent his attention from straying in all undesirable directions. When the scattered rays of awareness are gathered together and made to rest calmly and steadily on the Self, he attains realization. He then directly 'sees' the Self to be of the nature of blazing Awareness itself.[5] In this Supreme Principle he 'sees' the seeker, the seeking, and the sought to be interchangeable terms. This gives him an access of joy. In the absence of a better expression, we may say that he feels it 'within his self'.

In what sense is it a new joy? Is there not a kind of joy felt when a coveted sense-object is acquired? Yes; but that joy is limited and perishable. Surely, there was a period of anxious waiting before we could possess the object. Its retention being doubtful, there is bound to be a secret fear that it may be suddenly lost in the future. Besides there is no guarantee of enjoyment though the object might remain intact before us. What pleasure do we get from a collection of paintings if we happen to lose our eyesight ? The organ through which objects could be enjoyed being lost, their very presence can occasion greater misery than their previous nonpossession. In contrast to such 'conditioned' pleasures, the bliss of the Self stands without a parallel. It does not come to us through the senses, but directly from the comprehensive Principle that makes the senses and their objects function. How does this contact come ? Where is the 'limb' that can reach It ?

The reply is that the Buddhi or judging faculty itself blossoms into the necessary sensitive 'limb' when mental purity reaches its peak. At present, our mental movements are made through internal 'jets' as it were. They are: desire ; words uttered mentally to frame desire ; pictures raised up of objects, relations, and sensations representing the fulfilment of desire ; a sense of waiting ; anxiety on that score ; accusation of people who seem to be blocking our way ; consciousness of sin committed ; fear of its recurrence and of the future being blighted ; and so on. Cosmic creative energy, flowing through us as awareness, becomes conditioned by these 'jets'. The result is a condensation in the shape of endless painful situations. As the nature of the thoughts is, so is the experience of joy or sorrow when the time for fructification arrives.

IV

What happens when meditation is practised correctly ? Unwholesome memory tangles are eliminated. Creative energy flowing through all the 'jets' is slowly and systematically centred on Perfection Itself as a fact in the immediate present. Meditation is, thus, an intensely active and total effort of the personality. The beginner has to lift himself into it through graded steps. He has to start with a threefold distinction, viz. himself as the meditator, his process of meditation, and lastly, the goal of it, looked upon as the Self or simply as Liberation. The 'meanings' connected with these three usually take the shape of a mental proposal: 'I, so-and-so, direct my attention this way, to realize the glory of the Self'. This is technically called 'Form', Sva-rupa as against 'Meaning or Essence', Artha. Here, 'I' 'attention' and 'the Self' call up various 'associations' in keeping with the antecedents and cultural advance of the meditator. After some diligent practice, most of the wayward jumpings of thought can be controlled. Still a minimum sense of internal split and of separation from the Ideal is sure to persist, impeding the full expressiom of delight. This is because 'memories' of meanings basically surrounding the three terms, 'seeker', 'seeking', and 'Goal' have not been consciously integrated with the concept of the Self. Any thought-movement stirred up with the mental speech, 'I the seeker', must register a sense of smallness or bondage. Similarly, 'seeking' must suggest a tedious process, and 'Goal' a desirable, yet at present unattained, Entity. This must create an undercurrent of pain or restlessness, however minute, untill 'memories' dependent upon inwardly spoken words are disentangled and suitably harmonized.[6] To do this, a further heaving of the personality will be required. That will be the last step, so far us as fusion of values is concerned. After that, the meanings not only of the three terms, 'seeker', 'seeking', and 'Goal' but also of all other terms and entities of the internal as well as external worlds will undergo a permanent transformation. The limit is reached when they all stand revealed as natural, variegated, and fully enjoyable 'scintillations' from the priceless Jewel—the Self, looked upon as 'individual' or 'Supreme'.

Attention may, and will, yet call up images and deal with objects corresponding to them, as they appear. But there will be no sense of compulsion to accept them or reject them in a special way, as before. As they pass, the internal Judge of values will habitually give each of them the adoration previously reserved for the Self imagined to be fundamentally different from them. Adoration and delight naturally go together. Delight is no more an experience expected to come in the future as the result of any action done in the present. It is contacted in the present moment itself, and in every succeeding moment as it arrives.

At this stage, the three main terms of the 'Form', Sva-rupa, lose their previous power to rouse up totally separate meanings. For they all now mean only the Self. 'Form' has thus fulfilled its function. Being no more operative in any special way, it is said to have 'disappeared' and, as it were, 'dissolved'. This is, technically, an attainment of the 'Formless'. Positively paraphrased, it reads: 'The meaning, or Self, alone shines'. Whether this comprehensive value has emerged can be verified only by one's own inner Judge. That Judge is the special sensitive 'limb', evolved and strengthened through disciplines. It is about this that scriptures have spoken in various contexts.

One point more may be touched upon here. It is related to the last expression in Gaudapada's statement, viz. that the sage 'never deviates' from the Truth. In his commentary, Acharya Sankara says in effect: A person who is ignorant of the Truth is likely to mistake his mind to be the Self. He may think that his self is caught up in movement matching his mental fluctuations. He may also identify his self with the body etc. So he may interpret bodily movements as deviation from Atman and say. Oh, 'I am now fallen from the Knowledge of the Self!' On the contrary, when his mind is concentrated now and then, he may feel happy, thinking. 'I am now one with the essence of the Truth!' But the knower of the Truth never makes any such statement. For he sees directly that Atman is ever one and changeless and that it is impossible for it to deviate from its own nature. The consciousness, 'I am the Supreme Truth' never leaves him.

We may very usefully remember here the long description of the Sthita-prajna or the man of steady illumination, given in the second chapter of the *Gita*. We may remember too the special mention elsewhere that he will be absolutely free from fear, and unruffled in the midst of great sorrows. Acharya Sankara comments: 'Sorrows, such as may be caused by weapons like a sword and so on'.[7] Who can forget that the teacher of the Gita is a military hero, choosing of his own accord to act as an unarmed charioteer in the midst of the terrible conflict at Kurukshetra?

FOOTNOTES

1. Educative value of philosophic discipline

1. Yatha hi paśvādayaḥ ... daṇḍodyatakaram puruṣam abhimukham upalabhya māṁ hantum ayam icchati iti palāyitum ārabhante, harita-tṛṇapūrṇa-pāṇim upalabhya tam prati abhimukhībhavanti.
—Śaṅkara in his introduction to Brahma Sūtra 1.1.1.
2. Anubandhaṁ kṣayaṁ himsām anapekṣya ca pauruṣam, Mohād-ārabhyate karma yat-tat-tāmasamucyate.
—Gītā, 18.25.

2. Goal and plan of inspired guides

1. The Dhammapada, 43.
2. sīla, samādhi, or citta, paññā. Buddha by Oldenberg, 2.3. p.288
3. "... dhīra ... yoga-kṣemam-anuttaram". The Dhammapada, 23.
4. ibid, 29.
5. ibid, 40.
6. ibid, 422.
7. Bhagavadgītā, 4.38.
8. Compl. Wks. of Sw. Vivekananda, 7. pp. 152-3.
9. ibid 5. on Evolution, 17.
10. ibid 1. Raja Yoga, ch. 4. Sūtra 1
11. ibid 1. Rāja Yoga ch. on Prāṇa, 3.p. 157.
12. The Gospel of Buddha by Paul Carus, Introduction to Parables.
13. St. Matt. 8.8
14. "...tam-asmi manasā gataḥ.. tato me tadgatam manaḥ..." Śānti Parvan, ch. 41.
15. Ācārya-kulād-vedam-adhītya yathāvidhānam guroḥ-karmātiśeṣeṇa..., and Śankara's commentary thereon.
16. bhūya eva tapasā brahmacaryeṇa śraddhayā samvatsaram samvatsyatha, 1.2.
17. 7. i. 2.
18. Bṛhaspatim tu vavre sa ... upādhyāyam ... (ch. 310) and sa mokṣam-anucintyaiva śukaḥ ... adhīhi putra ... Uvāca gaccheti tadā Janakam ... Sa te vakṣyati mokṣārtham nikhilena viśeṣataḥ ... ch. 311) Śānti Parvan.

3. Seeds and sowing for inner harvest

1. This is in accordance with the principle given in Yoga Sūtra 2.16: "Pain that is not yet come is to be avoided." Vyāsa explains: "The pain that is past has been spent up by experience. Hence it cannot fall within the sphere of the Avoidable. That which is present is being experienced at the time of its existence. So it too cannot be considered as the Avoidable with reference to any action to be taken a second later. Therefore that pain alone that has not yet come (but that may come within the field of experience in the absence of discrimination &c) troubles the yogi who is sensitive like the eye-ball; it does not trouble any other. Hence that alone is the Avoidable pain. It is the cause of this Avoidable pain that is discussed".
2. After enumerating virtues to be cultivated by the earnest seeker, Yoga Vāsiṣṭha says: "The practice of some one of these pure virtues leads to the gain of all the four (mentioned). Every one of these separately leads to the others. Therefore diligently apply yourself to one of these for your success in getting them all". (Mumukṣu Khaṇḍa. 16, entitled Sadācāra-nirūpaṇam).
"Ekasminneva vai teṣām abhyaste vimalodaye,
Catvāro'pi kilābhyastā bhavanti, sudhiyām vara! 21.
Eko'pyeko'pi sarveṣām eṣām prasara-bhūr-iha;
Sarva-saṁsiddhaye tasmād yatnenaikam samāśrayet. 22.
3. Ālasyam yadi na bhavej-jagatyanarthaḥ
Ko na syād-bahu-dhanako bahuśruto vā?
Ālasyād-iyam-avaniḥ sa-sāgarāntā
Sampūrṇā nara-paśubhiśca nirdhanaiś-ca!
ibid, 5.30
4. Ābālyād-alam-abhyastaiḥ. Śāstra-sat-saṅgamādibhiḥ,
Guṇaiḥ puruṣa yatnena Svārthaḥ samprāpyate yataḥ,
Iti pratyakṣato dṛṣṭam Anubhūtam śrutam kṛtam,
Daivāttam-iti manyante Ye hatās-te kubuddhayaḥ ibid, 5.28-29.
5. Yad-daivam tāni karmāṇi Karma, Sādho! mano hi tat;
Mano hi puruṣas-tasmāt Daivam nāstīti niścayaḥ.
Eṣa eva mano jantur Yad-yat-prayatate hitam;
Kṛtam tat-tad-avāpnoti Svata eva hi daivataḥ,
Mana'ś-cittam vāsanā ca Karma daivam ca niścayaḥ,
Rāma! Dur-niścayasyaitāḥ Saṁjñās-sadbhir-udāhṛtāḥ.

Evam-nāmā hi puruṣo Dṛḍha-bhāvanayā yathā
Nityam prayatate, Rāma! Phalam āpnotyalam tathā.
Evam puruṣakāreṇa Sarvam-eva Raghūdvaha!
Prāpyate netareṇeha, Tasmāt-sa śubhado'stu te! ibid, 9.18-22

6. Vāsanaugheṇa śuddhena Tatra ced-adya nīyase,
Tat-krameṇa śubhenaiva Padam Prāpsyasi śāśvatam.
Atha ced-aśubho bhāvas-Tvām yojayasi saṁkaṭe,
Prāktanas-tad-asau yatnāt Jetavyo bhavatā balāt. ibid, 9. 26-27.
7. Śubhā'śubhābhyām mārgābhyām Vahantī vāsanā-sarit;
Pauruṣeṇa prayatnena Yojanīyā śubhe pathi. ibid, 9. 30.
8. Jantoś-cittam tu śiśuvat Tasmāt-tac cālayed-balāt. 9. 32.
Samatā-sāntvanenāśu Na drāg-iti śanaiḥ śanaiḥ.
Pauruṣeṇaiva Yatnena Pālayec-citta-bālakam. 9. 33.
9. Prāktanaś-caihikaś-cobhau Puruṣārthau phaladrumau
Saṁjātau puruṣāraṇye, Jayatyabhyadhikas-tayoḥ. ibid, 6. 25.

4. Unified outlook through proper discipline

1. Ā-adhyāya-parisamāpteḥ āsurī sampat prāṇiviśeṣaṇatvena pradarśyate, pratyakṣīkaraṇena ca śakyate asyāḥ parivarjanam kartum iti. Śaṅkara Bhāṣya: Gītā, 6.6 Pravṛttim ca, pravartanam, yasmin puruṣārtha-sādhane kartavye ... tām, tad-viparītām, yasmād anarthahetoḥ nivartitavyam sā nivṛttiḥ, tām ca janāḥ āsurāḥ ... na jānanti ... aśaucā anācārā māyāvinaḥ anṛta-vādino hi āsurāh. ibid, 7.
2. Cf. the drift of 'Bhogaiśvarya-gatiḥ' and 'Bhogaiśvarya-prasaktāḥ' in Gītā, 2.43 and 44; also of 'cintām-aparimeyām' 'Kāma-bhogārtham anyāyenārtha-sañcayān (īhante; na dharmārtham),' 'Mām, ātma-para-deheṣu pradviṣantaḥ' in ibid, 16. 11-18; and 'Karśayantaḥ śarīrastham ... karaṇasamudāyam, Mām ca tat-karma-buddhi sākṣi-bhūtam; Mad-anuśāsana-akaraṇam eva Mat-karśanam in ibid, 17.6.
3. Īśvare sannyāsasya adhikatara-phala-hetutva-upapatteḥ. ibid, 6. introduction.
4. Yathā hi skandha-śākhānām
Taror-mūlāvasecanam,
Evam ārādhanam Viṣṇoḥ
Sarveṣām ātmanaś-ca hi. Bhāgavatam. 8.8.5. 49.
5. Teṣām ... nivṛtta-sarva-bāhyaiṣaṇānām ... prītiḥ, snehaḥ

tat-pūrvakam Mām bhajatām ... prayacchāmi Buddhiḥ. śamyagdarśanam... yena... Mām parameśvaram ātmabhūtam ātmatvena pratipadyante ... antaḥ-karaṇāśayaḥ tasmin eva sthitaḥ san, jñānadīpena, viveka-pratyaya-rūpeṇa (mithyā-pratyaya-lakṣaṇam mohāndhakāram nāśayāmi) ... Bhakti-prasāda-snehābhiṣiktena, Mad-bhāva-abhiniveśa-vāteritena, brahmacarya-ādi-sādhana-saṁskāravat-prajñāvartinā, virakta-antaḥkaraṇa-ādhāreṇa-viṣaya-vyāvṛtta-citta-rāga-dveṣakaluṣi-tanivātāpāvāraka-sthena, nitya-pravṛttaikāgrya-dhyānajanita-samyag-darśana-bhāsvatā jñāna-dīpena. Gītā Saṅkara Bhāṣya, 10.10.2.

6. Cf. dakṣaḥ, pratyutpanneṣu kāryeṣu sadyo yathāvat pratipattum samarthaḥ. He is able to decide rightly on the spot in matters demanding prompt attention. ibid, 12.16
7. Sarveṣām api anna-rasa vikāratve Brahmavamśatve ca aviśiṣṭe, kasmāt puruṣa eva gṛhyate? Prādhānyāt. Kim punaḥ prādhānyam? Karmajñāna-adhikāraḥ ... 'Puruṣe tvevāvistarām-ātmā; sa hi prajñānena sampannatamo, vijñātam vadati, vijñātam paśyati, veda śvastanam, veda lokālokau, martyenāmṛtam īkṣati ityevam sampannaḥ.' Tait. ii.1
8. Tasya ca bāhyākāra-viśeṣeṣu anātmasu ātmabhāvitā buddhiḥ, anālambya viśeṣam kamcit, sahasā antaratma-pratyagātma-viṣayā nirālambanā ca kartum aśakyā iti dṛṣṭa-śarīra-ātma-sāmānya-kalpanayā, śākhā-candra-nidarśa-navat, antaḥ praveśayannāha tasya idam eva śiraḥ. ibid,
9. Nābher-adhastād-yad-aṅgam tat puccham pratiṣṭhā ... Etat-prakṛtyā uttareṣām prāṇamayādīnām rūpakatva-siddhiḥ mūṣā-niṣikta-druta-tāmrapratimāvat. ibid.
10. Cf. Jñānam śāstrokta-padārthānām parijñānam, vijñānam tu śāstrato jñātānām tathā eva svānubhava-karaṇam; tābhyām jñāna-vijñānābhyām tṛptaḥ sañjāta-alam-pratyaya ātmā antaḥkaraṇam yasya saḥ ... aprakampyo bhavati. Śaṅkara Bhāṣya, Gītā, 6.8.

5. Scope of personal exertion

1. Śāstraiḥ sad-ācāra-vijṛmbhita-deśa dharmaiḥ
Yat-kalpitam phalam atīva cira-prarūḍham
Tasmin-hṛdi-sphurati copanameti cittam

Aṅgāvalī tad-anu pauruṣam etad-āhuḥ.
Yoga Vāsiṣṭha, Mumukṣu Khaṇḍa, 6.40.
Aśubheṣu samādhiṣṭham
Śubheṣu evā'vatārayet
Prayatnāt cittam ityeṣa
Sarva-śāstrārtha-saṅgrahaḥ.
ibid.7.12.
Kriyayā spanda-dharmiṇyā
svārtha-sādhakatā svayam
Sādhu-saṅgama-sac-chāstra-
tīkṣṇayo'nnīyate dhiyā.
ibid, 7.27.

2. Sarvaiḥ kleśa-karma-āvaraṇaiḥ vimuktasya jñānasya ānantyam bhavati. Tamasā-abhibhūtam āvṛtam anantam jñāna-sattvam, kvacid-eva rajasā pravartitam udghāṭitam grahaṇa-samartham bhavati. Tatra yadā sarvaiḥ āvaraṇa-malaiḥ apagatam bhavati, tadā bhavati asya ānantyam. Jñānasya ānantyāt jñeyam alpam sampadyate yathā ākāśe khadyotaḥ. Vyāsa on Yoga Sūtra, 4.31.
3. Yathā hi śaradi ghana-paṭala-muktasya caṇḍarciṣaḥ paritaḥ pradyotamānasya prakāśa-ānantyāt alpam prakāśyam iti... ata eva sarvān dharmān jñeyān mehati varṣati prakāśanena iti Dharma-megha ityucyate. ibid, Vācaspati's gloss.
4. Pratyaya-viveka-nimnasya sattva-Puruṣa-anyatākhyāti-mātra-pravāhiṇaḥ cittasya tat-chidreṣu pratyaya-antarāṇi 'asmi' iti vā, 'mama' iti vā jānāmi' iti vā, 'nā jānāmi' iti va. Kutaḥ? Kṣīyamāṇa-bījebhyaḥ pūrva-saṁskārebhyaḥ iti. Vyāsa on Y.S. 4.27.
5. Tasya praśānta-vāhitā saṁskārāt. Y.S. 3. 10. Nirodha-saṁskāra-abhyāsa-pāṭava-apekṣā praśāntā-vāhitā cittasya bhavati. Tat-saṁskārā-māndye, vyutthāna-dharmiṇā-saṁskāreṇa nirodhadharma-saṁskāro'bhibhūyate. ibid. Vyāsa.
6. Aśuddhi-āvaraṇa-mala-apetasya prakāśātman buddhi-sattvasya, rajas-tamobhyām anabhibhūtaiḥ svacchaḥ sthiti-pravāho Vaiśāradyam... Tadā, yogino bhavati adhyātmaprasādaḥ. Bhūtārtha-viṣayaḥ, krama-ananurodhī sphuṭaḥ prajñālokaḥ. Tathā ca uktam:
Prajñā-prasādam āruhya
Aśocyaḥ socato janān
Bhūmiṣṭhān iva śailasthaḥ

Sarvān prājño'nupaśyati.

—Vyāsa on Y.S. 1.47.

6. Catchwords for correcting perspective

1. Aho! dīptimato'pi viśvasanīyatā asya vapuṣaḥ. Athavā upapannam etadasmin ṛṣi-kalpe rājani. Kutaḥ:

Adhyākrāntā vasatir-amunāpyāśrame sarvabhogye,
Rakṣā-yogād-ayam api tapaḥ pratyaham sañcinoti;
Asyāpi dyām-spṛśati vaśinaś-cāraṇa-dvandagītaḥ.
Puṇyaḥ śabdo munir-iti muhuḥ kevalaṁrājña-pūrvaḥ.
phalāni upaharataḥ.... sa-praṇāmam parigṛhya, 'Ājñām icchāmi.' 'Vidito bhavān āśramasadām ihasthaḥ. Tena bhavantam prārthayante.' 'kim ājñāpayanti ?' Act 2.

7. Uplifting power behind words and acts

1. Compl. Wks. of Sw. Vivekananda Vol. 1, Karma Yoga, P. 27.
2. Particularly as this is the season when her birthday is celebrated.
3. This and the following quotations are taken from "Sri Sarada Devi" (1940 Madras Edition) Conversations, Series 3. P. 487.
4. ibid, pp. 477-78
5. Series 2, pp. 381, 415, and 458.
6. ibid, p. 405.

8. Scriptural aids to end 'afflictions'

1. Vicārayācārya-paramparāṇām
   Matena satyena sitena tāvat
   Yāvad-viśuddham svayam eva buddhyā
   Hyananta-rūpam param abhyupaiṣi.
   Yoga Vāsiṣṭha, Mumukṣu, 19.35
   Yathā samvit-tathā cittam
   Sā tathāvasthitim-gatā
   Parameṇa prayatnena
   Nīyate'nya-daśām punaḥ.
   Mad-buddhārtho jagat-śabdo
   Vidyate param-āmṛtam

Tvad-buddhārthas-tu nāstyeva
Tvam-aham-śabdakād-api.
ibid, Utpatti, 40.13 & 61.

2. Kāmasya ne'ndriya- prītir-
lābho jiveta yāvatā,
Jīvasya tattva-jijñāsā
Nā'rtho yaś-ceha karmabhiḥ.
Bhāgavata 1.2.10

3. Sati mūle, tad-vipāko jāti-āyur-bhogāḥ.
Yoga Sūtra, 2.13.

Satsu kleśeṣu, karmāśayo vipāka-ārambhī bhạvati, na ucchinna-kleśa-mūlaḥ. Yathā tuṣā'vanaddhāḥ śāli-taṇdulā a-dagdha-bīja-bhāvāḥ praroha-samarthā bhavanti, na apanīta-tuṣā, dagdha-bīja-bhāvā vā, tathā kleśā-'vanaddhaḥ karmāśayo vipāka-prarohī bhavati, na apanīta-kleśo, na prasaṁkhyāna-dagdhakleśa-bīja-bhāvo vā iti. Sa ca vipākas-trividho, jāti, āyur-bhoga iti. Vyāsa.

4. Sukha-duḥkhe ca rāga-dveṣa-anuṣakte, tadavinirbhāga-vartinī, tad-abhāve na bhavataḥ. Na ca asti sambhavo na ca tatra yas-tuṣyati vā udvijate vā tat ca tasya sukham vā duḥkham vā iti. Tad-iyam ātma-bhūmiḥ kleśa-salila-avasiktā, karma-phala-prasava-kṣetram iti...prasaṁkhyānadagdha-bīja-bhāvo na phalāya kalpate, iti. ibid, Vācaspati.

5. Pradhāna-puruṣayoḥ 'saṁyogo' heya-hetuḥ. Saṁyogasya ātyantikī nivṛttiḥ hānam. Hanopāyaḥ saṃyag-darśanam. Tatra hātuḥ svarūpam upādeyam vā heyam vā na bhavitum arhati. Vyāsa on Y.S 2.15

6. Tasyaiva hetoḥ prayateta kovido
Na labhyate yad-bhramatām uparyadhaḥ,
Tal-labhyate duḥkhavad-anyataḥ sukham
Kālena sarvatra gabhīra-raṁhasā.
Bhāgavatam, 1.5.18

7. Tato'nyathā kiṁcana yad-vivakṣataḥ
pṛthag-dṛśas-tat-kṛta-rūpa-nāmabhiḥ
Na kutracit-kvāpi ca duḥsthitā matir-
labheta vātāhata-naur-ivāspadam.
ibid, 1.5.14

8. Atra sargo, visargaś-ca,

Sthānam, poṣaṇam, ūtayaḥ,
Manvantareśānukathā,
Nirodho, muktir-āśrayaḥ.
Daśamasya viśuddhyartham
Navānām iha lakṣaṇam,
Varṇayanti mahātmānaḥ
Srutenārthena cāñjasā. ibid, 2.10.1-2.

9. Cf. Jagato'rthe tathātmanaḥ... 4.39; Lokānām varadā bhava, 11.35 varam yam manasecchatha tam prayacchāmi jagatām upakārakam. ibid, 37.

10. Ārādhitā saiva nṛṇām
bhoga-svargā' pavargadā...
Tato vavre nṛpo rājyam
Avibhraṁśyanya-janmani,
Atra caiva nijaṁ rājyaṁ
Hata-śatru-balam balāt.
So'pi vaiśyas-tato jñānaṁ
Vavre nirviṇṇa-mānasaḥ.
Mametyaham iti prājñaḥ
Saṅga-vicyuti-kārakam. ibid, 13.

11. Yac-ca kiṁcit-kvacid-vastu
Sad-asad-vā'khilātmike!
Tasya sarvasya yā śaktiḥ
Sā tvam kiṁ stūyase mayā? ibid, 1.82.

12. Yā śrīḥ svayaṃ sukṛtinām
bhavaneṣu', alakṣmīḥ
Pāpātmanām, kṛta-dhiyām
hṛdayeṣu buddhiḥ,
Śraddhā satām, kula-jana-
prabhavasya lajjā,...
ibid, 4.5.

13. Yā devī sarvabhūteṣu... cetanā... nidrā... kṣudhā... mātā... kṣānti... śāntirūpeṇa, &c. ibid, 5.

14. Kalā-kāṣṭhādi-rūpeṇa
pariṇāma-pradāyinī.. ibid, 11.9.

9. Picturesque reminders

1. Viśiṣṭ ṁśa-samarthatvam

Upamāneṣu gṛhyate,
Ko bhedaḥ sarva-sādṛśye
Tūpamānopameyayoḥ?
Dṛṣṭānta-buddhāv-ekātma-
jñāna-śāstrārtha-vedanāt
Mahā-vākyārtha-saṁśuddhā
Śāntir-nirvāṇam ucyate.
Yoga Vāsiṣṭha, Mumukṣu Khaṇḍa, 19.1-2.
Svānubhūteś-ca śāstrasya
Guroś-caivaika-vākyatā
Yasyābhyāsena tenātmā
Santatenā' valokyate.
ibid, 13.2

2. Cf. Arthā'valokane dīpād-
ābhā-mātrād-ṛte kila
Na sthāna-taila-vartyādi
Kiṁcid-apyupayujyate.
The light of the sense (of something) is compared with a lamp in its brightness only, not in respect of its stand, oil or wick. ibid, 19. 65.
Akāraṇe kāraṇatā
Yad-bodhāyopamīyate
Na tatra sarva-sādharmyam
Sambhavaty'upamā-śramaiḥ.
In teaching about Brahman which is beyond change, illustrations like that of gold and ornaments, or of clay and pots, have been usually employed. However much we try, these illustrations can never have total applicability to Brahman. ibid, 19. 63.
3. Ātmā'vabodhana-samartham api svabhāvena sarva-prāṇinām jñānam bāhya-viṣaya-rāga-ādi-doṣa-kaluṣitam ... na avabodhayati nityam sannihitam api ātma-tattvam, malā'vanaddham iva ādarśam vilulitam iva salilam. Śaṅkara Bhāṣya, Muṇḍaka, 3. 1.8.4.
4. Āśramāḥ trividhāḥ... Hīnā nikṛṣṭā, madhyamā, utkṛṣṭā ca dṛṣṭiḥ darśana-sāmarthyam yeṣam te, manda-madhyama-uttama-buddhi-sāmarthy'opetāḥ-upāsanā upadiṣṭā iyam tad-artham, manda-madhyama-dṛṣṭy'āśrama-ādi-artham, karmāṇi ca. Na ca ātmā eka eva advitīya iti niścita,-uttamadṛṣṭy-artham. Dayālunā Vedena anukampayā, sanmārgagāḥ santaḥ katham imām uttamām ekatvadṛṣṭim prāpnuyur-iti. Māṇḍūkya Kārikā 3. 16. Śaṅkara Bhāṣya.

5. Cf. the significance of Kaṭha, 2.24. samāhitacittaḥ samādhāna-phalād-api upaśānta-mānasaḥ. Śaṅkara Bhāṣya.
6. Cf. Muṇḍaka, 1.1.8 Tapasā jñānena, utpattividhi-jñatayā ... Brahma cīyate, upacīyate utpādayiṣad-idam jagat, aṅkuram iva bījam ucchūnatām gacchati, putram iva pitā harṣeṇa... annam ... avyākṛtam ... utpadyate ... Hiraṇyagarbho Brahmaṇo jñāna-kriyā-śakti-adhiṣṭhito jagat-sādhāraṇo avidyā-kāma-bhūta-samudāya-bījāṅkuro jagadātmā ... Śaṅkaraṛ Bhāṣya.
7. Cf. Ūrddhva-mūlam avāk-śākham
   Vṛkṣam yo veda saṁprati
   Na sa jātu janaḥ śraddhyāt
   Mṛtyur-mā mārayād-iti.
   Taittirīya Āraṇyaka. Pra. I. Anu. 11.

   Ūrddhvam sarvotkṛṣṭam Brahma mūlam ... adhamā Brahmādi-stambāntā dehāḥ śākhāḥ; ayam ca saṁsāro vraścana-yogyatvāt Vṛkṣaḥ... He who knows this Tree, with the aid of his preceptor, will not entertain the notion he had, in common with other ignorant people, that death will one day knock him down. Because he will clearly see that he is in reality Brahman, ever free from birth and death. Sāyaṇa Bhāṣya.
8. Free reading of Śaṅkara Bhāṣya. Kaṭha, 6.1.
9. Muṇḍaka, 1.1.6
10. Kaṭha,6.2-4
11. Muṇḍaka, 1.1.7
12. Cf. Yo yad-guṇakam Brahma upāste sa tadguṇabhāg-bhavati ... Manaso hi sthāna-prayatnanāda-svara-varṇa-pada-vākya-viṣayā ... vṛttih. .. Yajuḥ &c. Taitt. Up 2.3. Śaṅkara Bhāṣya.

10. Synthesis through deeper reflection

1. Yaṁ labdhvā cāparaṁ lābham manyate nādhikaṁ tataḥ. Gītā 4.22.
2. Cf. Etad-buddhvā buddhimān syāt kṛta-kṛtyaśca. ibid, 15.20 These and other expressions quoted from the Gītā can be applied to the Ideal, Personal or Impersonal.
3. Cf. Samaṁ sarveṣu bhūteṣu tiṣṭhantam ... Samam paśyan hi sarvatra samavasthitam ... ibid, 13.27-28.

4. Yasmān-no'dvijate loko Lokān-no'dvijate ca yaḥ. ibid, 12.15.
5. Jihvāgre vartate Lakṣmīḥ;
Jihvāgre mitra-bāndhavāḥ;
Jihvāgre bandhana-prāptir;
Jihvāgre maraṇaṁ dhruvam!'
6. Lokāḥ: Karma-phalāni lokyante, dṛśyante, bhujyante iti, Janmāni... Īśa Up. 3. Śaṅkara Bhāṣya.
7. Raja Yoga by Vivekananda, 'Prāṇa', ch. 3.
8. Iha ced-aśakad-boddhum prāk-śarīrasya visrasaḥ. Kaṭha, 6.4.
9. Yogasudhākara of Śrī Sadāśivendra Sarasvati.
10. Nanu upādīyamānam api tapo dhātu-vaiṣamyahetutayā Yoga-pratipakṣa iti, katham tad-upāya ityata āha (Vyāsa:) Tat ca (citta-prasādanam-abādhyamānam-anena āsevyam iti manyate). Tāvanmātram eva tapaś-caraṇīyam na yāvatā dhātu vaiṣamyam āpadyate iti. Vācaspati, Yoga Sūtra, 2.
11. Tasya idam eva śiraḥ. Taitt. Up., Valli 2,1.
12. Cf. Titikṣā, with stress on 'sahanam...', cintā-vilāpa- rahitam as well as Śraddhā and Bhakti. Vivekacūḍāmaṇi. 25, 26 and 32.
13. Ayam prāṇamayaḥ puruṣavidho, mūṣā-niṣikta-pratimāvat; na svata eva. Śaṅkara Bhāṣya on Taitt. Up., Valli 2, 2; also Tenaiṣa pūrṇaḥ.
14. Mukha-nāsikā-niḥsaraṇo vṛtti-viśeṣaḥ (Prāṇaḥ) śira eva parikalpyate... pakṣādi-kalpanā. ibid,
15. Ekāṁśena: Ekāvayavena, ekapādena, sarvabhūta-rūpeṇa, Śaṅkara Bhāṣya on Gītā, 10.42.

11. Reflection and control of reactions

1. Dadhnaḥ mathyamānasya yo'ṇimā, aṇubhāvaḥ sa ūrdhvaḥ samudīṣati, sambhūyordhvaṃ navanīta bhāvena gacchati, tat-sarpir-bhavati... Evam eva annasyaudanāder-aśyamānasya, bhujyamānasya audaryeṇa agninā vāyu-sahitena, khajeneva mathyamānasya, Yo'ṇimā... tan-mano bhavati, mano'vayavaiḥ saha sambhūya mana upacinoti... Sā'nnopacitā manasaḥ śaktiḥ ṣoḍaśadhā pravibhajya puruṣasya kalātvena nirdidikṣitā... Yasyām satyām draṣṭā, śrotā, mantā, boddhā kartā, vijñātā, sarvakriyā-samarthaḥ puruṣo bhavati. Hīyamānāyām ca yasyām sāmarthyahāniḥ. Ch. Up, 6.6.1 and Śaṅkara's Bhāṣya,

2. ibid, 2-6.
3. Kāmaḥ saṁkalpo, vicikitsā, śraddhā, dhṛtir-adhṛtir-hrir-dhir-bhīr-ityetat-sarvam mana eva. Brh. Up. 1.5.3.
4. Na tvāṁ jighāṁsāmi careti yan-mām
   Ayam mahātmā matimān uvāca,
   Tasyaiva tad Rāma vaco'nurūpam,
   Idam punaḥ karma ca me'nurūpam! Kiṣkindhā, 24.8

   Vadho hi me mato nāsīt;
   Sva-māhātmyāvyatikramāt;
   Mamāsīd-buddhi-daurātmyāt-
   Prāṇa-hārī vyatikramaḥ
   Druma-śākhā' vabhagno'ham...
   Sāntvayitvā tvanenokto
   Na punaḥ kartum arhasi...
   Bhrātṛtvam āryabhāvaś-ca
   Dharmaś-cānena rakṣitāḥ;
   Mayā krodhaś-ca kāmaś-ca
   Kapitvaṃ ca pradarśitam! 10—12.
   Sañjāta-bāṣpaḥ para-vīra-hantā
   Rāmo muhūrtam vimanā babhūva! 24.
5. Pāpaṁ tavaiva tat-sarvam,
   Vayaṁ tu phalabhāginaḥ!
   Tat-śrutvā jāta-nirvedo
   Vicārya punarāgamam
   Munayo yatra tiṣṭhanti
   Karuṇā-pūrṇa-mānasāḥ.
   Munīnāṁ darśanād-eva
   Śuddhāntaḥ-karaṇo' bhavam.
   Ayodhyā, 6.74-76.
6. Īṣat-sahāsam-amalam paripūrṇa-candra-
   Bimbānukāri kanakottama-kānti-kāntam
   Atyadbhutam prahṛtam āttaruṣā tathāpi
   Vaktram vilokya sahasā Mahiṣāsureṇa 4.12.
7. Vidyāḥ Samastās-tava Devi bhedāḥ,
   Striyaḥ samastāḥ sakalā jagatsu... 11.6
   Yā śrīḥ svayaṁ sukṛtinām bhavaneṣu.
   ...sukṛtinām hṛdayeṣu buddhiḥ,
   Śraddhā satāṁ... Tāṁ tvāṁ natāḥ smaḥ... 4.5.

12. Spiritual ascent through art and worship

1. Compl. Wks. of Sw. Vivekananda, Vol. 4. Address on Bhaktiyoga, p. 15.
2. ibid 3. pp. 81-82.
3. Saumitre! nanu sevyatām tarutalam Caṇḍāṁśur-ujjṛmbhate. Caṇḍāṁśor-nisi kā kathā Raghupate! Candro'yam-unmīlati! Vatsaitad-bhavatā katham nu viditam? dhatte kuraṅgam yataḥ: Kvāsi preyasi hā! Kuraṅga-nayane Candrānane Jānaki!
4. Eko Devaḥ sarvabhūteṣu gūḍhaḥ Sarvavyāpī sarvabhūtāntarātmā etc.
5. Naicchan-muktipater-muktim tasmāt tāpamupeyivān... Bhavacchidaḥ pādamūlam gatvā yāce yad-antavat... Bhavacchidam-ayāce' ham bhavam bhāgya-vivarjitaḥ... Svārājyam yacchato mauḍhyān māno me bhikṣito bata... Īśvarāt kṣīṇapuṇyena phalikārān-ivādhanaḥ. Bhāg. 4.9. 29-35
6. Bhāg. 11. 14.26.
7. Yoga Sūtra, 1.39. Tatra labdha-sthitikamanyatrāpi sthitipadam labhate (Vyāsa).
8. Cf. Bhag. 11. 27.9 also 16-17.
9. ibid. 24; also 30-35.
10. ibid. 44.

13. Intention's penetrative power

*Complete Works, 3, 'The Vedānta'.

1. citi-śaktir-apariṇāminī, apratisaṁkramā, darśita-viṣayā śuddhā ca anantā (Vyāsa on Yoga Sūtra 1.2.)
2. Sri Ramakrishna the Great Master (Madras, 1952 edition). p. 375.
3. Vyājena hi tvayā Droṇa upacīrṇas-sutam prati;
Vyājena iva tato Rājan! darśitaṁ narakam tava.
Yena tvaṁ tathā Bhīmas-tathā Pārtho yamau tathā,
Tathaiva Draupadī Kṛṣṇā vyājena narakam gatāḥ.
Svargārohaṇa Parvan, 3.
4. Capalo'yam vaṭuḥ. Kadācit-asmad-prārthanām antaḥ-purebhyaḥ kathayet. Bhavatu, enam evam vakṣye: 'Vayasya! ṛṣi-gauravād āśramaṁ gacchāmi. Na khalu satyameva tāpasa-kanyakāyām mamābhilāṣaḥ'.

5. Alam asmān-anyathā sambhāvya. Rājñaḥ pratigraho'yam.'... 'Cakravāka-vadhūke! Āmantrayasva sahacaram; upasthitā rajanī.' 'Tāvat viṭapāntarito bhava!'
6. 'Yadi nāma sa rājarṣiḥ pratyabhijñana-mantharo bhavet, tadā tasmai idam ātmanāmadheyāṅkitam-aṅgulīyakam darśaya'... 'Anena sandehena vām ākampitāsmi'... 'Mā bibhīhi; atisnehaḥ pāpaśaṅkī'.

14. Vision that supplements and balances

1. Sayings of Sri Ramakrishna, No. 912.
2. Cf. the example in the beginning of Śaṅkara's Bhāṣya on the Gītā: Yasya tu ajñānāt, rāgādidoṣato vā, karmaṇi pravṛttasya, yajñena, dānena, tapasā vā viśuddha-sattvasya jñānam utpannam paramārtha-tattva-viṣayam, 'Ekam eva idaṁ sarvam Brahma, akartṛ ca', iti tasya karmaṇi, karma-prayojane ca nivṛtte api, loka-saṁgrahārthaṁ, yatna-pūrvaṁ yathā pravṛttiḥ tathā eva karmaṇi pravṛttasya, yat pravṛtti-rūpaṁ dṛśyate, na tat karma, yena buddheḥ samuccayaḥ syāt. Yathā Bhagavato Vāsudevasya Kṣātra-karma-ceṣṭitam na jñānena samuccīyate puruṣārtha-siddhaye, tadvat, phalābhisandhi-ahamkāra-abhāvasya tulyatvāt viduṣaḥ etc.
3. Na ca śakto'pi padārtha-viparyāsaṁ karoti. Kasmāt? Anyasya yatra kāmāvasāyinaḥ pūrva-siddhasya tatra bhūteṣu saṁkalpād-iti. (Vyāsa) Na khalu ete yatra kāmāvasāyinaḥ tatra bhagavataḥ Parameśvarasya ājñām atikramitum utsahante. (Vācaspati).
4. Yogena cittasya, padena vācaḥ
   Malaṁ śarīrasya ca vaidyakena
   Yo' pākarot tam pravaram munīnāṁ
   Patañjalim prāñjalir-ānatosmi.
5. The Master As I Saw Him.

15. Refinement of reactions

1. Ālūna-hṛdayāmbhojān mahāmoha-mataṅgajān
   Vidārayati śuddhātmā vicāro nāma kesarī.
   Yoga Vāsiṣṭha, Mumukṣu, 14.8.
   Mānase sarasi svacche vicāra-kamalotkaraḥ
   Nūnam vikasito yasya Himavāniva bhāti saḥ.

ibid, 16.
Dharma-bhittau bhṛśam lagnām
dhiyam dhairya-dhuram gatām
Adhayo na vidhunvanti
vātaś-citra-latām iva. ibid, 18.24.
Sat-saṅga-santoṣa śama vicāravati san-matau
Pravartante mantri-vare rājanīva jaya-śriyaḥ. ibid. 16.26.

2. Rathaḥ sthāṇur-dehas-turaga-racanā cendriya-gatiḥ
Parispando vāto vahana-kalitānanda-viṣayaḥ
Paro'ṇur-vā dehī jagati viharāmīty' anaghayā
Dhiyā dṛṣṭe tattve ramaṇam aṭanam jāgatam
idam. ibid, 12.22

This body of ours is the car and these organs are its horses. Our very breathings may be compared to the winds blowing on it and our mind, whose property is movement, to the reins for regulating the car's course. I, the embodied one, enjoying the bliss resulting from the proper control of this vehicle, am a spark of the Supreme Reality, sportfully moving in this world. Realizing thus, with the intellect pure and fully illumined, one finds it delighful indeed to sojourn in this world.

3. Tasmāt pauruṣam āśritya sac-chāstraiḥ sat-samāgamaiḥ
Prajñām amalatām nītvā samsāra-jaladhim taret. ibid, 6.24
4. Cf. the two stanzas prior to 12.22, which end with this refrain: 'ramaṇam aṭanam jāgatam idam'.
5. Cf. Śaṅkara Bhāṣya on Gītā, 4.1. 'This Yoga, treated of in the two preceding discourses (imam adhyāya-dvayena uktam yogam), I taught to Vivasvat... to infuse strength into the Kṣatriyas, the rulers of the world (jagat-paripālayitṛṇām kṣatriyāṇām bala-ādhānāya). It is only when possessed of the strength of this Yoga that they can protect Brahma, the spiritual Ideal and tradition. When the spiritual Ideal, comprising Teaching and Administration, Brahma and Kṣatra, is well upheld that becomes adequate for regulating the affairs of the world (Tena yoga-balena yuktāḥ samarthāḥ bhavanti Brahma parirakṣitum. Brahma-kṣatre paripālite jagatparipālayitum alam)
6. Kumāram prathama-vayasam ... aprāptaprajanana-śaktim, bālam eva. śraddhā. praviṣṭavatī... Tvam punaḥ punaḥ mayā pralobhyamānaḥ api priyān putrādīn, priyarūpān ca apsaraḥ

prabhṛtilakṣanān kāmān...teṣām anityatva-asāratvādidoṣān (cintayan),... tyaktavān asi, aho buddhimattā tava! Śaṅkara Bhāṣya, Kaṭha, 1.2 and 2.3.

7. Pratīcyeva ātma-śabdo rūḍho loke, na anyatra (to denote the inner spirit, not to denote any other).
Vyutpatti-pakṣe api tatraiva ātma-śabdo vartate
'Yac-cāpnoti yad-ādatte yac-cātti viṣayān iha
Yac-cāsya saṁtato bhāvas-tasmād-ātmeti kīrtyate'.
Tam, pratyagātmānam svam &c. S.B. Kaṭha, 4.1
8. This section is based on Gītā, 7.

16. Towards Fuller Vision

1. Sarva-śaktir-anantātmā
Sarva-bhāvāntara-sthitaḥ
Advitīyaś-cid-ityantar-
Yaḥ paśyati sa paśyati.
Yoga Vāsiṣṭha, Sthiti, 22.27.
Ātmānam itarac-caiva
Dṛṣṭyā nityā'vibhinnayā
Sarvam cij-jyotir-eveti
Yaḥ paśyati sa paśyati. ibid, 28.
Yan-nāma kiñcit-trailokyam
Sa evā'vayavo mama
Taraṅgo'bdhāvivetyantar-
Yaḥ paśyati sa paśyati. ibid, 33.
Śocyā pālyā mayaiveyam
Svaṣeyam me kanīyasī
Trilokī pelavety uccaiḥ
Yaḥ paśyati sa paśyati. ibid, 34.
2. Bṛh. Up, 1.4.7.
3. Māṇḍūkya Kārikā 4.55-56.
4. Dharma-adharma-ākhyasya hetoḥ ahaṃ kartā, mama dharma-adharmau, tat-phalam kālāntare kvacit-prāṇi-nikāye jāto bhokṣye: iti yāvad-hetuphalayor-āveśo... ātmani adhyāropaṇam taccittatā... tāvat... dharma-adharmayoḥ tat-phalasya ca anucchedena pravṛttiḥ. ibid, Śaṅkara Bhāṣya.
5. Manasedam śarīram hi
Vāsanārtham prakalpitam

Kṛmi-kośa-prakāreṇa
Svātma-koś iva svayam.
Na tad-asti ca yan-nāma
Cetaḥ saṅkalpam-ambaram
Na karoti na cā'pnoti
Durgam apyatiduṣkaram.
Yoga Vāsiṣṭha, Sthiti, 45.7-8.

6. In this third section many passages from Śaṅkara Bhāṣya on Bṛh. Up. 1.4.7 have been strung together, e.g.. Na tu sarvagatasya niravayavasya dig-deśa-kālāntara-apakramaṇa-prāpti-lakṣaṇaḥ praveśaḥ kadācid-apyupapadyate. Na ca parād-ātmano'nyaḥ asti draṣṭā, 'na anyad-ato'sti draṣṭṛ, na anyad-ato'sti śrotṛ' ... upalabdhyarthatvāt ca sṛṣṭi-praveśa sthiti-apyaya-vākyānām. Upalabdheḥ puruṣārtha-śravaṇāt ... Yāvad-ayam veda, 'paśyāmi, śṛṇomi, spṛśāmi' iti vā, svabhāva-pravṛtti-viśiṣṭam veda, tāvat añjasā kṛtsnam ātmanam na veda. Katham Punaḥ paśyan veda ?... sa yathā kṛtsna-viśeṣopasaṁhārī san kṛtsno bhavati... evam kṛtsno hyasau svena vasturūpeṇa gṛhyamāṇo bhavati... Kim na vijñātavyam evam anyat? Na... jñātavyatve api, na pṛthak-jñanāntaram apekṣate ātmajñānāt... Jñā nalābhayor-ekārthatvasya vivakṣitatvāt...
7. Sri Ramakrishna the Great Master, p. 381.
8. Japo jalpaḥ śilpam sakalam api mudrā-viracanā
Gatiḥ prādakṣiṇya-kramaṇam aśanādy-āhuti-vidhiḥ
Praṇāmaḥ saṃveśaḥ sukham akhilam ātmārpaṇa-dṛśā
Saparyā-paryāyas-tava bhavatu yan-me vilasitam!
Saundaryalaharī, 27.
9. Sri Saradadevi (Madras Edn. 1940). p. 391.
10. ibid, p. 400.
11. ibid, pp. 424-425.
12. ibid, p. 458.
13, ibid, p. 105.
14. ibid, p. 18
15. Sarvā hi ghṛnā ātmano'nyad-duṣṭam paśyato bhavati, ātmānam eva atyanta-viśuddham nirantaram paśyato na ghṛṇā-nimittam arthāntaram asti iti prāptam eva; tato'na vijugupsate' iti. Śaṅkara Bhāṣya, Iśa, 6.

17. Creation of Interest and Certainty

1. Stanzas 321 to 329. 'dṛśyam pratītam pravilāpayan svayaṁ...

pramādataḥ pracyuta- kelikaṇdukaḥ sopānapaṅktau patito yathā tathā... pramādān-na paro'sti mṛtyur-vivekino brahmavidaḥ samādhau...'

2. Y.S. 1.14. Sa tu dīrghakāla-nairantarya-ṣatkārāsevito dṛḍhabhūmiḥ.
3. Yadi divasair-māsair-vā samādhi-siddhiṁ vāñchhet, tadā 'Vidyamānāścatvāra eva vedāḥ; tān-adhyetuṁ ' gatasya māṇavakasya pañca divasā atītāḥ; nādyāpyasau samāgataḥ' iti mūḍhavacanānusāryevāyaṁ yogī syāt. Ataḥ saṁvatsarair-janmabhir-vā dīrghakālaṁ yoga āsevitavyaḥ. Yogasudhākara of Srí Sadāśivendra Sarasvati, Vāṇivilas Edition, Series No. 11.
4. Satkāraḥ ādaraḥ. Anādare laya-vikṣepakaṣāyādayaḥ prasajjeran. Tasmād-ādareṇāsevitavyaḥ. ibid.
5. Cf. Ṛtambharā prajñā and Dharmameghaḥ samādhiḥ 1.48 and 4.29 respectively of Yoga sūtra.
6. Cf. the types of 'sacrifices' mentioned in Gītā 4.
7. ... na duḥkhena guruṇāpi vicālyate. Gītā 6. 22; quoted by Yogasudhākara while commenting on Y.S. 1.14. Note Saṁkara's comment: 'pain, such as may be inflicted by a sword-cut, etc'.

8-10. Teachings of Sri Ramakrishna (Mayavati Edn.) Nos. 460, 463 and 768.

18. Awakening and Grouping of Talents

1. Gītā, 10.41
2. Comp. Wks. of Sw. Vivekananda, 3. 'The Work. Before Us'.
3. ibid. 'Vedānta and Indian Life'. This passage is quoted to show how men of vision judge aright the trend of world forces. The lecture was delivered by Swamiji soon after his return from the West.
4. Based on a few of the manifestations mentioned in Gītā, 10.20-40.
5. The story is given in detail in Mahābhārata, Karṇa Parvan, 26.27 (Southern Recension, edited by P. P. S. Sastri, B.A. Oxon., M.A.),
   Kāñcanaṁ divi tatrāsīd-antarikṣe ca rājatam:
   Āvasam cābhavad-bhūmau tadā teṣām Parantapa! 24.24.
   Kāñcanaṁ Tārakākṣasya divyam-āsīn mahātmanaḥ.
   Rājataṁ Kamalākṣasya; Vidyunmāles-ca thāyasam. 28.

6. Yathā varṣa-sahasreṣu sameṣyāmaḥ parasparam...
Ekībhāvaṁ gamiṣyanti purāṇyetāni cānagha!
Samāgatāni caitāni yo hanyād-Bhagavan! naraḥ
Devo vā dvipadām śreṣṭhas-sa no mṛtyurbhaviṣyati. 17-20.

One of their sons got another boon which made the water of a certain tank capable of restoring to life any of their soldiers slain in battle!

Sasṛje tatra vāpīm tām mṛta-sanjīvinīm prabhuḥ... 36-38.

7. Cakraṁ cakre candramasaṁ tārakā-maṇi maṇḍitam,
Divākaraṁ cāpyaparaṁ cakraṁ cakre'mśumālinam, 26.8

8. Sārathitvaṁ kariṣyāmi Śaṅkarasya mahātmanaḥ.
Sarvathā rathinaḥ śreyān kartavyo rathasārathiḥ...
Evam uktvā jaṭābhāraṁ samyamya prapitāmahaḥ...
Pratoda-pāṇir-bhagavān āruroha ratham tadā 27.19-22.

9. Ayaṁ cāpyavamāno me na kartavyaḥ kathaṁcana
Āpṛcche tvā'dya Gāndhāre yāsyāmi viṣayam prati;
Na cāhaṁ sūta-putrasya sārathyam-upajagmivān. 23.55-56.
Rathino'bhyadhiko vīraḥ kartavyo rathasārathiḥ... 29.2
Tataḥ Karṇasya durdharṣaṁ syandana-pravaram mahat
Āruroha mahātejās-Śalyas-simha ivācalam. 21.

10. Romain Rolland's Life and Gospel of Vivekananda, Part 2.C.4

19. Formula of Rousing and Refining

1. Cf. Gītā 2.62-64, and Śaṅkara Bhāṣya thereon: Śāstrācāryo padeśāhita-saṁskāra--janitāyāḥ smṛteḥ syāt vibhramo, bhramśaḥ, smṛtyutpatti-nimittaprāptau anutpattiḥ...kāryākārya-viṣaya-vivekāyogyatā antaḥ-karaṇasya buddheḥ nāśa ucyate.. Tāvat eva hi puruṣo yāvat antaḥ-karaṇaṁ tadīyaṁ kāryākārya-viṣaya-viveka-yogyam, tad-ayogyatve naṣṭa eva puruṣo bhavati... puruṣārthāyogyo bhavati.

2. Cf. citta-nirodhe, cittavat niruddhāni indriyāṇi, na itarendriyavat upāyāntaram apekṣante. Yathā madhukara-rājānam makṣikā utpatantam anūtpatanti, niviśamānam anu-niviśante, tathā indriyāṇi citta-nirodhe niruddhāni ityeṣa pratyāhāraḥ... Tac-ca paramā tu, iyaṁ vaśyatā yaccitta-nirodhe niruddhāni indriyāṇi, na itarendriyavat prayatna-kṛtam upāyāntaram apekṣante yoginaḥ. Vyāsa Bhāsya on Yoga Sūtras, 2.54-55.

3. Cf. Tataḥ ca kāryeṇa liṅgena devādi-pūjayā sattvādi-niṣṭhā

anumeyā... Evam kāryato nirṇītaḥ satvādi niṣṭhaḥ... Śaṅkara Bhāṣya, Gītā, 17.3-4.

4. Eṣa tvām abhinava-kaṇṭha-śonitārthī
Śārdūlaḥ paśum-iva hanmi ceṣṭamānam;
Ārtānām bhayam apanetum ātta-dhanvā
Duṣyantas-tava śaraṇam bhavatvidānīm!
...kiñcin-nimittād-api manaḥ-saṁtāpāt āyuṣmān mayā viklavo dṛṣṭaḥ. Paścāt kopayitum āyuṣmantaṁ tathā kṛtavān asmi. Kutaḥ;
Jvalati calitendhano'gnir-
Viprakṛtaḥ pannagaḥ phaṇam kurute,
Prāyaḥ svam mahimānaṁ
Kopāt pratipadyate jantuḥ.
Act 4.27 and 31.
5. Inspired Talks of Sw. Vivekananda.
6. Mano hyavidyā. Vivekacūḍāmaṇi, 169.
7. ibid, 168.
8. ibid, 176.
9. Cf. Ātmanaḥ, parasmāt puruṣād-akṣarāt satyādeṣa uktaḥ Prāṇo jāyate... Chāyā iva dehe, manokṛtena, manaḥ saṁkalpecchādi-niṣpanna-karmanimittena (āyāti). Praśna Up. 3. 3. Śaṅkara Bhāṣya.
10. Vivekacūḍāmaṇi, 172.
11. Cf. ibid,
Vairāgya-Bodhau puruṣasya pakṣivat
Pakṣau vijānīhi vicakṣana tvam,
Vimukti-saudhāgra-latādhirohaṇaṁ
Tābhyāṃ vinā nānyatareṇa siddhyati. 374.
Etad-dvāram ajasra-mukti-yuvateḥ...
Svārājya-sāmrājya-dhuk...376
Na deśa-kālāsana-dig-yamādi-
Lakṣyādyapekṣā'pratibaddhavṛtteḥ
Saṁsiddha-tattvasya mahātmano'sti;
Sva-vedane kā niyamādyavasthā? 529.

20. Graded Forms and Levels of Aid

1. Complete Wks. of Sw. Vivekananda, 7. 168.
2. ibid, 3.302.

3. ibid, 5.257.
4. ibid, 6.36.
5. ibid, 1.130. These and other valuable ideas of the swami have been collected and published in a booklet 'Education', by the Sri Ramakrishna Math, Mylapore, Madras.
6. Teachings of Sri Ramakrishna, 236.
7. Gītā, 6.29-32.
8. Teachings of Sri Ramakrishna, 184.
9. ibid, 185.
10. The Gospel of Sri Ramakrishna, Pp. 441-2.
11. ibid, Pp. 290-1.
12. Sri Ramakrishna, the Great Master, p. 188.
13. ibid, P. 370
14. ibid. P. 296.
15. ibid. P. 384.

21. Opening up of Inner Springs

1. More or less on the model: 'Abhivādaye... (Rāma Śarmā) nāmā aham asmi, Bhoḥ!'... Dīrgha-āyuṣmān bhava, somya, (Rāma Śarman)'
2. Muṇḍ. Up. 1.2.13. Cf. Also 'dadyād-abhītiṁ sahasā mahātmā... Tattvopadeśam kṛpayaiva kuryāt... Ayam svabhāvaḥ svata eva yat-paraśramāpanoda- pravaṇam mahātmanām...' Vivekacūḍāmaṇi 38.-42.
3. Vivekacūḍāmaṇi, 43.
4. Cf. 'upadraṣṭā-anumantā ca', Gītā, 13. 22.
5. Na hi ātmā nāma kasyacit kadācit aprasiddhaḥ, prāpyo, heya, upādeyo vā. Aprasiddhe hi tasminātmani, asvārthāḥ sarvāḥ pravṛttayaḥ prasajyeran. Na ca dehādi-acetana-arthatvam śakyaṁ kalpayituṁ. Na ca sukhārtham sukham, duḥkhārtham vā duḥkham; ātma-avagatyavasāna-arthatvāt ca sarvavyavahārasya. Tasmād-yathā sva-dehasya parichedāya na pramāṇa-antara-apekṣā tataḥ api ātmanaḥ antaratamatvāt, tad-avagatim prati na pramāṇa-antara-apekṣā... (Ātma-) jñāne yatno na kartavyaḥ, kiṁ tu anātma-buddhi-nivṛttau eva. Śaṅkara Bhāṣya on Gītā, 18.50
6. Cf. Na hi a-jita-adhara-bhūmiḥ anantarabhūmiṁ vilanghya prānta-bhūmiṣu samyamaṁ labhate. Tad-abhāvāt ca kutaḥ tasya

prajñālokaḥ? Bhūmeḥ asya iyam antara-bhūmiḥ ityatra yoga eva upādhyāyaḥ. When one plane has been conquered by samyama, it is applied to the next immediately following. None who has not conquered the lower plane can jump over the plane immediately following and then achieve samyama with reference to the plane further off. And if this samyama cannot be achieved, how can the 'visibility of the Cognition' come?... As to which is the next immediate plane after a certain plane, it is the practice of Yoga alone that will teach this. Vyāsa on Yoga Sūtra, 3. 6, Cf. Also Vācaspati: Jitaḥ pūrvo yogaḥ uttarasya yogasya jñāna-pravṛtti-adhigamahetuḥ. When the preceding state of Yoga is conquered, it becomes the cause of the knowledge of the nature and activity of the next.

22. Coordinated insight and service

1. Jāgarite hi puṇyāpuṇya nimitta-sukhaduḥkhā-dyanekāyāsānu bhavāt śrānto bhavati, tataś-caāyasthānām karaṇānām aneka-vyāpāra nimitta-glānānāṃ sva-vyāpārebhya uparamo bhavati. Chāndogya 6.8.1 Śaṅkara Bhāṣya.
2. Nānyatra sva-rūpāvasthānāt śramāpanodaḥ syād-iti yuktā prasiddhirlaukikānām svam hyapīto bhavati iti. ibid.
3. Yathā śakuniḥ, pakṣī, śakuni-ghātakasya hastagatena sūtreṇa prabaddhaḥ, pāśito,... bandhanamokṣārthī san prati-diśam patitvā, anyatra bandhanād- āyatanam, āśrayam... aprāpya, bandhanam evopāśrayate, evam eva... sa mana-ākhyopādhirjīvaḥ avidyā-kāma-karmopadiṣṭāṁ... sukhaduḥkhādilakṣaṇām jāgrat-svapnayoḥ patitvā... anubhūya, anyatra sad-ākhyāt-svātmanaḥ... viśramaṇa-sthānam alabdhvā,... prāṇena,-sarvakārya-karaṇāśrayeṇopalakṣitā prāṇa ityucyate sadākhyā parā devatā-tām devatām prāṇākhyām evopāśrayate... jīvasya satyasvarūpaṁ jagatomūlam... ibid, 8.2.
4. Eṣa mahānyagrodho, bījasyāṇimnaḥ sūkṣmasya adṛśyamānasya kāryabhūtaḥ sthūla-śākhā skandhaphala--palāśavān tiṣṭhati utpannaḥ sannuttiṣthati iti-ataḥ... sata evāṇimnaḥ sthūlaṁ nāmarūpādimat-kāryaṃ jagad-utpannam... Tat Satyam, Sa Ātmā, Tat Tvam Asi. ibid. 6.12.2.
5. Viparyayasya aśuddhirūpasya kṣayo... Yathā sādhanāni anuṣṭhī-yante tathā tathā tanutvam aśuddhir-āpadyate... Kṣaya-kramānu-rodhinī Jñānasyāpi dīptir-vardhate... ā-viveka-khyāteḥ. Yoga Sūtra 2.28. Vyāsa Bhāṣya.

6. Vācaspati says that 'Vā', meaning 'Or' or 'option' in 'Or by expulsion and retention of Prāṇa', in Y.S. 1.34, does not apply to cultivation of maitrī etc. mentioned in 1.33. These latter 'must be present with all the means. Vā-śabdo vakṣyamāṇopāyāntarāpekṣo vikalpārthaḥ, na maitryādibhāvanāpekṣayā; tayā saha samuccayāt.
7. Satyaṁ yathārthe vāṅg-manase; yathā-dṛṣṭaṁ, yathānumitaṁ, yathāśrutaṁ tathā vāṅg-manase iti; paratra sva-bodha-saṁkrāntaye vāg-uktā sā yadi na vañcitā... bhavet... sarva bhūtopakārārtha-pravṛttā, na bhūtopaghātāya. Y.S. 2.30. Vyāsa.
   Yathā Droṇācāryeṇa sva-tanayāśvatthāmā-maraṇaṁ. Āyuṣman! Satyadhana! Aśvatthāmā hata, iti pṛṣṭasya Yudhiṣṭhirasya prativacanaṁ hastinamabhisamdhāya satyam: hato'śvatthāma iti; tad idam uktasyottaraṁ na Yudhiṣṭhirasya sva-bodham saṁkrāmayati. For example, Yudhiṣṭhira was asked by Droṇācārya with reference to the death of his son: My dear one, your wealth is truth. Is Aśvatthāman dead? The reply was: It is true that Aśvatthāman is dead! This reply of the king who meant the death of Aśvatthāman, the elephant, and not of Droṇa's son of the same name, did not convey to the hearer's mind what was in the mind of the speaker. Vācaspati.
8. Satyam parāpakāra-phalaṁ satyābhāsaṁ, natu satyam ityāha-Yathā satya-tapasaḥ taskaraiḥ sārthagamanam pṛṣṭasya sārthagamanābhidhānam iti. Vācaspati. Tasmat parīkṣya sarvabhūtahitaṁ satyam brūyāt. Vyāsa.
9. Mastaka-nyasta-bhārāder-duḥkham anyair-nivāryate,
   Kṣudhādi-kṛta-duḥkhaṁ tu vinā svena na kenacit.
   Pathyam-auṣadha-sevā ca kriyate yena rogiṇā
   Ārogya-siddhir-draṣṭāsya, nānyanuṣṭhita-karmaṇā. 54.55.
10. Satyaṁ, dharma-kāryam-anatipālyaṁ devasya. Tathāpi idānīmeva dharmāsanād-utthitāya punaruparodhakāri Kaṇva-śiṣyāgamanam asmai notsahe nivedayitum. Athavā a-viśramo'yam loka-tantrādhikāraḥ. Kutaḥ:—
    Bhānuḥ sakṛd-yukta-turaṅga eva;
    rātrindivaṁ gandhavahaḥ prayāti;
    Śeṣaḥ sadaivāhita-bhūmi-bhāraḥ;
    ṣaṣṭhāmśa-vṛtter-api dharma eṣaḥ.
    Raja: Sarvaḥ prārthitam artham adhigamya sukhī saṁpadyate jantuḥ. Rājñāṁ tu caritārthatā duḥkhottaraiva.

Autsukya-mātram-avasādayati pratiṣṭhā,
Kliśnāti labdha-paripālana-vṛttir-eva;
Nā'tiśramā' panayanāya yathā śramāya
Rājyaṁ sva-hasta-dhṛta-daṇḍam-ivātapatram. Act 5.

24. Attainment, Delight, and Non-swerving

1. Draṣṭṛ-darśana-dṛśyānām madhye yad-darśanam sthitam. Sādho! tad-avadhānena svātmānam avabuddhyase. Yoga Vāsiṣṭha. Utpatti Khaṇḍa, 9.75
2. Tattvam-ādhyātmikam dṛṣṭvā tattvam dṛṣṭvā tu bāhyataḥ / Tattvī-bhūtas-tad-ārāmaḥ tattvādapracyuto bhavet. Māṇḍūkyā Kārikā 2.38
3. Loke api ekasmād-guroḥ śṛṇvatām kaś-cit yathāvat pratipadyate, kaś-cit ayathāvat, kaś-cit viparītam, kaś-cit na pratipadyate; kimu vaktavyam atīndriyam ātmatattvam? Śaṅkara Bhāṣya, Kena, 2.1.
4. Vasantavat loka-hitaṁ carantaḥ. Vivekacūḍāmaṇi 37.
5. Cf. the expressions used in stanzas 18 to 22 in Gītā vi, along with Saṅkara Bhāṣya; viniyataṁ cittam... ekāgratām āpannam, hitvā bāhyacintām... svātmani sthitim labhate... dṛṣṭa-adṛṣṭa-viṣayebhyaḥ... tṛṣṇā yasya yoginaḥ nirgatā... yasmin kāle... cittam uparatim gacchati, niruddham, sarvato nivārita-pracāram... yogānuṣṭhānena... samādhi-pariśuddhena antaḥ-karaṇena, ātmānam Param caitanya-jyotiḥ svarūpam... upalabhamānaḥ sve eva ātmani... tuṣṭim bhajate... sukham... anantam... buddhyā indriya-nirapekṣayā... indriya-gocara-atītam, aviṣaya-janitam... ātma-svarūpe...
6. It will not be difficult to see the implications of the Yoga Sūtras, Smṛti-pariśuddhau sva-rūpa-śūnyā iva artha-mātra-nirbhāsā nirvitarkā (I. 43) and Tadeva artha-mātra-nirbhāsam sva-rūpa-śūnyam iva samādhiḥ (3.3).
7. Yathā atattva-darśī kaś-cit cittam-ātmatvena pratipannaḥ, citta-calitamanu calitam ātmānam manyamānaḥ, tattvāt calitam dehādi-bhūtam ātmānam kadācit manyate pracyuto'ham ātma-tattvād idānīm iti. Samāhite tu manasi, kadācit, tattvabhūtam prasannātmānam manyate idānīm asmi tattvī-bhūta iti. Na tathā ātmavid-bhavet. Ātmanaḥ eka-rūpatvāt, pracyavana-abhāvāt ca. Cf. also Śaṅkara's comment on Gītā 6.21, Ayam vidvān

ātma-svarūpe sthitaḥ tasmād-eva tattva-svarūpāt na pracyavate. Ātma-lābham prāpya duḥkhena-śastra-pāta-ādinā, guruṇā mahatā api na vicālyate (6.22).

Cf. the description of the man of self-control and real Peace, given in Yoga Vāsiṣṭha, Mumukṣu Khaṇḍa, 14.75. for example: 'He whose thoughts shine like the cool moon-beams, whose mind remains unruffled when confronted with fighting or death, even as at the prospect of festivity—he indeed is called a self-controlled man of Peace'.

Tuṣāra-kara-bimbābham mano yasya nirākulam.
Maraṇotsavayuddheṣu sa śānta iti kathyate.